Water in the
21st-Century West

Water in the 21st-Century West

A *HIGH COUNTRY NEWS* READER

Char Miller, editor

Oregon State University Press

Corvallis

The paper in this book meets the guidelines for permanence and
durability of the Committee on Production Guidelines for Book
Longevity of the Council on Library Resources and the minimum
requirements of the American National Standard for Permanence of
Paper for Printed Library Materials Z39.48-1984.

Library of Congress Cataloging-in-Publication Data
Water in the 21st-century West : a High country news reader / Char
Miller, editor.
    p. cm.
  ISBN 978-0-87071-566-2 (alk. paper)
  1. Water conservation--West (U.S.) 2. West (U.S.)--Environmental
conditions. 3. Water use--Social aspects--West (U.S.) 4. Water use--
Political aspects--West (U.S.) 5. Water use--Environmental aspects-
-West (U.S.) 6. Water-supply--Social aspects--West (U.S.) 7. Water-
supply--Political aspects--West (U.S.) 8. Water-supply--Environmental
aspects--West (U.S.) I. Miller, Char, 1951- II. High country news.
  TD223.6.W475 2009
  363.6'109780905--dc22

                                                          2008053106

First published in 2009 by Oregon State University Press
Printed in the United States of America

Oregon State University Press
121 The Valley Library
Corvallis OR 97331-4501
541-737-3166 • fax 541-737-3170
http://oregonstate.edu/dept/press

Contents

VI. Toxic Terrain

VII. Urban Pressures

Dry Spell

Char Miller

It seems like old times: during the spring and summer of 2008 newspaper headlines were shouting of drought; city, county, and state governments prepared for water shortages; governors schemed to build bigger dams, larger reservoirs, and longer canals, concrete solutions to which grassroots activists rose up in opposition. Not much has changed in the arid West— its early-twenty-first-century environmental politics appear to resemble those that have defined regional political life since World War Two.

Appearances can deceive; resemblances are not replicas: the challenges facing the contemporary West are of a different order than those that preceding generations confronted. Then the central dilemma was how to capture water and channel it to water-guzzling farms and thirsty urbanites living in booming Denver, Salt Lake, or Phoenix, Los Angeles, or San Diego. Billions of federal and state dollars were poured into the California Aqueduct, the Central Utah and Central Arizona Projects, as well as into innumerable dams, reservoirs, and tunnels to move water across watersheds, through mountains, and over deserts to irrigation spigots and suburban faucets hundreds of miles away. Until the 1960s, this form of water management went largely uncontested: it was a happy time, affirmed former Bureau of Reclamation Commissioner Floyd Dominy: "This is the stage I like to describe as having no naysayers," he told the *High Country News* in 2000. "If we proposed a project, it was endorsed, and it got built."

The consensus did not hold; by the mid-1960s, a reenergized environmental movement began challenging dam projects throughout the West, drawing considerable media attention and public applause. The movement's arguments for the preservation of wild and scenic rivers, assertions that often gained powerful support from tribal peoples fighting to protect their rights to water and riparian habitats, proved

1

persuasive in and out of court, stymied Dominy's ambitions, and bottled up the legislative process. By the early 1970s, soaring construction prices combined with a spike in legal costs to shut down the Big Dam Era, forcing communities to reconsider their strategies for growth and development.

That's being charitable: most consumers—rural and urban—operated on the assumption that water supplies were still plentiful and infinite. Conservation measures rarely were implemented on farms, in factories, or on the ubiquitous lawns rolling out from tract homes in cookie-cutter subdivisions. This see-no-evil pattern of behavior paid little heed to two factors: the rapid increase in the West's urban population and a changing climate. More than eighteen million people had moved into the West between 1960 and 1990, a flood that has yet to abate, and most have found shelter in its swelling mega-cities and fast-growing midlevel towns. Their numbers have intensified the demand for water at the same time that a warming climate has generated less precipitation; although the West has had long experience with drought, until the 1980s the dry years were manageable in part because of a smaller human imprint. That is no longer true: the environmental dilemmas, social pressures, and political debates about water have escalated as more and more people have relocated to this land of little rain. Never has the West's future seemed so insecure.

Tracking these critical tensions in the physical and cultural landscape has been the mission of *High Country News* since its inception. Founded in the early 1970s in response to the intensifying changes then buffeting the region, from overgrazing and clearcutting, strip mining and slant drilling, to escalating recreational use of national forests and parks, it has made sense of this welter of forces that are demographic, environmental, and social in their origin and implication. Its goal has been to speak to and for "People who care about the West," and it has demonstrated its commitment to the region by developing into the single most important forum for environmental journalism in the United States. That's one reason why it has been showered with awards for its in-depth analyses, why its reporters have scooped up prizes, why its readers and subscribers are so fervent in their support of the independent bi-weekly published in tiny Paomia, Colorado. These signature achievements are especially striking amidst the demise of the fourth estate in early twenty-first-century America: large city dailies and small-town weeklies have shrunk in size, journalists have become an endangered species, and coverage has been homogenized, pabulum for the people.

There is nothing bland about *High Country News*, as is evident in its rigorous assessment of the manifold trials facing its home ground, portions of which are republished in *Water in the 21st-Century West*. No issue, after all, has occupied a greater share of its coverage over the past four decades than water, no surprise give how essential that liquid is to all life. Yet as it has pursued its flow through ecosystems, natural and human, and tallied up the costs and benefits that have come in the wake of our ability to dam up, siphon off, consume, and recycle white gold, *High Country News* has made it abundantly clear why the contemporary West is in such a perilous state.

Our peril seems to be intensifying, to judge from gyroscopic weather patterns and the heightened attention they have begun to receive in the media and legislative assemblies. That is reason enough to open this volume with a segment devoted to *High Country News'* coverage of climate change, a subject that it has tackled with its typical flair for turning the planetary local. In January 2006, citizens of Aspen, Colorado, "a genteel company town ... that ... owes its life to the climate," met to discuss how even a small rise in local temperatures entailed a decrease in snow and thus ski conditions; tourism, the economic driver throughout the Rockies, would surely suffer. Downstream worries have been no less intense: calculating spring runoff is a key measure of reservoir levels and of the capacity of cities and farms to water themselves. But a significant decline in snowpack makes a mess of governmental initiatives to build more dams: if the West becomes drier, what will fill them up? That law of diminishing returns underscores a different dilemma confronting scientists studying Pacific Coast marine life: as nutrient-rich ocean currents, responding to changes in temperature, swing away from traditional nesting grounds such as the Farallon Islands off San Francisco, auklets and other species suffer unprecedented die-offs; should biologists refrain from intervening, letting nature take its course? Does global warming, in short, call into question the preservationist ethos of modern environmentalism?

Those queries beg another: "what outcomes we are willing to accept?" To this there is no easy answer, and the question haunts many of the essays in this collection. That is especially true in *High Country News'* reports on dams. These big-ticket items have been key components in the creation of cheap water and low-cost hydropower that have driven the West's astonishing growth since the 1940s. Yet as they backed up water on the Snake and Columbia, Elwha, Klamath, and Colorado, the Missouri and Rio Grande, turning these and other watersheds into organic machines, dams also provoked an endless stream of lawsuits. Controversy swirled around their environmental impact—salmon proved an especially effective marker species; its migratory flow between river and ocean, and back again, has been badly disrupted by these massive structures. Endangered too have been the lives of those whose lifecycles pulse to the salmon's rhythmic movement: native peoples throughout the West have fought in the judicial system and court of public opinion to unleash these penned-up waterways. The pressure to decommission dams built up across the 1990s, forever bracketed by concerns that tearing dams down would undercut the building blocks of regional prosperity. Still, the drive to restore salmons runs—made all the more compelling due to the 2008 crash in the numbers of adults heading upstream—has made some headway, often on less-significant streams and tributaries. Even so, doubters remain as to the virtue of the project; breaking though their resistance, said Dick Goin, a longtime proponent of freeing the Elwha, is like "explaining a sunrise to a blind man."

Requiring just as radical a shift in perception is the newfound power that Native Americans are wielding in western water politics. After more than a century of abuse in which, through treaty, thievery, and threat, reform and reclamation, the region's indigenous peoples were stripped of their connections to the rivers that sustained their lives and livelihoods, the tide has shifted. Making use of Supreme Court decisions such as *Winters v. U. S.* (1908), and such federal legislation as the Wild and

Scenic Rivers Act (1968), Clean Water Acts of the 1970s, and Endangered Species Act (1973), as well as long-ignored nineteenth-century treaties, the Yakama, Pima, and Maricopa, the Navaho and Nez Perce, have secured fundamental concessions to remove dams, harvest more salmon, or gain a larger share of irrigable water. Some of these victories have been substantial, others Pyrrhic: for every salmon run resurrected there have been mirage-like claims to all the Colorado's flow; if in exchange for a billion-dollar salmon project, Columbia basin tribes settle out of court, their former environmentalist allies charge them with selling out. With that allegation's sting comes an acknowledgement of clout gained, authority achieved. Once the most-disadvantaged people in the West, Native Americans have become regional power brokers, a transformation of inestimable significance.

No triumph is ever unalloyed. Whoever determines the flow and distribution of water, for instance, sets up a charged political landscape, with winners and losers jostling for position. Every new acre-foot of water that one user secures comes at another's expense. Weighing these costs becomes exponentially more complicated when set within the larger hydrological system. Does pumping groundwater in Flagstaff adversely impact a string of high-desert springs some seventy miles away, damaging the life chances of the oft-rare biota that these small oases nourish? What rights does a rural county have to a voluminous aquifer beneath it, when a fast-growing, nearby city—call it Las Vegas—decides that it can better utilize the underground reservoir? If western law, which is predicated on "first in time, first in right," with first in time depending on who initiated the "beneficial use" of water, then a poor place like Lincoln County, Nevada, which lacks the capital to mine its waters, may not have as strong a legal claim as a financially flush metropolis. And what happens when regional supplies get tight, a specter that haunts alike builders and developers, agribusiness and urban water managers? What to do when finally hydrologists are able to convince once-skeptical state courts and agencies that there is a direct connection between ground- and surface-water? By 2005, Idaho had used relevant scientific data to craft innovative legislation that enabled it to buy out farmers' water rights, boosting the Snake River's flow to support salmon migration. Other conservation reforms designed to make a state more water wise include the holy grail of water-management schemes, desalinization, although its energy costs and salt-residue disposal problems diminish its economic viability. Much more cost effective is grey water, created from recycled and/or treated effluent, a process that many towns and cities have started implementing for outdoor landscaping. Going one step farther is arid Cloudcroft, New Mexico, sited high in the Sacramento Mountains: it has developed a system to purify wastewater to meet federal drinking-water standards. Even under drought conditions, that may be a tough sell, an acquired taste.

But given how toxic some of the West's water has become, the implementation of intense purification procedures may become standard fare. Developing an equally intense political response to this blooming toxicity is as critical in the West, long a dumping ground for its own and others' wastes. Its lengthy mining history has proved a double whammy: mine tailings have poisoned any number of wells and aquifers and abandoned shafts have become attractive sinkholes into which to dump contaminated soil, nuclear wastes, and fifty-gallon drums of chemicals. Then there was the massive investment of federal dollars in the region during World War Two, producing a host of manufacturing plants, factories, military bases. Although these brought high-paying jobs and a rapid influx of people, with these social goods came costs that the neighborhoods surrounding these facilities have absorbed. Plumes of ammonium perchlorate have been discovered in western groundwater, streams, and rivers; mercury saturates the Great Salt Lake and swirls up with forest-fire smoke; and medical researchers have been tracking upticks in associated cancers and other health problems. Local battles over remediation, often led by people of color, the poor, and disadvantaged have erupted in Colorado and Nevada, California and Utah, struggles that have captured national attention, accelerating demands for greater environmental justice and social equity.

These contests, so reminiscent of the protracted fight across much of the twentieth century between residents of Owens Valley and Los Angeles over control of the eastern California watershed, is a stark reminder that political power and economic clout often are centered far from key battlefields. That distance, like imbalances in influence and wealth, can make it difficult to combat underground pollution or underhanded water grabs. In this context, street-level protests can rally communities but not necessarily affect outcomes. Lawsuits can level the playing field to a degree, especially in the wake of federal legislation regulating water quantity and quality, endangered species, wilderness preservation, and habitat restoration, among other environmental initiatives. It was a combination of these factors that compelled Los Angeles, for example, to reduce its take of Mono Lake's waters so that its level will rise enough to protect California Gull nesting colonies and damp down dust storms swirling out of the dried-out lakebed.

What LA giveth, it can take away: or try to. Its imperial reach is exemplified in the aqueducts and pipelines that its water purveyor, the Metropolitan Water District, controls; these stretch out several hundred miles to the east to the Colorado River and snake even farther north through the San Joaquin Valley to tap the Sacramento River Delta. But nature can trump human claims: oscillating amounts of snow and rain in the Sierra mountains has complicated the delivery capacity of the massive Clinton-era CALFED water project designed to meet water demands north and south; and have sparked federal-court rulings that more water must remain in the Central California river systems to maintain the endangered Delta smelt. Southern California's allocation of this stream flow has been cut sharply, and as of 2008 the region has been forced for the first time to enact stringent conservation measures.

Can fast-sprawling Las Vegas, with its improbable desert location, be far behind? Patricia Mulroy, the director of the Southern Nevada Water Authority, has proved a deft player in western water politics. She restructured the agency, extended its powers across the booming Las Vegas valley, and focused on sopping up water rights and storing surplus water in regional aquifers, not building dam infrastructure. It helps to have money, buckets of it courtesy of the gaming industry, but the odds that this most-arid city can buy its way out of drought while maintaining

(handwritten margin note: Major differences between first and last par) its current growth pattern are long indeed. That same pressure troubles Denver and Salt Lake City. As millions have poured into these Sunbelt metroplexs, their demand for all things water has exploded. Denver for one banked on its ability to bore through the Rocky Mountains to transfer water out of the Colorado's northern tributaries, a gamble that worked until a federal judge ruled otherwise. Suburbanized Salt Lake's unquenchable thirst for the Wasatch Mountains' water has been contested as well and on two counts—upstream wildlife needs and reduced downstream flow into the shrinking Great Salt Lake.

Whatever the lake's size, this salty expanse, which Terry Tempest Williams has dubbed the "liquid lie of the west," and the surrounding swell of its human population, points to a larger issue facing the entire region: how to calculate sustainable levels of economic growth and human habitation in a region of finite—some might say shrinking—water supplies? And even if calculable, how to regulate the inflow of people and the movement of water to them? No place on earth has yet to figure that out; no place on earth needs to do so more than the American West.

Climate of Change

ꙮ

Save our Snow

Michelle Nijhuis

On an evening in early January, the back streets of Aspen are slathered with ice; not slush, not snow, but a beefy layer of solid ice. It's slick stuff, but Aspenites are thankful for what it represents. Without a reliably cold winter, this storied ski resort would have no champagne powder, no steep-and-deep expert runs, and no reason for tourists to fill its plentiful hotel rooms, restaurants, and theatres from Thanksgiving through March. Aspen, in short, is a genteel company town, and that company owes its life to the climate.

So it's no real surprise that on this frigid night, local citizens are packing into a well-appointed auditorium on the edge of town, doffing their down jackets and settling in for the evening. They've come to hear what global climate change means for them, and for their collective economic future.

This is no lightweight lecture. Gerald Meehl, a lanky scientist from the National Center for Atmospheric Research in Boulder, Colo., has spent most of his career testing and refining computer models of future climate. Though global climate models are fiercely complex, they've long yielded only very coarse forecasts, treating the Rocky Mountains, for instance, as a vague hump in the middle of the continent. In recent years, climate scientists have produced much clearer snapshots of the future, and Meehl describes some of these views for the citizens of Aspen.

Aspen's wintertime average temperatures, he says, are projected—according to conservative estimates—to rise a little less than 1 degree Fahrenheit in the next twenty years. That might not sound like much, but it is equivalent to the warming that Aspen experienced over the last half-century, when the typical number of frost-free days in town increased by about a month.

In the dark auditorium, the intake of breath is audible.

By mid-century, Meehl adds, the predicted rise in local average temperatures hovers between 2.7 and 3.6 degrees Fahrenheit.

At a community meeting the next morning, a team of researchers supplies more details. Mark Williams, a snow scientist from the University of Colorado, translates the previous evening's grim predictions into the local argot: skiing conditions. Aspen, whose main street sits about 7,900 feet above sea level, has an advantage over lower-lying ski towns, he says, because typical wintertime temperatures on its mountains are far below freezing. "We have a technical term for this," he says. "It's butt-cold." If average temperatures do rise as projected over the next century, he says, there will be far fewer frosty days in town, but his preliminary results show that all except the lowest slopes of the Aspen ski areas will remain skiable.

This forecast, other researchers at the meeting report, makes some ski-area managers heave a sigh of relief. They might have to make more snow, shave a few days off the ski season, or even pack skiers into the gondola to carry them over the bare slopes near the bottom of the mountain. But with money and luck, Aspen ski areas will be open for Christmas in 2100.

Yet many listeners aren't reassured by this apparent good news: Isn't there an increased likelihood of extreme drought years? Where will the water come from for extra snowmaking? What if floods, storms, or disease disrupt the global economy, and tourism in Aspen slows to a trickle? What if, as lower-elevation ski areas near the coast lose their snow, fewer people learn to ski, and the sport itself becomes obsolete?

It's a messy discussion. There are countless subtleties and caveats, and few straightforward answers. But this conversation, by its very existence, is modestly astounding. There's no discussion here of whether global warming is "real," and caused in large part by human activities; the scientists, and their small knot of listeners, obviously accept both conclusions. The morning's most pressing question—and it's a big one—is how this small town can possibly change its forecast.

On Thanksgiving weekend of 2004, during a long drive to Salt Lake City, Aspen city attorney John Worcester tuned in to the Rush Limbaugh

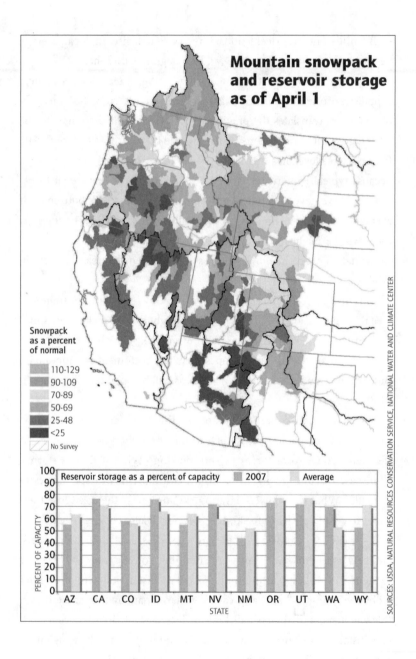

Mountain snowpack and reservoir storage as of April 1

Snowpack as a percent of normal

110-129
90-109
70-89
50-69
25-48
<25
No Survey

Reservoir storage as a percent of capacity   2007   Average

PERCENT OF CAPACITY

AZ   CA   CO   ID   MT   NV   NM   OR   UT   WA   WY

STATE

SOURCES: USDA, NATURAL RESOURCES CONSERVATION SERVICE, NATIONAL WATER AND CLIMATE CENTER

show. Limbaugh, as it happened, was discoursing on the lack of evidence for global warming. "Like a lot of people who tend to disagree with him, I took it on faith that he was full of crap," says Worcester. "But then I realized that I really didn't know much about global warming myself."

Worcester, who trained as a chemical engineer before becoming a lawyer, decided to give himself another education. "I wanted to be able to take an honest position on the issue," he says. When he returned home, he downloaded a copy of the latest Intergovernmental Panel on Climate Change report—widely considered the most authoritative scientific source on climate change—and read the scientists' summaries of their findings.

He learned that, over the twentieth century, the globe's average surface temperature increased by more than 1 degree Fahrenheit, a rate of warming greater than in any other century for the last one thousand years. The 1990s were the warmest decade of the entire millennium in the Northern Hemisphere, and the early 2000s have continued to break various temperature records. "There is new and stronger evidence that most of the warming observed over the last fifty years is attributable to human activities," the IPCC reported. The panel also predicted that global average temperatures will rise anywhere from 2.5 to 10.4 degrees Fahrenheit between 1990 and 2100—a rate of warming very likely without precedent in the last ten thousand years.

Such numbers convinced Worcester, as they have many others, that global warming deserves serious attention. Yet Worcester didn't call his senator, or visit his representative's local office, or put on a suit and tie and storm Capitol Hill. Instead, he stayed home.

Worcester surmised that his town probably had more to worry about than many other places in the country. Temperatures in snow-covered areas are expected to rise more quickly than those in lower-lying places, and Aspen's climate and snow-dependent economy make the community particularly vulnerable to change. Though federal attempts to deal with global warming were bogged down in partisan politics, Worcester became convinced that progress could, and should, be made on the local level. "The more reading I did," he says, "the more it dawned on me that the city of Aspen really ought to be addressing the problem."

Worcester enlisted the assistance of John Katzenberger, who, as the director of the nonprofit Aspen Global Change Institute, convenes international meetings of climate experts in Aspen each summer. Worcester and Katzenberger devised a city program called the Canary Initiative, named for the proverbial canary in the coal mine. It included a $120,000 scientific assessment of the particular impacts of global warming on the city, a $20,000 inventory of the greenhouse-gas emissions produced by Aspen as a whole, and a full-time staffer to help the town and its citizens reduce their contribution to global warming. When Worcester took the idea to the city council, it wasn't a hard sell. "The council understood immediately that this is a global problem," he says, "but that we have the inclination, and the resources, to do something about it."

With the Canary Initiative, Aspen joined a growing roster of communities grappling with global warming on the local level. Before it began its search for solutions, though, Aspen had to understand its own role in changing the climate—and that required an unsettling look in the mirror.

"Because of the kind of community we are—for the most part, we have very clean air, clean water, and everything looks wonderful—we could have gone on forever saying, 'We're fine,'" says Mayor Helen Klanderud. "Well, maybe we're not as environmentally fit as we should be."

Thirteen years ago, Portland, Oregon, became the first city in the country to adopt a strategy to reduce its carbon dioxide emissions. Last summer, the city and its surrounding county attracted national attention by shrinking their overall annual emissions almost to 1990 levels. City- and countywide emissions have now declined for four consecutive years. By 2010, they expect their emissions to be 10 percent lower than they were in 1990, exceeding the demands of the international Kyoto Protocol agreement, which the United States has refused to join.

The reductions, Portland officials say, have been surprisingly painless. Some, like those that resulted from energy-efficiency measures, immediately saved money for local governments and residents. Others, like those that accompanied light-rail construction or land-use planning programs, were side benefits of already popular efforts. "We believe all actions to date have been low to no cost," says Michael Armstrong, conservation program manager for the city's Office of Sustainable Development.

During the national debate over the Kyoto Protocol in the late 1990s, the Energy Information Administration estimated that compliance with initial protocol targets would cost the nation as much as $437 billion. Portland's results suggested a very different, and much more pleasant, future.

Following in Portland's footsteps, towns and cities throughout the West—and around the country—have adopted similar emissions-reduction programs. Most of these communities are part of a program called Cities for Climate Protection (CCP), an effort of an international association of local governments with the unflattering name of ICLEI (which stands for the International Council for Local Environmental Initiatives, and is pronounced "ick-lee").

Usually, one enthusiastic city leader or employee, such as Aspen city attorney John Worcester, convinces his or her town to tackle the issue. CCP members follow a well-established template: First, they assess the sources of their emissions. Then they set their own reduction goals, make a plan, and, with the assistance of software and guidance from ICLEI, begin the complex business of shrinking their emissions.

As in Portland, local emissions reductions usually come in modest, pragmatic packages. Efficient LED bulbs replace conventional traffic signals; a few gasoline-electric hybrids join the city fleet; the city council votes to purchase wind power for municipal operations; a handful of [*things that can be done*] families receive public funding to get new insulation or doorjambs. Some cities purchase carbon "credits" by donating to organizations such as the nonprofit Climate Trust, which in turn uses the donations to fund emissions-reduction efforts or to plant and preserve trees, which absorb carbon dioxide. These actions are far from dramatic, but their impacts, when multiplied over several years and hundreds of cities, do add up. Plus, their appeal is so broad as to make them almost apolitical: no one has ever lost an election because she fought for better household insulation, or knocked $100,000 off the city's annual electric bill with a new set of traffic signals.

On the national stage, global warming remains one of the bitterest, most polarizing political issues of our time. But on the local level, the debate loses its hysterical edge, and the whole issue starts to seem refreshingly—well, refreshingly boring. And there, in those long, dull columns of carbon dioxide equivalents and kilowatts and dollars saved, lies this nascent movement's political strength.

Since the CCP program began in 1993, it has grown to 166 member cities in the United States, and more than seven hundred cities worldwide. In the United States alone, its members' annual reductions in emissions are now equivalent to about twenty-three million tons of carbon dioxide, a load roughly equal to the entire annual greenhouse gas production of the Philippines. ICLEI estimates that these efforts also net more than $535 million in yearly savings. "There's not one city we've worked with that has not seen some level of cost savings," says Michelle Wyman, the executive director of ICLEI's U.S. office. "It's guaranteed."

The list of member cities in the West includes many progressive strongholds—Portland, Seattle, Berkeley, Boulder, and Aspen, among others—where the majority of citizens are already aware of, and worried about, the effects of global warming. But the program also appeals to more conservative sensibilities.

Ray Martinez, the former mayor of the Colorado university town of Fort Collins, is a former sergeant in the city police force and a longtime Republican. When a citizen advisory group first proposed that Fort Collins join the Cities for Climate Protection in the late 1990s, he was skeptical. "I knew that much of the science was still being debated," he says. "But I realized that it doesn't really matter what climate change might mean one hundred years from now—what matters are things like whether your kid has respiratory problems from the particles in the air. What matters is creating clean air today."

The bulk of Fort Collins's greenhouse-gas emissions—about 47 percent—come from electricity generation, with transportation a close second. Emissions are still on the rise, partly because of the city's population growth, but through its participation in CCP, Fort Collins kept an estimated 241,000 tons of carbon dioxide—equal to 9 percent of its total output—out of the atmosphere in 2004, according to its most recent report. Purchases of renewable energy, promotion of recycling programs, and the installation of an additional methane gas collector at its wastewater treatment plant all contributed to the savings. With the help of grant funding, Fort Collins also runs a program to encourage energy efficiency in businesses and institutions, ranging from the local Ben and Jerry's franchise to Colorado State University. The local public school district recently invested in natural lighting, solar panels, and other energy-saving features for a new high school building, making it one of the most efficient high schools in the country.

"Some mayors, in some cities, still see [emissions reduction] as a political disaster, as something that takes an environmental, liberal view," says Martinez, who stepped down because of term limits last spring. "But I say, just look at the money it saves. Isn't that part of the Republican platform, to save taxpayer dollars?"

The Cities for Climate Protection program isn't without its problems and risks. It's entirely voluntary, and commitment to it varies. Tracking emissions and reductions, even with the help of groups like ICLEI, requires time, money, and attention, and the universe of options for action can, at times, seem overwhelmingly large. And while cost savings and emissions reductions come easily at first, they can soon begin to require more up-front investment and political chutzpah. "You can't do it all by just changing light bulbs," says ICLEI outreach officer Susan Ode. "You have to do things that seem more dramatic. Going to the next level does require some kind of courage."

It can also require patience. Some measures, such as the purchase of renewable energy, may need the approval of only a handful of city leaders. Others, such as changing commuter habits or shrinking household energy use, require sustained public education campaigns, and a much more significant commitment by the citizenry.

But supporters say such campaigns also help turn a global issue into a local one. "They begin informing people," says Randy Udall, a regional energy expert and the director of the nonprofit Community Office for Resource Efficiency in Aspen. "People will say, 'Jesus, you mean that when I drive my car, I'm putting a pound of this stuff out every mile, and some of it will be there a century from now? Wow.' "

For some Western leaders, evangelism within their own city limits isn't enough. In 2002, just before the Olympic Winter Games opened in Salt Lake City, Mayor Rocky Anderson promised that the city government's greenhouse-gas emissions would drop to 7 percent below 1990 levels by 2012—the goals that would have been set for the United States had it signed the Kyoto Protocol. City operations are already more than three-quarters of the way to their goal, thanks to the use of methane emissions from its city landfill and wastewater-treatment plant for electricity generation, the purchase of wind power, and other measures. The city is now signing up local businesses for an energy-efficiency program, and will soon expand its efforts to individual residents, aiming to extend the government's accomplishments to Salt Lake as a whole.

In February of last year, on the day the Kyoto Protocol became law for the 141 countries that signed it, Seattle Mayor Greg Nickels, Democrat, upped the ante. The Pacific Northwest was in the midst of one of the driest winter months on record, and Seattle's water and hydropower supplies were threatened. Climate change, Nickels remembers, "suddenly went from being an issue that was somewhere else, a long time from now, to one that's here and now."

Not only would his entire city meet Kyoto targets, he said, but it would also challenge other cities and towns throughout the country to do the same. He announced the "U.S. Mayors' Climate Protection Agreement," and said he wanted 141 mayors to sign up before the meeting of the U.S. Conference of Mayors the following June.

He got what he wanted, and more: as of February 17 of this year, 205 mayors had signed the agreement, each pledging to "strive to meet or exceed Kyoto Protocol targets" in their city operations and communities. The liberal West Coast and the Northeast boasted the heaviest participation, but the list also includes the mayors of Norman, Oklahoma; Bellevue, Nebraska; Billings, Montana; Laredo, Texas, and many other more conservative burgs.

Seattle is making good on its promises at home. Its city-owned utility, Seattle City Light, announced late last year that it had reduced its net greenhouse-gas emissions to zero, thanks in part to its purchase of wind power and divestment from coal. The utility's reductions, combined with various energy-efficiency measures, have helped overall city operations cut their greenhouse gas production to more than 60 percent below 1990 levels. To help chart a path toward Kyoto targets for the city as a whole, Nickels appointed an eighteen-member commission of local business, nonprofit, and government leaders; their recommendations are due to the mayor this month.

For the most part, these local efforts operate independently from the increasing number of statewide emissions-control plans and policies. But both Seattle and Salt Lake City have made some inroads into state politics. Nickels actively supported Washington's Clean Car Act, passed last spring, which adopts California's standards for greenhouse-gas emissions from new vehicles. This past December, news of Salt Lake City's accomplishments and cost savings encouraged Governor Brian Schweitzer of Montana, Democrat, to call for the creation of a climate-change advisory group in his state.

The influence of local efforts may reach even further: cities such as Seattle, Salt Lake, and Portland, with their demonstrable results, could help break the national political impasse on climate change, leading to a more coherent approach to reducing emissions. "Ultimately, what we want to do is shape national policy," says Nickels. "We want to see the federal government step up and rejoin the community of nations."

Nickels says he hasn't spoken with President Bush or anyone in the White House about his campaign, but he recently received an award from the federal Environmental Protection Agency for climate protection, an honor he says is a bit ironic. "I'm kind of tempted to go to the ceremony and say 'You know, if you guys were doing your job, if the federal government were doing its job, there would be no place for leadership from me,'" he says. "But I may not do that."

This past December, at the United Nations Climate Change Conference in Montreal, ICLEI organized a parallel event for mayors, city staffers, and activists. More than three hundred people attended, including both Nickels and Pam O'Connor, the mayor of Santa Monica, California, an early supporter of Nickels' effort. The Canadian newspaper *The Globe and Mail* gushed over Nickels, calling him a "national folk hero" with "the quintessentially American way of coming up with the right idea at the right time."

The municipal leaders issued a declaration committing their cities to an ambitious set of long-term emissions-reduction targets: 30 percent below 1990 levels by 2020, and 80 percent by 2050. On Dec. 8, just before the end of the U.N. conference, the city of Montreal hosted an address by former U.S. President Clinton, who applauded the mayors and their nuts-and-bolts approach. "My plea is that ... we do what we would do if we were all mayors," Clinton said. "If you can't agree on a[n international] target, agree on a set of projects so everybody has something to do when they get up in the morning."

The U.S. delegation to the Montreal conference, meanwhile, stuck to its opposition to mandatory targets for greenhouse-gas reductions. The chief U.S. negotiator at the conference even walked out of an informal discussion on emissions reductions. The best the delegation could muster was to agree to nonbinding talks about international action on climate change beyond the year 2012, when Kyoto expires.

K. C. Golden, a former special assistant to the mayor of Seattle who attended the conference, says the mayors' efforts helped buoy the spirits of the international community. "People throughout the world have been very down at the mouth about continuing the [Kyoto] process while the United States—the world's largest emitter of greenhouse gases—sits on the sidelines," says Golden, now the policy director for the nonprofit group Climate Solutions. "But in Montreal, state and local leaders were able to say, 'It's worth the effort—we'll meet you down the road once we get past this impasse at the national level.' I think they've been instrumental in creating enough confidence on the international level for the process to continue."

Last month, on Valentine's Day, the Aspen Canary Initiative presented its citywide emissions inventory to the town council. The next evening, the city's global-warming project manager, Dan Richardson, delivered the results to the public.

The good news, Richardson reported to a handful of listeners—on the other side of town, bestselling novelist Ann Patchett was speaking to a sellout crowd—is that Aspen's greenhouse-gas pollution isn't nearly as bad as it could be. Over the past several years, the city has made major investments in renewable energy, public transportation, and recycling, and implemented stringent, energy-efficient building codes; in the process, it has already kept a substantial dose of greenhouse gases out of the atmosphere.

As part of the Canary Initiative, the Aspen city government has made a legally binding commitment to reduce its operations' emissions by 1 percent each year, and it now offers bonuses to employees of city departments that meet their reduction goals. Mayor Klanderud's signature on the U.S. Mayors' Climate Protection Agreement made a nonbinding but citywide commitment to Kyoto targets. Over the next several months, town officials and residents will help develop a so-called Canary Action Plan, also likely to include specific—and perhaps more ambitious—reduction targets.

But the inventory contained bad news, too. It showed that, despite its progressive measures, Aspen's per-capita emissions in 2004 were almost twice the national average. The town's commercial and private air traffic, which accounts for a whopping 41 percent of the total emissions, topped the list of contributors. Second was ground transportation, producing about 25 percent of emissions; the majority came from vehicles traveling to and from Aspen on crowded Highway 82, the main artery for Aspen's service workers, many of whom live in more affordable communities down the valley.

Most cities don't include air travel in their emissions inventories, so Aspen's was unusually thorough. But even when the analysis removed air travel and commuter and tourist driving, Aspen's per-capita emissions remained well ahead of the average U.S. citizen's. "I've seen the enemy, and it is me," Richardson told his listeners.

To compensate for its airport emissions, Aspen could pay for the capture of methane, a powerful greenhouse gas, from nearby coal mines, or support other climate-friendly projects in surrounding towns. The Aspen Skiing Company may soon encourage its visitors to buy "Green Tags," which—for the price of about $20 per 1,000 miles of flying—fund various emissions-reductions projects. Yet offsets, no matter how numerous, won't change the fact that Aspen is an isolated ski town without enough affordable housing for its workers; a lot of people burn a lot of fuel flying and driving to it.

So Aspen, and many other towns, are likely to face dilemmas in coming decades. The scale of these dilemmas could be monumental—especially considering that even the goals set out by the Kyoto Protocol are not enough to stop current warming trends, according to most scientists. Restoring climate stability will require much more dramatic reductions, probably similar to those the mayors called for in Montreal: 30 percent below 1990 levels by 2020, and 80 percent by 2050. Getting there will surely require a lot of conservation and innovation, and not a little risk.

"It's not just resort economies that will have to change," says Auden Schendler, director of environmental affairs for the Aspen Skiing Company. "We, as a society, are going to have to change how everything operates. We're going to have to address some of the stickiest issues."

The challenges are great. But so are the rewards. In the midst of one of the global-warming meetings in Aspen, University of Colorado snow scientist Mark Williams points out two curves on a graph. One is the projected snow cover at the base of Aspen's mountains in 2100, assuming the world does little to change its ways. The second, far above, represents skiing conditions in a time of stringent international greenhouse-gas limits. Fewer emissions equal more snow, and better skiing: in Aspen, at least, this is an equation everyone can understand.

March 6, 2006

Michelle Nijhuis is contributing editor to *High Country News*.

Into Thin Air?

Matt Jenkins

The dream of the infinitely expanding West is getting beaten over the head with an empty bucket. Flows in the Colorado River, which is now entering its eighth straight year of drought, will be less than half of average this year. In the Sierra Nevada, snowpack is just 46 percent of normal. And those numbers are likely to get even worse in the future, as droughts are amplified by global warming.

Now, water managers in the region are contemplating how to react, and new dams have been pitched as one possible response. In California, Governor Arnold Schwarzenegger, Republican, announced on Jan. 9 that "with California's booming population, and with the impact that global warming will cause to our snowpacks, we need more infrastructure." Just two days later, California state Senator Dave Cogdill, Republican, picked up the battle standard and introduced a bill to raise $4 billion in bond money for two new dams, saying, "We have to act now."

Indeed, global warming is already changing the West's waterscape. Average temperatures in the region have increased by about 2 degrees Fahrenheit since the 1970s. A greater portion of each year's precipitation is falling as rain rather than snow, and snowpack—which serves as a natural, slow-release reservoir—is melting earlier than it used to; both changes are intensifying the pulse of winter and spring runoff.

Cogdill, who represents parts of the largely agricultural San Joaquin Valley, says that the continued loss of snowpack and the intensified bursts of seasonal runoff could exceed the storage capacity of California's existing dams. "If you don't do something about our ability to manage that water," he says, "more and more of it will run into the ocean, and late in the year we'll be in a real deficit."

New dams can catch excess bursts of water when they come out of the mountains, then spread those flows throughout the year. But it is becoming clearer that, for the West as a whole, more dams may not stem future water crises. New climate projections are hinting that, in the future, the region won't just be warmer. It will also be drier.

Any effort to build more dams will be shadowed by the curse of diminishing returns. For one thing, there simply aren't many places left to put a dam, either in California or in the West as a whole. One of the two proposed California dams would be built at Temperance Flat, in the Sierra foothills near Fresno, to catch floodwater in the San Joaquin River. Yet possible dam sites are so limited that the dam would have to be built in an existing reservoir called Millerton Lake. The second, Sites Reservoir, would be built in the hills on the western edge of the Sacramento Valley, and would hold water from the Sacramento River.

A very big question lurks behind the new-reservoir endeavor: while the dams are being pitched as part of a strategy to increase the reliability of California's water supply, the reliability of the river flows needed to fill the new reservoirs is far from clear. In the case of Temperance Flat, for example, flow data from the past fifty-seven years indicate that a dam could catch a considerable amount of water.

But past performance is no guarantee of future results. What will happen to river flows depends, in large part, on how much precipitation falls in a warming world. Michael Dettinger, a U.S. Geological Survey researcher at the Scripps Institute of Oceanography, has helped lead the way in assembling large "ensembles" that provide a composite view of various climate projections. Earlier projections, released about seven years ago, indicated that total precipitation in the West might actually increase with global warming. "Back then, the [climate-simulation model] that got most of the focus made the West just incredibly wet: it doubled the amount of precipitation, and more in some places," Dettinger says. Now, "a lot of people think that was virtually a computer bug."

In the years since, an increasing number of scientists have focused their efforts on climate change, largely in support of the most recent Intergovernmental Panel on Climate Change assessment, released this spring. "It's still unsettled," says Dettinger, "but as people have tinkered with their models and made the models better, there's been a general drift to it getting drier" in California, and in the Colorado River Basin.

There is still considerable uncertainty in climate and water projections, and the Colorado River serves as an outsized example of the challenges facing researchers and water managers. Denver Water supplies 1.2 million people and gets about half of its water from the Colorado River. "The question is, does Denver have to recalculate what the firm annual yield of our water rights is because of global warming?" says Chips Barry, Denver Water's manager. "And the answer is, maybe. How do you do that? The answer is, I haven't got the foggiest idea, because you can assume things all over the map."

Climate scientists are working to puzzle out the reasons behind the sometimes-contradictory projections generated by what they call "dueling models." Temperatures are incontrovertibly rising. Less clear is how temperature will affect precipitation, how evaporation will affect runoff, and how both factors will affect the total volume of river water that can, in turn, be stored behind dams. And on the Colorado River, where future projections are especially bleak, "the question that's out there," says Dettinger, "is, 'Is that going to be a large reduction in runoff, or a less-large reduction in runoff?' "

Marty Hoerling, a Boulder, Colorado-based meteorologist for the National Oceanic and Atmospheric Administration, has projected that, because rising temperatures and increasing evaporation will reduce runoff, the average annual flow in the Colorado River over the next quarter century may be just ten million acre-feet. That is the same amount of water that was in the Colorado during the four worst years of the current drought. It left existing reservoirs half empty; more alarming, it is a third less than the amount of water that is already being used every year.

A recent paper by Niklas Christensen and Dennis Lettenmaier, at the University of Washington, projects more modest decreases in flow. But the disparities between various projections leave water managers without a good sense of just how bad a scenario to prepare for. "We bring in these climate scenarios and say, 'Gee, you should do this and you should do that,' " says Lettenmaier. "[Water managers] look at it and say, 'Five years ago, there was this scenario, and now there's a different one.' We're all over the map."

In the absence of a more precise view of the future, some municipal water managers are trying to maximize the flexibility in their existing systems. Marc Waage, the water resources director for Denver Water, says the agency is focused on " 'no-regrets' planning, where you take incremental steps that work well in a variety of different future scenarios, even though you don't know which one of those scenarios is going to happen." That strategy aims to create a diverse portfolio that includes existing reservoirs, increased water recycling, and water-efficiency improvements. That, says Waage, "will tend to work well under a number of different scenarios, so it makes sense to continue until we know more."

The Metropolitan Water District of Southern California supplies water to eighteen million people in Los Angeles and San Diego. Roger Patterson, an assistant general manager for the district, says that although Metropolitan hasn't ruled out the possibility of considering new dams, "people are trying to get the most out of the infrastructure we've already put in place." Metropolitan has already been doing that by leasing water from farmers to supplement its own supplies. Farms use about 80 percent of the water in the West, and water transfers, says Patterson, are "a prime mechanism" for helping cities get through droughts. He says that building additional canals, to more tightly link the various water systems in California, could help expand the range of possibilities for transferring water from farms to cities.

But an increased reliance on water transfers puts the squeeze on the region's farmers. And that, more than anything else, may be driving the push for more dams—which could provide an alternative supply for cities and take the heat off farms. The dam bill in California "is really about providing enough [water] so the water currently being used by the AG community is not at further risk of either being severely reduced or eliminated altogether," says Sen. Cogdill. "The costs being projected right now range from $325 to $350 per acre-foot. Given the fact that most of the ag community in this state relies on water that's considerably cheaper than that, you're probably going to be seeing more of this water allocated for urban municipal uses and for environmental benefits."

Cities, however, will be looking closely at cost and—now, more than ever—reliability. Farmers will be increasingly plagued by the fact that they get their water at such low prices. Urban water agencies have been regularly leasing water from farmers for considerably less than $325 an acre-foot, and it will take a lot to convince an urban water manager to buy into a dam whose supplies are both more expensive, and less reliable, than water that can be bought off the farm.

The same pressure is building in Colorado, where the agencies that supply Denver's growing suburbs are increasingly reliant on buying farm water. "The people and water supplies in our district are in the crosshairs," says Eric Wilkinson, the general manager of the Northern Colorado Water Conservancy District, a major irrigation district north of Denver. "Irrigated agriculture within our district is basically the supply of choice for growing municipalities." Last year, the district proposed that Denver's suburbs build a new $4 billion reservoir on the Yampa River, a tributary of the Colorado.

That might buy some breathing room for farmers, but with projections of lowered Colorado River flows in the future, it could be a losing bet for everyone at the table. Eric Kuhn, the general manager of the Colorado River Water Conservation District in Glenwood Springs, Colorado, has closely followed the evolving climate science. "All of the studies [for the Colorado River] point the same direction, which is less water and less flow," he says. "Why would you build more dams when the existing dams don't fill?"

April 30, 2007

Matt Jenkins is a *High Country News* contributing editor.

Unnatural Preservation

M. Martin Smith and Fiona Gow

Armored in a rain slicker and floppy hat against guano-bombing waterfowl, Russ Bradley pokes about for signs of life on a craggy island paradise just off the California shore. One might expect the search to be easy, given the hundreds of thousands of common murres, ashy storm petrels, Brandt's cormorants, Leach's storm petrels, Western gulls, double-crested cormorants, glaucous-winged gulls, black oystercatchers, pigeon guillemots, rhinocerous auklets, tufted puffins, bald eagles, peregrine falcons, and Cassin's auklets that summer on the Farallon Islands, twenty-seven miles off San Francisco in the Pacific Ocean.

During the past three years, however, Bradley has been checking on the breeding sites of the black, burrow-nesting Cassin's auklet, and he's been finding abandoned eggs; dead, black, cue-ball-sized chicks; and skinny, faltering fledglings. "Most of the chicks have died," says Bradley, a research biologist with PRBO Conservation Science, a nonprofit, founded as the Point Reyes Bird Observatory, that has spent the last forty years counting and observing the hundreds of thousands of birds that nest yearly on the Farallons. "This was as complete a failure response as we'd ever seen before. And we'd been following this species for thirty-five years."

The apparent culprit: ocean currents, redirected by rising sea temperature, have swept out of range the millions of tiny krill that the adult birds scoop into their beaks, chew into purple smelly goo, and then spit up for their young. In other words, this unprecedented starvation wave may be a result of global warming.

Bradley is one of the experts who knows most about the auklet die-off. Just the same, he's adamant in his belief that he should not attempt to save any of the dying chicks. To do so, he says, would be considered unnatural and unscientific. "You definitely grimace when you see the guy next door who hasn't done so well and has died at a very young age,"

Bradley says. "We try to maintain ourselves as scientists. But we really feel for the birds."

In the world of natural preservation, it's not just scientists who take Bradley's don't-mess-with-Mother-Nature stance. Since the 1960s, the idea that natural preservation consists mostly of letting nature take its course—absent human-caused environmental disturbance—has been doctrine among public parks bureaucrats, biologists, environmentalists, rangers, and other members of the vast landscape of individuals and organizations involved in preserving America's natural environment. When naturalists have intervened to save species, as in the forty-year struggle to save the bald eagle, their efforts have been driven by the goal of returning life to its wild state, so that a damaged ecosystem can tilt back into balance. For the most part, naturalists have not sought to save nature purely from itself. With global warming, however, this hands-off approach is rapidly becoming quaint and out-of-date.

As the planet grows hotter, and the consensus mounts that the temperature is not turning back down, there may be a lot less meaning in the idea of preserving "naturalness" than has been the case. After all, in the not-too-distant future, the state of nature will in many cases be something nobody's ever seen.

So far, however, public-land managers have responded by doing almost nothing, according to a new report by the U.S. Government Accountability Office, the agency that evaluates federal programs. By and large, the GAO says, officials who manage U.S. public lands have simply ignored a 2001 Department of Interior directive ordering them to identify and protect resources that might be threatened by climate change.

This is no minor failure. An emerging scientific consensus says that unless the National Park Service, the U.S. Forest Service, the U.S. Fish and Wildlife Service, the Bureau of Land Management, the National Oceanic and Atmospheric Administration, state fish and game departments, and private environmental organizations re-direct their missions to deal with climate change, they'll oversee the advance of nationwide environmental catastrophe. The character of public wildlands will be drastically—and permanently—altered.

So professional preservationists, and the environmental movement as a whole, are left with unnatural choices: They can intervene aggressively to maintain habitat threatened by planetary warming—installing sprinkler systems around California's giant sequoias, to name one suggestion floated by scientists. In the process they would become something akin to farmers and pet fanciers.

They can intervene aggressively to provide huge migration paths northward for heat-threatened plants and animals. Because this would require them to help dramatically change existing ecosystems, it would turn the current conservation ethic on its head.

Or they can decide to continue to use the traditional hands-off approach—and thereby allow millennia-old ecosystems to die off and be replaced in ways that would never have happened naturally, if not for global warming.

In January 2001, just as Bill Clinton handed the White House keys to George W. Bush, the Department of the Interior issued a broad order to the Forest Service, the U.S. Fish and Wildlife Service, the Bureau of Land Management, and the other agencies that manage one-third of the nation's surface land as well as numerous marine sanctuaries. The order was at once simple and fiendishly complex: the agencies should "consider and analyze potential climate change effects in their management plans and activities."

It was a reasonable directive. Trees on millions of acres of forests in Glacier National Park have fallen to a beetle infestation apparently linked to climate change. At the Florida Keys National Marine Sanctuary, coral reef bleaching—a phenomenon that, if prolonged, would undermine the area's marine ecosystem—may be connected to warmer sea temperatures. On the 2.6 million acres of U.S. land managed by the BLM in northwestern Arizona, a recently intensified cycle of drought, wildfire, and flooding has caused desert scrub and cactus to be replaced by grasslands.

According to a GAO report released this summer, however, the bureaucracies that manage public land throughout the United States were provided no guidance of any kind on how to deal with climate change, and park and other natural resource managers did not attempt to deal with the problem on their own.

Since 2001, of course, these federal departments have been ultimately directed by George W. Bush, who has famously not concerned himself with climate change. But the GAO report, and interviews with National Park Service scientists and managers around the country, strongly suggest that government stewards of parks, wildlife, and public land simply don't understand the problems they face in an era of climate change. "Resource managers we interviewed ... said that they are not aware of any guidance or requirements to address the effect of climate change, and that they have not received direction regarding how to incorporate climate change into their planning activities," the GAO report said.

The Department of the Interior, which oversees many of the bureaucracies that manage public land, seems unclear on the very concept of addressing the effects, rather than the causes, of climate change. In its official response to the GAO report, the department had an associate deputy secretary rebut the criticism that the agency has "made climate change a low priority" by, essentially, changing the subject. In its response, the Park Service highlighted what it viewed as its successes—none of which were successes in protecting parks, forests, and rangeland from global warming's effects. Instead, the agency's response letter said, "We have made a high priority on developing renewable energy resources; improving energy efficiency and the use of alternative energies at our facilities across the nation."

The officials who manage America's natural resources deserved the GAO's scathing critique. But there are roadblocks beyond bureaucratic intransigence that keep naturalists from effectively grappling with global warming's effects. Though researchers have identified some species, regions, and ecosystems already threatened by global warming, science is mostly ignorant of climate change's impacts; until recently, there was little experimental research in the field. Science doesn't yet have information as basic as how much heat or dryness it takes to kill a tree, or whether foggy coastal and less foggy inland California will become warmer or cooler due to global warming.

Beyond the lack of scientific data is a fundamental philosophical problem: to preserve public wildlife during a time of significant climate change, managers will have to do things that run counter to the current ethic of "natural preservation."

"Conservation and land management agencies like the Park Service are confronted with a collapse of the paradigm they've operated under, which is [that] the future will be more or less like the past, and nature needs to be managed only on the margins, where we correct for the minor injustices humans inflict on the natural environment," says David Graber, chief scientist for the Pacific West region of the National Park Service, whose office is at Sequoia and Kings Canyon National Park. "We're facing a period of dramatic uncertainty. What managing nature would mean is a dramatic unknown. We don't know what our goals would have to be. "We're literally talking about things that have only been talked about for months, rather than years."

Global warming undermines almost all the rules that environmental stewards have lived by.

With a warming planet, invasive species are no longer merely exotic pests that hitch ship passage from other continents. They're native grasses, shrubs, beetles, bacteria, and viruses that have had new "native" habitat opened for them to invade, courtesy of higher average temperatures. The millions of acres of forests that have been recently killed by beetles— which now thrive in the recently warmer northern winters—are but one apparent testament to this emerging phenomenon. "The west side of the park used to have much colder winters, which slowed the beetles. But winters for the past fifteen or so years have not been as cold," notes Judy Visty, natural resource management specialist at Rocky Mountain National Park. "Pine beetles are wreaking havoc."

With planetary warming, forest fires and droughts in the western U.S. have transformed into something more significant than mere components of a historic cycle of life. Scientists now predict that escalating droughts, tree die-offs, and fires could cause western forests to contribute more carbon dioxide to the atmosphere than they extract.

Research into California's giant sequoia indicates that with warmer average temperatures, these monarchs of the forest may slow and then stop producing seedlings. And "if the fog, or if the ocean currents were to change, [the coastal redwood] would be in real trouble," says Ken Lavin, interpretive specialist at Muir Woods National Monument.

Many global warming-induced changes aren't yet as noticeable as forest die-offs, but are notable nonetheless. Mountain lakes disappear along with the glaciers at Montana's Glacier National Park. The pika, a cool-weather-loving mountain rodent, is vanishing from the Sierra Nevada. Rising seawater threatens to salinize the freshwater ecosystems of the Everglades and submerge beach habitat along the Northern California coast. And an increasingly hot and dry climate is projected to kill 90 percent of the trees at Joshua Tree National Monument.

For most people, these events are the canaries in the ecological coal mine, portending the far-off day when climate change may have life-and-death implications for humanity. For conservationists, however, these embattled plants and animals—and all the other species global warming will kill or push to new habitats—*are* the coal mine. Conservationists need to think hard and fast *now*: Do we rush to rescue climate-imperiled species before it's too late? Or do we let nature take its course, quietly watching the disappearance of species that we have spent decades restoring and protecting?

"It may be that soon one-third of the species I'm seeing outside my window might not be able to find habitat here. Maybe half of them will be new species that find the new climate here amenable," says Graber. "Am I going to fight the new species? Am I going to welcome them?"

The questions are agonizing for naturalists such as Graber. For nearly a half-century, preserving native species and fighting invasive ones has been the reason for his existence. That goal is enshrined in the job descriptions of thousands of people running the vast natural-industrial complex made up of parks, preserves, refuges, private nature conservatories, and millions of other acres of protected U.S. wildlands.

The ecological movement wasn't always so sure of itself. There are other possible, sensible-sounding approaches to maintaining nature preserves. New York's Central Park and San Francisco's Golden Gate Park are horticultural fabrications, with scant relationship to the natural world that came before. Locals seem to like them just fine. In fact, the idea of "preserving" nature as a pleasing aesthetic spectacle, as opposed to the restoration and maintenance of authentic ancient ecosystems, drove park management well into the twentieth century.

Then, in 1962, the Secretary of the Interior set up a special advisory board on wildlife management, led by ecologist A. Starker Leopold, that went about researching and discussing exactly what America's parks should be. The board came up with a revolutionary idea, summarized in a pamphlet known universally in the nature bureaucracy as the "Leopold Report." It is best known for five evocative words summarizing what became the American scientific community's consensus on what nature preserves should be: "a vignette of primitive America."

That phrase has evolved to mean that public-land managers should endeavor to preserve plants, animals, and other natural features so they remain within the range that they exhibited before Europeans first arrived in North America. Any meddling that occurs in protected areas, therefore, must be in the service of a perceived previous natural order.

"It instituted in the Park Service in a way a kind of respect for nature that was apart from gardening," Graber says. "Before the Leopold Report, I called it cowboy biology. We made it up as we went along. If Yellowstone wanted more buffalo, they got them."

Under the new regime, it became necessary to prove that such a bison introduction would be "natural."

Notwithstanding some controversies—such as "natural" wolves versus "introduced" ranchers in the Yellowstone area—this approach has met with monumental success. Nearly a century after Congressman William Kent introduced the legislation that created the National Park Service, the 295-acre ravine he donated to create Muir Woods National Monument remains much as it was a millennium ago, filled with redwoods, ferns, and ladybugs.

"We don't move anything unless it falls on someone," notes Muir Woods interpretive specialist Lavin.

Another impressive legacy of the new ethos lies twenty or so miles to the west. At the turn of the century, egg hunters and pelt gatherers had reduced the wildlife-rich Farallons to a relatively barren state. Since they became protected as the Farallon National Wildlife and Wilderness Refuge in 1969, the islands have become the largest seabird colony outside Alaska and Hawaii. Northern fur seals, which once populated the Farallons by the tens of thousands, were hunted to extinction there following the Gold Rush. They, too, have returned in force. A single pup was born on the islands in 1996. Last year, there were one hundred pups.

The starving Cassin's auklets, however, point to a possible future when this let-it-be strategy will no longer produce the desired results.

Strategies that do something effective—that don't just let nature succumb to climate change—are hard to come by.

Two hundred and fifty miles southeast of San Francisco, new studies resulting from decades of research show that giant sequoia saplings are thriving less robustly in the warming central Sierra Nevada. So do officials in Sequoia National Park build sequoia sapling greenhouses? Do they install sprinkler systems around the great sequoia monarchs? Or do they prepare a new habitat farther north, removing other species to make space for sequoia saplings? Should such moves even be contemplated, given the still-fledgling nature of predictive climatology?

And what of the rest of the trees in the West— the ones doomed to die from drought, fire, and beetle infestation?

Scientists studying forest diebacks say one response to the dying might be to thin forests, so that individual trees are hardier and more beetle resistant. It remains to be seen how well this would go over with an environmental movement accustomed to opposing logging. Other controversial ideas include intensive breeding and genetic engineering to create insect-resistant tree species, combined with the aggressive use of herbicides and pesticides.

Wildlife managers have long believed that local plant species should be kept genetically pure. But climate change may ultimately call for a sophisticated type of wildlife gardening, in which heat-loving southern plant species are brought north and encouraged to crossbreed with cold-loving cousins.

Already, a massive die-off of piñon pine trees in the Southwest is being called a "global warming type event." Again, selective logging might be one answer, scientists say: if fewer trees share scarce water, they just might survive in the new climate.

But for plant species that simply can't survive in their old habitat, some scientists are floating the idea of a forced march north.

Animals whose habitat dwindles as the climate changes might just scurry elsewhere, explains Nathan Stephenson, a research ecologist at the Western Ecological Science Center at Sequoia and Kings Canyon National Parks. But trees cannot get up and walk away. "The National Park Service has to decide: are we going to assist species migration?" says Stephenson.

Helping plants and animals migrate north isn't just a matter of leasing fleets of flatbed nursery trucks. Many species under threat aren't easy to dig up and put in a pot. Soil microorganisms, fungi, butterflies, and other small creatures critical to the functioning of ecosystems may also find their traditional homes unlivable. Assisting species migration would mean setting aside broad swaths of wild land to provide an uninterrupted pathway north for entire habitats.

"I've had a number of conversations with land managers, identifying all the land in California that could conceivably be used as refugia, and what would be the appropriate species to go where. The magnitude of the problem is mind-boggling," says Graber, the Park Service scientist. "There is a vocal minority of people in the conservation community who believe that things should unfold on their own. The theory being, we don't know what we're doing, and we're bound to screw things up.

"What we're talking about is an order of intrusion greater than anything we've done in the past."

Already the nonprofit Nature Conservancy is considering buying land and ecological easements to create north-south habitat-migration superhighways. "We need to take into account this vulnerability to large vegetation shifts," says Patrick Gonzalez, a forest ecologist who works with The Nature Conservancy under the title "climate change scientist." "One way in which we're using that data is in the establishing and maintaining of corridors that link areas in the network."

Doing this on any sort of meaningful scale, however, would require making the preservation of American grasses, trees, and rodents an expensive national priority. And it would mean treating habitat-choking urban sprawl as even more of an environmental calamity than is currently recognized.

Putting America on this sort of ecological wartime footing—to prepare for an environmental future that nobody can fully predict—will likely prove a hard sell in Washington. Almost as difficult will be convincing the environmental community to abandon a hard-won national consensus about what it means to preserve the natural world.

The vast bureaucracies that manage public land already have to answer to myriad bickering constituencies. Some of global warming's greatest impacts will appear without warning, as ocean temperatures and currents, extended growing seasons, extinction of microorganisms, or any combination of these factors cause cascading effects, such as the ones that are apparently killing the Farallon Islands auklet chicks. Saving species in such a quickly changing environment may not allow for policy meetings, comment periods, revised management plans, and alternate implementation strategies. It might just mean deciding at a moment's notice to mash up buckets of krill stew and spoon-feed auklet chicks—now and forevermore.

Although there are reams of conclusive science on the "whether" of global warming—it is definitely occurring—there's very little precise information on when, and where, and what will happen next. Before park officials begin loading ferns onto flatbeds or launch the mother of all tree-thinning operations in the Colorado Rockies, they need scientific backing to be sure what they're doing has some hope of preserving life on earth.

Such science is scarce.

Despite the vast swath of death wrought across the West by drought, heat, and bark beetles, science still doesn't know exactly what it takes for nature to kill a tree. At Muir Woods, to note an extreme example of this area of human ignorance, there's no record whatsoever of a mature redwood dying a "natural," non-human-induced death.

And though there's been vast observational research on the effects of global warming, there's not much experiment-derived knowledge about what a warmer planet will do to particular habitats. "I think one of the big challenges of planning is the amount of uncertainty. We don't even know if it's going to get warmer and drier or warmer and wetter, and if you don't even know that, it starts to get really hard," says Stephenson, the USGS forest ecologist. "Often people have talked about desired future conditions. Now, you talk about switching to undesired future conditions. We know we don't want to completely lose our forest; perhaps we don't care if we don't have species abundance. And that does really bring you to a really general approach to try to increase resilience to ecosystems."

But it's hard to talk about making an ecosystem resilient if one doesn't know what it takes to kill it in the first place. Science is just now getting down to the brass tacks of cooking and parching trees to death on purpose, in a recently christened 500-ton welded stainless-steel-and-glass habitat-cooking oven.

The oven used to be known as Biosphere II, an artificial enclosed ecosystem originally intended for space research. The University of Arizona recently agreed to lease this giant terrarium near Phoenix from its owner, a land developer. The university will rededicate Biosphere II for research on how organisms react to climate change.

Finally, scientists can write an accurate recipe for baked dead tree.

"Wow, that [must] sound like a really dopey experiment," says University of Arizona natural resources professor Dave Breshears, who's on the faculty of the Institute for the Study of Planet Earth. "But we don't really have the right kind of quantitative information. We've got a drought, and we've got bark beetle infestations, and have higher densities than before and warmer temperatures. And it's hard to unravel the effects of those."

There are scientists who hold the reasoned belief that, given the lack of useful information, any decision to abandon the traditional approach to natural preservation is bound to be rash. Eric Higgs, director of the School of Environmental Studies at the University of Victoria, British

Columbia, fears land managers may wreak havoc if they begin meddling with, rather than preserving, wild habitat.

"How is it we find respectful ways of intervening, of removing invasive species, or planting or translocating species? How do we do that in our deeply respectful way?" Higgs wonders. "We want future generations to say, 'They didn't get it all right, but they got some of it right.' Leopold certainly made many mistakes, but he was an individual who kind of had it right. I'd like to think that contemporary restorationists would blaze that kind of trail."

With that in mind, National Park Service trailblazers all over America are holding meetings, conferences, and symposia to incorporate climate change into a scheduled revision of overall park policy. The Park Service has created a Task Force on Climate Change to figure out what, if anything, to do about threatened park resources.

Officials with the Golden Gate National Recreation Area along California's north-central coast, for example, are preparing to study the question with a series of global warming-themed staff meetings scheduled throughout next fall.

The agency is still sidestepping some of what's at stake, however. When asked what it was doing to preserve wildlands in the face of global warming, the Park Service's climate change coordinator boasted of a program called Climate Friendly Parks, which seeks to reduce parks' carbon footprint by doing things like installing low-flow toilets. Addressing the threat to ecosystems by reducing parks' resource consumption is like treating a cancer patient by telling her to cut back on food additives. Scientists are well aware of this apparent lack of direction in the agency's response to climate change.

"There's kind of a chaotic feeling right now. Everyone understands the situation is really problematic. We need to start. We can't wait to act until things start dying," Graber notes. "But we don't know what to do." Leigh Welling, the Park Service climate change coordinator, puts it a different way.

"It's a scary thought," says Welling, "Managers are looking at their job and saying, "Oh jeez, how do I do my job?' "

Some naturalists have a one-word answer to that question: differently.

One of the predictions of global warming is that there will be changes in the wind patterns and ocean currents that move nutrients to places where creatures can reach them. "In May of 2005, and roughly the same time of year in 2006, we had highly unusual wind patterns and ocean currents that were atypical," said Ellie Cohen, executive director of PRBO Conservation Science, the organization that monitors birds on the Farallon Islands.

If those new patterns become the norm, some of the bird species that now blanket the Farallons could perish. Others, however, might thrive. Will preserving a semblance of the status quo turn conservationists into something closer to gardeners or zookeepers?

"It may be that at some point ecologists and conservationists decide the level of intervention may have to be higher than anything we've ever considered before," says Cohen. "Are we willing to go on the Farallon Islands to feed Cassin's auklet chicks until they're big enough to survive?"

And if not, what outcomes are we willing to accept?

February 4, 2008

M. Martin Smith and *Fiona Gow* are journalists living in San Francisco.

Dammed Up

❧

Floyd Dominy:
An Encounter with the West's Undaunted Dam Builder

Ed Marston

Ed Marston: Floyd Dominy, you are famous for building Glen Canyon Dam and creating Lake Powell behind it. Is that your proudest achievement?

Floyd Dominy: Yes, I think so. I was in the federal government for thirty-seven years, in water and land development, but I expect the Glen Canyon Dam and the creation of the most wonderful lake in the world, Lake Powell, is my crowning jewel. But I would say that any discussion of Glen Canyon Dam has to start with the understanding of the law of the river on the Colorado. Glen Canyon Dam was part of a major undertaking to develop the upper basin in the Colorado, and that law of the river, of course, was established back in the twenties. There's a lot of idle talk, I think, about maybe we can amend the law of the river and make it a little more friendly to the upper basin.

Marston: And the river in question is the Colorado River, and it's a seven-state compact.

Dominy: That's right.

Marston: It's almost a treaty between foreign nations.

Dominy: Exactly. Now, that compact was arrived at after several years of very violent and rough negotiation between the seven states. I don't think you can do better if you renegotiated it today, for this reason: at the time it was negotiated, the ratio in population didn't go strictly against the upper basin as bad as it does now.

Marston: You mean there're so many more people in California than there are up here.

42

Dominy: Right. For example, in the twenties, the upper basin had eight congressmen and the lower basin had thirteen. Today, the upper basin has thirteen and the lower basin has sixty-three. And the other thing about it is that California wanted something in 1920.

Marston: It wanted ...

Dominy: It wanted the Hoover Dam.

Marston: And now it has the Hoover Dam.

Dominy: And it wanted the All-American Canal. They were spending millions of dollars developing that Imperial Valley, and, of course, the water supply they wanted on the coast. And they wanted the federal government to help them. Well now, they've got that; they've got Hoover Dam; they've got the All-American Canal, so I don't think our region would come out very well if they tried to renegotiate that compact.

Marston: What position did you occupy when Glen Canyon Dam was built?

Dominy: Well, I started out, I was the associate commissioner when it was first under way.

Marston: And what year was that?

Dominy: Well, it got under way very soon after 1956, when it was authorized. It's amazing how things change. In 1956, when the project was authorized, it was under construction in a matter of weeks. Today, we'd still be writing environmental impact statements.

Marston: Yes, these are the good new days. That brings me to a quote I wanted to read to you from the writer of *Cadillac Desert*, Marc Reisner. He said: "Dominy drove Reclamation, in John McPhee's phrase, 'like a fast bus.' Some of his passengers admired and others hated him, but both camps were scared half to death. Dominy was General Patton with General MacArthur's ego doing Mulholland's work, which he considered the Lord's." Does the federal government today lack a Floyd Dominy?

Dominy: I was a dominant man, no question about it. As a matter of fact, some people said my name should be "Dominate," not "Dominy." I was dedicated. I knew that we needed to develop the waters of the West if we were going to develop the West. Sure, I was a little rough at times, but I think, of course, Reisner's book is prejudiced all the way through. He doesn't give me the benefit of a doubt on any of his judgments.

Marston: But that quote isn't exactly a slam.

Dominy: No, I understand that, I understand that, and I accept that as a fairly realistic quote. I loved to argue with Congress.

Marston: Whereas other … bureaucrats of a similar station would have kowtowed to Congress.

Dominy: Most of them didn't have the energy that I had before a congressional committee, and I wasn't above challenging the Secretary of Interior and the Bureau of Budget and Management. If they hadn't gone along with certain things I wanted, I sometimes went direct to Congress.

Marston: And where did your power come from? What enabled you to do that while others running Housing and Urban Development couldn't do that?

Dominy: Well, I think they could have if they'd had the courage to do it. See, when I went to the Bureau of Reclamation, I already knew more about that program than anybody in it.

Marston: You came as an outsider?

Dominy: Yes, because I was born and reared in the Nebraska dryland area. I grew up on a subsistence farm, without plumbing and so forth, and I was county agent in one of the most drought-stricken areas of the West during that critical period in the thirties. So I knew the value of water. I knew the problems that farmers had in making a living in the arid West. I had all that in my background when I stepped into the Bureau of Reclamation as a land-development specialist.

Marston: So what enabled you, even with that knowledge, to rise through the ranks so quickly?

Dominy: Well, I did my homework. In 1954, President Eisenhower had a Democratic Congress, and the whole picture changed for the commissioner of the Bureau of Reclamation. Before, he had Western members on that committee who were devoted to helping him. But the Democrats changed it and put us under a different committee. Now we were put over into the Public Works subcommittee, and there wasn't a single Western member on that committee. And I went to the Commissioner of Reclamation when I was the chief of the irrigation division ...

Marston: So you were a couple of rungs down.

Dominy: Oh, yes. I wasn't even assistant commissioner. And I went to him and I said, "Look, you can't bring the regional directors in here to testify. We can't just answer the questions, we've got to make a speech, we've got to sell Reclamation. This group is not friendly to Reclamation. They want all the money to go to the Corps of Engineers and the eastern part of the United States."

Marston: So this wasn't an environmental battle, this was a battle for pork.

Dominy: Right. And he brushed me off and didn't accept my recommendation. So I did my homework. I thought I'd be a backstop. I had been for years. I knew every line and item in that budget. I made several trips out West to make sure that I was—that I could support the budget on each project. And then the day came when we went before the committee and they [the congressmen] said, "Well, they don't have room for you." So I wasn't up there, and the roof fell in. And the committee was so antagonistic to Reclamation that after a couple of days they said, "Well, you're not answering our questions, you're not giving us the information we need. We're going to adjourn the hearing. You go back to your ivory tower and study your lesson, and we'll bring you back after a while." Well, that's when the Western congressmen and senators, of course, became very excited. And they began to wonder, "Where the hell's Floyd Dominy?"

Marston: How come they knew you at all?

Dominy: Because I was a backstop. I had answered the questions.

Marston: Oh, I see. So there were suits in front of you, but you were feeding them.

Dominy: Right, right. And then also, I had testified before the Interior and Insular Affairs Committee on the amendatory repayment contracts. This was the first job I had in Reclamation of any significance, when I was in the irrigation division. Commissioner Strauss and all the rest of them, they didn't want to go up and defend those amendatory contracts because it was making Reclamation look bad. The old projects hadn't worked out. There were financial difficulties. And I carried them up to Congress and told them, I said, "This project needs to have not forty years' repayment period, but one hundred forty years' repayment period." [On] one project the congressmen said, "Well, this looks like infinity." I said, "That's right, it will never pay out." "Well then, why don't we abandon it?" "Well, we don't abandon it because we have a viable community out there. We've got a small city, we've got a viable environment, if you let those settlers pay what they can afford to pay, which is very little." I already had that background, and the Western congressmen and senators had seen me in action in that program. So, to make a long story short, the Interior secretary called me down to ask: "Is Bureau of Reclamation in as bad a shape up on the hill as I'm being told it is?" Well, I told him, "I don't think it's a proper question to address to me," and I refused to answer. But he said, "Well, look, my phone won't quit ringing about how bad this thing is up there. The relationship of the Bureau to the Congress; and all the Western congressmen and senators are saying you seem to be the man to take care of it." He said, "Can you?" And I said, "Yes, of course I can, but I can't do it as chief of the irrigation division. You've got to give me a title of at least assistant commissioner, and you've got to give me the responsibility that I can handle it."

So that's how it happened. In 1957 they made me an associate commissioner, and Commissioner Dexheimer was told to stay out of my way, and I really ran the Bureau for two years before I was made commissioner.

Marston: That's when the dams got built.

Dominy: Oh yes, yes. The Yellowtail Dam on the Bighorn and all the others, the Trinity Dam in California. This is the stage I like to describe as having no naysayers. If we proposed a project, it was endorsed, and it got built.

Marston: It's probably no secret to you that some people today think these dams are a terrible mistake, including Glen Canyon. In fact, you just debated—was it this fall again that you debated David Brower, formerly of the Sierra Club?

Dominy: Yes.

Marston: Were the dams terrible mistakes? And do you think this new generation—not that I include Brower in that—do they have a chance to take those dams down?

Dominy: First of all, let me say, I don't think we destroyed the Gunnison River [in Colorado] by building three wonderful hydroelectric dams. Before, it was a closed river. Now the public has access to those three reservoirs, with far more fishing and boating and recreational activities than was ever there in its natural state. Glen Canyon Dam, for example, in addition to its main function of providing the regulated water supply for the upper basin projects, it also has opened up for three million visitors a year, a land that probably had twenty or thirty visitors before. Rainbow Bridge gets three hundred thousand or more a year now, when it had only fifteen thousand in fifty years. The Colorado River float trip was limited to about a six-week period, haphazardly, when it was available in the flood season. Now you've got twenty thousand people a year going down it every year.

Sure, we've changed the environment of the river, but that doesn't mean we've made it worse. I happen to think that *Homo sapiens* is what the Endangered Species Act ought to be addressed to. I'm no fan of the Endangered Species Act. The thing that they're talking about now is that we've destroyed the humpback chub, because he can't live in clean water. Well, hell, all the archaeological digs around the world prove every day that various species have been evolving—flora and fauna—and expiring over the years.

Marston: Well, Mr. Dominy, let's go from rhetoric to practicalities. Do you think there is a chance to breach some of these dams? Including some of the ones that you built and are proud of having built?

Dominy: They certainly have no chance of breaching Glen Canyon Dam. If you took Glen Canyon Dam out of there, you'd destroy the viability of all those uppe

basin projects. You'd destroy the viability of the 110,000-acre irrigation projects of the Navajos. You'd destroy the viability of the San Juan-Chama that delivers 150,000 acre-feet of water into New Mexico for Albuquerque and that area.

Marston: Why would you destroy the viability of projects that are upstream of Glen Canyon Dam?

Dominy: Because you have to have that storage to meet the law of the river. Don't you remember that in 1936 the Colorado River flowed only four and a half million acre-feet in the whole year?

Marston: So you mean all those upstream projects would have to forgo their diversions in order to provide the lower basin with water?

Dominy: Right. You can't possibly meet the law of the river without getting a big sponge to hold up your plentiful years, to squeeze out during your dry years.

Marston: Well then, let me put you on the spot. Richard Ingebretsen is the Utah doctor who wants to breach Glen Canyon Dam. And he is incredibly proud of a napkin with a sketch by you showing the best way to breach the dam. Now my question to you is: Why do you hang out with these people? Why do you spend time debating a Dave Brower; what is the chemistry here?

Dominy: Well, I like people. I think the book that John McPhee wrote, he quotes me as saying that I like people, I like cab drivers, I like pimps, I like anybody. I like to associate with people. And I like to debate my position on issues with people.

Marston: Let me be the devil's advocate. Could it be that the kind of vitality that you and your movement shared in the fifties and sixties has shifted to a different vision, that dam-breakers are the keepers of a vision just as you had a vision fifty years ago?

Dominy: Well, it may be.

Marston: And that you're attracted to that?

Dominy: I can only say that I don't think the so-called environmentalists of today are necessarily right. I'm an environmentalist. I'm a different kind of environmentalist. I believe that nature can be improved upon. I do it right here in Virginia. I built a dam on my little farm in Fairfax fifty years ago. There was no fish there, nothing, and now it's the finest little fishing hole for that neighborhood. When I bought this farm up here, it didn't have any fish on it, it had no water supply at all. I built nine ponds, and four of them are wonderful fishing holes. And they're used by the ducks and the Canadian geese and, sure, I've changed the environment. I think I've improved on it.

Marston: A relatively small scale compared to Morrow Point Dam.

Dominy: Yes, but the principle is the same. Let's take a look at the carrying capacity of the Colorado River, for human use, between Lake Mead, [Nevada] and Rock Springs, Wyoming. In its natural state, how many people can it support for recreational activities? Maybe a couple of thousand. Now we have millions using it because of man-made structures.

Marston: So do you think the environmental movement is a nostalgia movement for back when there were fewer people and nature could be handled a little more gently?

Dominy: Yes, I think so.

August 28, 2000

Ed Marston (emarston@hcn.org) is former publisher for *High Country News*.

River of Dreams

Adam Burke

The Elwha River is talking, and Dick Goin is talking, too. We're on the riverbank, about a quarter mile from where the Elwha meets the ocean on the north coast of the Olympic Peninsula. Upriver, the Olympic Range crouches—7,000-foot peaks cradling glaciers and soft-shouldered lowlands bearing a patchwork of lush forests and clear-cuts. Downriver lies the cobble-strewn stretch of delta where the Elwha empties into the Strait of Juan de Fuca.

The smell of salty surf, the cry of gulls above the murmuring Elwha, the shimmering surface of the river reflects in Goin's eyes.

It is not clear if he sees any of it. Goin is looking into the past, at biblical volumes of pink salmon flooding the lowland tributaries of the Elwha.

"When I was a lad in the late thirties, there would be several hundred thousand salmon. From the mouth to the dam and from bank to bank it was like maggots; it was just crawling. You couldn't see the stream bottoms."

Back then, when salmon returned to spawn and die in the Elwha, they were more than a spectacle; they were a godsend. Goin's family had abandoned a failing farm in Iowa and moved west to escape the Dust Bowl. But the Great Depression followed them. Making ends meet was difficult everywhere, even on the lush and fertile Olympic Peninsula.

"The game was pretty well already all shot down, and so it was what we could raise—a couple of hogs—and what we could grow in some awfully rocky soil. Salmon were an extremely important part of the diet for lots of people."

Though he didn't realize it, the river's abundance was fading even then. In 1908, well before Goin's time, dam construction on the Elwha had destroyed the salmon fishery in all but the lowest five miles of the river. A second dam was built at Glines Canyon, several miles above the first dam, in 1926.

At a more gradual pace, the undammed lower reach was unraveling too, because the dams prevented sediment and gravel from replenishing productive spawning beds.

"It dawned on me when I was about sixteen or seventeen that I was seeing less fish each year. But I wasn't alarmed about it, because there were still so many, and so few people utilizing them."

Now, at seventy, Goin is retired from his career as a machinist for the now-defunct Rayonnier Pulp Mill. He spends many days on the river, helping tribal and state biologists keep tabs on the few returning salmon and steelhead. Goin views his volunteer work as repayment to Elwha salmon for the years of nourishment they provided him and his family.

And the Elwha gives him hope.

"The Elwha is the only river that just has one thing wrong with it," Goin says. "It doesn't have logging, it doesn't have development, it doesn't have degradation through chemicals; it has one thing only and that's the dams. Up above them is an absolutely pristine watershed where the natural situations can take place unimpeded by anything."

Goin believes that removing both the dams will restore the Elwha to its former glory. But not everyone shares his optimism.

"We have an awful lot of locals who don't believe that there were that many fish in this river because they didn't see it," says Goin. "What we're talking about here is explaining a sunrise to a blind man."

Even so, in 1992, the U.S. Congress saw the light and passed the Elwha River Restoration Act, authorizing the Interior Department to acquire the dams and remove them, if necessary, to restore the river. It was a rare, quicksilver moment for resource management, when all parties, even those who had benefited from years of cheap hydropower, gave their blessings to the legislation.

But as any civil-rights activist knows, it's one thing to pass a law, and another to implement it. Today, the two Elwha dams remain standing while Congress slowly comes up with the money needed for their removal.

The restoration of the Elwha is a beacon of possibility for western rivers. But its roller-coaster history is also a reminder that patience, tenacity, and luck, as well as money, are needed to take down the dams.

Time is also required. And time is the one thing the river's salmon may not be able to afford.

The Olympic Peninsula is a 6,200-square-mile thumb on the Northwest landmass of the United States. Hulking mountains sit in the center of the peninsula, large and high enough to house glaciers. Rivers run out of these mountains in all directions.

The Elwha descends northward roughly forty-four miles to the ocean. The upper reaches of the Elwha contain miles of ideal salmon habitat. Lower down, the river has cut through resistant basalts, forming a series of chutes and canyons.

Historically, young salmon spent up to two years in the deep holes and riffles of the Elwha, and then migrated out to sea. Several years later, the fish returned to their birthplace to spawn and die.

The Elwha's rough water and steep, narrow cataracts encouraged chinook to grow larger and more powerful before returning to spawn. The one hundred-pound Elwha chinook were legendary among natives, early explorers, and settlers.

Equally remarkable were the returns of pink salmon, estimated at over a quarter million fish. The river supported all five species of Pacific salmon native to the Northwest, and ten anadromous—or ocean-going—fisheries altogether. The Elwha's productivity was on par with the salmon-rich rivers of Alaska.

"These days, you can go to other Olympic rivers in the fall and get just a glimpse of how it was on the Elwha," says writer and naturalist Tim McNulty. "When salmon were running, there were eagles in the trees, and ravens, and bear coming down, river otter, raccoons at night, winter wrens—all kinds of wildlife. It was a moveable feast."

And salmon were the main course. Juvenile salmon fed not only birds and mammals, but resident fish stocks. Spawned-out adult carcasses hosted insects and microbial life, and enhanced plant growth. Scientists have even found marine carbons in riparian trees where salmon spawned.

In the lowlands, salmon were a central part of the diet, economy, and culture for the Lower Elwha Klallam Tribe.

"The Elwha was our mother watershed. Some believed that we originated from the salmon people, that our spirit came back through the salmon," says Rachel Kowalski-Hagaman, a Lower Elwha Klallam woman. "We learned about life on the Elwha, we practiced our religion on the Elwha. She was our home."

But in 1908, these life cycles were abruptly altered when Thomas Aldwell and his Olympic Power Company started building the first dam on the river.

Aldwell had arrived from Canada in 1890, part of a full-tilt rush to develop the Northwest. Land was free for the claiming. Coastal forests were shipped to San Francisco. Canneries lined the coastline, the industry moving northward as it wiped out one salmon run after another. Seattle was booming.

One hundred and twenty miles from Seattle (as the crow flies), and accessible only by boat, Port Angeles was still a backwater. Doctors visited patients by horseback and canoe. Settlers eked out hardscrabble lives canning and salting fish, staking claims, and farming rocky soil. A few hundred Lower Elwha Klallam Indians camped on the beach, and made their living fishing with nets. It was the frontier Aldwell was looking for— ripe with industrial potential waiting to be harnessed.

Logging operations of the time were primitive; fir, spruce and cedar were felled with hand tools and the giant timbers hauled along greased roads by teams of oxen.

Aldwell understood that Port Angeles would need an industrial engine to tap the riches of the forest. But it took him almost two decades to realize that the land he owned on the Elwha River could be that engine.

When a visitor from Oregon described how he'd powered a pulp mill with a small dam, Aldwell had a brain wave: "A pulp mill! I was thinking of the canyon on my claim ... the volume of the river and steep walls of the canyon ... Suddenly the Elwha was no longer a wild stream crashing down to the strait; the Elwha was peace, power and civilization," Aldwell recounts in his autobiography, *Conquering the Last Frontier.*

Aldwell's Elwha Dam would mean more than power for Port Angeles mills. The tiny town could become a portal, where the vast timber resources of the peninsula were processed into lumber. The project attracted investors, and by 1916, Aldwell had convinced the wealthy Zellerbach family of San Francisco to purchase the dam and open a mill in Port Angeles.

Hydropower meant amenities, income, and trade for peninsula residents. Within a few years the citizens of Port Angeles and other towns had electricity in their homes.

But the project had gotten off to a rocky start. Instead of anchoring the dam to bedrock, Olympic Power attached it to canyon walls on either side. In 1912, the base blew out, and an almost-full reservoir emptied in a matter of hours.

Olympic Power plugged the hole with tons of concrete, and rafts of conifer branches on the inside, but even today people question the safety of the dam, and water still leaks from it.

The dam also violated a state law requiring that all dams facilitate fish passage. The spectacle of thousands of fish dashing themselves against the concrete barrier provoked outrage from Native Americans and whites alike. Citizens wrote angry letters to the state fish commissioner, demanding that the law be enforced.

Instead, state officials suggested Aldwell's obstruction could facilitate a hatchery operation. Though not a legal alternative to the fish passage, the hatchery was built at the base of the dam and run by the state, only to be abandoned after several years. Meanwhile, the Washington Legislature had altered the fish-passage law to accommodate the hydro projects across the state.

In 1920, the federal government institutionalized what Aldwell had accomplished illegally. The Federal Power Act established hydropower as the "highest and best use of watersheds," and formed the Federal Energy Regulatory Commission (FERC) to license private hydro development.

In 1926, FERC licensed a second private dam upriver to Northwest Power and Light in what became Olympic National Park in 1938. The Glines Canyon Dam, at 210 feet, was twice as high as the Lower Elwha

Dam, and more than doubled the power output from the Elwha. The license for Glines Canyon Dam was good for fifty years—an eternity.

That eternity ended in the mid-1970s, when the first generation of FERC dams exhausted their fifty-year operating permits. The Elwha projects were complicated—there were safety concerns, the lower dam had never been licensed, and the Glines dam was in a national park. It took almost a decade for Crown Zellerbach, the corporation that now owned both dams and the Port Angeles mill, and FERC to feel their way through the unfamiliar process of dam relicensing. Ultimately, FERC determined that the dams were linked, and the procedure would work toward a single license for both.

In spite of these delays, executives at Crown Zellerbach expected a perfunctory process. Orville Campbell was in charge of the relicensing procedure: "The company had used the dams for some fifty years," says Campbell. "There was no reason to believe FERC wouldn't give us another fifty."

But while the dam owner worked toward relicensing, times were changing. Business-as-usual ran headlong into powerful new environmental laws and the ghosts of millions of vanished salmon. On the Elwha, the Department of Fisheries estimated that the loss of the salmon runs had cost the people of Washington $500,000 annually.

Native American rights had finally received some federal attention. In 1974, federal Judge George Boldt ruled that treaty rights guaranteed tribes half of the historic levels of fish in Northwest rivers. The "Boldt decision" gave the Lower Elwha Klallam a powerful new weapon to press their case for fish passage on the river.

"They claim that the dams were cheap power," says tribal member Kowalski-Hagaman. "They have never [provided] cheap power. The taxpayers have paid for that power. The ecosystem has paid for that power. Lower Elwha Klallam people paid for that power. The dams basically displaced our tribe."

Then, Bruce Brown's 1982 book *Mountains in the Clouds: A Search for the Wild Salmon* captured the public imagination and systematically confirmed what locals were witnessing with their own eyes. River by river,

Brown correlated salmon declines on the peninsula with intense resource development: logging, construction, chemical pollution, overfishing, diking, and riprap had destroyed many of the once-abundant runs. Hatcheries had failed to make up for the losses.

As the public became aware of the irreplaceable value of wild salmon, the Elwha emerged as a rare opportunity to turn back the clock. Much of the river was pristine and largely protected within Olympic National Park. Salmon advocates like Dick Goin returned to the problem of the dams again and again. Federal agencies and the Lower Elwha Klallam Tribe were also pushing for Elwha salmon recovery. But it took one key strategist in the 1980s to change the way FERC would look at dam relicensing on the Elwha.

Richard Rutz, a wilderness activist in Seattle, learned about the Elwha almost by accident. While they were poring over maps looking for potential wilderness areas, a fellow conservationist told Rutz the story of Elwha salmon and the dams.

As he looked into the Elwha further, Rutz saw what others before him had missed: that the Glines Canyon Dam (now inside Olympic National Park) was illegal, that federal law mandated environmental review of all dam relicensing, and that the power created by the dams was replaceable.

"The license holders had come to believe that these licenses were theirs by right. They didn't think they needed to do anything in order to get [the licenses] again," Rutz recalls.

Though not a lawyer, in 1984 Rutz wrote a legal intervention in the FERC relicensing process for four environmental groups. The intervention argued for dam removal and complete restoration of the Elwha watershed. By 1986, FERC had allowed the Seattle Audubon Society, Friends of the Earth, Olympic Park Associates, and the Sierra Club to become interveners in the relicensing process.

When FERC opened the doors to these groups, it opened the floodgates to contemporary environmental values. It would not be able to close them again.

Rutz's intervention became a rallying point for those who opposed a new license for the Elwha dams. Prominent environmental lawyers quickly agreed to represent the case in court. Then, the Lower Elwha Klallam Tribe, the National Marine Fisheries Service, U.S. Fish and Wildlife Service, and National Park Service put their weight behind dam removal.

But this coalition needed more than a legal foothold—it needed a reasonable public face, as well. The spotted owl wars were sending shockwaves through the Northwest's logging industries. A plan to bring back salmon at the expense of hundreds of jobs in Port Angeles would be politically difficult. In fact, the local congressman proposed a bill to relicense the dam.

By this time, Crown Zellerbach's assets had changed hands: James River Corporation owned the dams, Daishowa America owned the mill and the rights to Elwha hydropower from both dams. Jim Baker, an activist who worked with the Northwest Energy Coalition, suggested that Daishowa could easily conserve the twenty megawatts of electricity the dams provided by retrofitting new motors and improving efficiency. The proposal showed that dam removal could be a solution for all sides, and it ended the push for a quick fix from Congress.

With an aggressive public outreach campaign, a constructive, win-win solution on the table, a strong legal case and legal muscle to back it up, proponents for dam removal pressed their case.

The interveners filed a lawsuit with the Ninth Circuit Court of Appeals. Federal agencies were also in court, disputing which had jurisdiction over a private dam inside a national park boundary. Then, to everyone's surprise, FERC made salmon restoration its top priority in its draft Environmental Impact Statement (EIS) for relicensing.

While environmentalists view the draft EIS as a "real wake-up call" for the dam owners, Orville Campbell, who was still working on behalf of both companies to relicense the dams, disagrees: "Even though it indicated we were going to have to mitigate the projects, the draft EIS indicated to us that FERC was headed toward granting our license."

In spite of how messy things appeared on the surface, political leadership in Congress recognized an opportunity. Tom Jensen, a U.S. Senate committee lawyer who worked with Senator Bill Bradley, Democrat-New Jersey, began to visit with the various parties.

"The potential for a solution was obvious," Jensen recalls. "It was a very small amount of electricity used by one mill. The Elwha was in a national park, and we had the possibility of restoring a genetically unique salmon run in pristine habitat. It kept us believing that we could get to a deal."

The companies, too, had begun to recognize the value of letting go of the dams. "I began to see that holding onto the dams might not be in our best interest," says Campbell. "We are in the business of making paper, not producing power."

It took a year and a half to hammer out legislation. Congressman Al Swift, Democrat-Washington, and senators Brock Adams, Democrat-Washington, and Bradley carried the bill through their committees and onto the floors of the U.S. House and Senate.

The Elwha River Restoration Act passed in a legislative photo finish—on the final day of the congressional session October 7, 1992. With some grumbling, President George Bush signed it into law.

The Act authorized the Interior Department to acquire the dams for $29.5 million, and remove them if necessary to restore the river. It guaranteed replacement power to the mill from Bonneville Power Administration, and a clean water supply for Port Angeles.

"It was a great day for the tribe," says Lower Elwha Klallam attorney Russ Bush. "Some of the elders had gone to Washington, D.C., to testify. And now it looked like we were going to have salmon back. The tribe had a ceremony on the reservation to commemorate the event."

But even with a law in place and a river-friendly Clinton administration in office, Elwha salmon had to wait for politics. First the 1994 Gingrich revolution put a crimp in Elwha funding. Then, Senator Slade Gorton, the powerful Washington Republican who chaired the Senate Interior Appropriations subcommittee, scuttled appropriations for Elwha several years in a row.

"The goodwill and collaboration we had created that allowed the bill to pass then got squandered for a period of time, when Slade Gorton changed positions and went from being a sponsor of the bill to being an opponent," says Jensen.

First Gorton blocked funding because he said there was no local support for dam removal, and later he wanted a guarantee that the Snake River dams in eastern Washington would not be breached.

But a diverse panel of community leaders in Port Angeles persuaded Gorton that there was local support for removing the Elwha dams. The Elwha Citizens' Advisory Committee held meetings for several months in 1994, and eventually concluded that the modest amount of power wasn't worth the loss of the state's finest salmon runs.

"In the early nineties, Port Angeles was plastered with anti-dam removal signs," says Joe Mentor, a former Senate aide and board member of Olympic Park Associates, who helped mediate the advisory committee. "This committee worked through the difficult questions and came up with a dam-removal strategy it could support."

After several lost years, Gorton abandoned his attempt to link Elwha restoration to guarantees that the Snake River dams would not be breached. Then, project coffers started to fill, and the federal government was able to buy the two dams in February of 2000, the first step toward dam removal.

Currently, funding for the Elwha project is halfway there, with about $70 million of the $140 million needed to complete the project appropriated. This year, the Bush administration approved the entire $25.8 million budget request from the National Park Service for Elwha, and the U.S. House followed suit.

"They've learned from Gorton's mistakes on Elwha, and they know that the project has broad support," opines Shawn Cantrell, who for ten years has coordinated the Elwha effort in Seattle for Friends of the Earth. "They're not going to call a lot of attention to the fact that it's funding a dam removal, but they're not going to fight it either. They probably just want to push it on through and not leave any fingerprints on it."

Plans for dam removal are on schedule for late 2004. The Park Service is negotiating now with the city of Port Angeles on a plan to protect the city's municipal and industrial water supplies during restoration.

According to Brian Winter, who heads the restoration project for the Park Service, the river will do much of the restoration itself, gradually transporting downstream seventeen million cubic yards of sediment and gravel that has backed up behind the reservoirs. The Park Service will revegetate the area that is now underwater with native plant species, and it will work with state and tribal hatcheries to protect the Elwha's native salmon stocks.

Within ten years after dam removal, scientists estimate, salmon numbers in the Elwha will go from three thousand to three hundred ninety thousand.

But the glacial pace of funding may not suit the fish. Several stocks are already extinct, or functionally so, and even the strongest runs are on life support, maintained by state and tribal hatchery operations. The legendary Elwha chinook, plagued by parasites and lack of habitat, now number in the hundreds.

The dark irony of a free Elwha without native salmon stocks has activists braced for another roller-coaster, should restoration funding become snagged in Congress again.

"There are many things which could cause delay down the road. We're just staying alert so that as soon as these things surface, we deal with them head on," says Cantrell. "It's not over till the dams come out."

For others, dam removal won't be the significant moment. "The day I'm really waiting for is the day I can hike up above where the dams are now, and watch the first living torpedo come up the river looking for its ancestral spawning grounds," says Jim Baker. "That's the day when I'll really feel like it was all worth it."

Activists are divided over whether the fight to save the Elwha, with its national park location and broad support, signals anything about the potential to take down other dams. Rutz prefers to see the Elwha on its own terms.

"We've always maintained that this is a unique situation with unique factors," he says. "That's true of every river."

But Baker, who went on from the Elwha to the Snake River fight, insists that the Elwha is in some ways a blueprint. He allows that the Snake River dams are on a different scale in terms of their size, federal status, and the amount of hydropower they generate. Nevertheless, he maintains that what has been missing from the Snake fight thus far is not persuasive arguments or citizen support for dam breaching, but political leadership.

What most everyone can agree on is that the Elwha has helped usher in a new era for watersheds where the value of dams is no longer a given. Salmon returning to the upper reaches of the Elwha will make it a laboratory for recovery efforts throughout the Northwest.

"When we give the fish a chance, the incredible vitality of those animals is going to show us what habitat means," says Tom Jensen. "Without an example like Elwha, we'll never be able to do anything other than speculate from our various positions about what we ought to do on the Columbia, or the Snake, or elsewhere in the range of the fish."

Dick Goin agrees. Goin views the issue with the simple wisdom of a man who just turned seventy this year: It's time to open the door for these fish, and get out of the way.

"I know I will never see the abundant runs that I saw when I was a boy. But I'll be satisfied enough to go and see them and to know that the fish are in the upper Elwha again. When salmon are in their own river, things are whole again, and all the good things that come with salmon can start to happen."

September 24, 2001

Adam Burke is an independent radio producer based in Paonia, Colorado.

The Terrifying Saga of the West's Last Big Dam

Joshua Zaffos

The war on terror has a new front in southwestern Colorado. Outside the fast-growing city of Durango, the government has allocated $2 million for terrorism security at the Animas-La Plata Dam construction site. How will that money specifically ward off al-Qaida operatives and increase homeland security?

"If I tell you too much, I'd have to kill you," project manager Patrick Schumacher told *The Durango Herald* last September, making a point with grim humor. "It's a direct result of 9-11."

Of course, he was joking—or was he? Dams stand as potential terrorist targets. But the Animas-La Plata Project, better known as A-LP, isn't even built yet. Still, for many critics, nothing is more terrifying than the prospect of A-LP itself.

Congress originally authorized the Bureau of Reclamation to build the Animas-La Plata Dam and pumping project in 1968. The project entailed pumping water from the Animas River one thousand feet over a divide into the La Plata River, then storing it in a series of reservoirs and sending it to farmers through forty-eight miles of canals and pipelines for low-value crops like alfalfa. The Rube Goldberg nature of the scheme and the hundreds of millions of dollars it would have cost infuriated river lovers and fiscal conservatives, who fought A-LP in its various forms for the next three decades.

By 1995, the dam had still not been built, and *U.S. News and World Report* called the project the "last surviving dinosaur from the age of behemoth water schemes."

The Bureau of Reclamation determined that the project's costs astronomically outweighed its benefits—A-LP would return only 36 cents for each dollar spent—yet the agency continued to back the plan. In some college courses on resource management, the Animas-La Plata Project became a textbook example of bureaucratic survival strategies. The lesson: a government agency, in this case the Bureau of Reclamation, often does anything it can to ensure its survival and continue an outmoded mission, despite high costs to the taxpayer.

Dam proponents unwilling to concede failure scaled back the original plan in the late nineties and, as environmental critics put it bluntly, "wrapped the dam in an Indian blanket." The redefinition meant that water from the project would go to two Ute Indian tribes, which had nineteenth-century water rights, but no water.

The tribes will likely use their new water to grow their own low-value crops, or else sell it to coal-fired power plants that pollute the desert skies with sulfur and carbon dioxide. There were other changes in the new operating version of A-LP: it reduced its take of water from the Animas River to limit negative impacts on endangered fish, proposed an off-site reservoir, and cut the La Plata River out of the project.

Water from the dam will still go to non-Indians for irrigation as well as to meet the growth explosion in southern Colorado and northern New Mexico, where population is projected to increase as much as 50 percent over the next twenty-five years.

These changes to the project convinced Congress to finally allocate money for actual construction. The Bureau of Reclamation won approval for a $338 million project budget in 2000, and went to work blasting and digging in 2002. By last July, the agency announced cost projections had raised the project's cost closer to $500 million, and these overruns could jump higher, since construction is still underway.

Frustrated by thirty-five years of resistance and scrutiny, and hoping to avoid further embarrassment and holdups, Reclamation Commissioner John Keys told reporters last December, "I just don't want any more land mines." The remark probably referred to figurative obstacles, but Reclamation still got $2 million for anti-terrorism protection. That expense pales in comparison to the $160 million overrun so far.

The projected total cost of a half-billion dollars for the project—not including four decades of court battles and environmental studies—makes this dam a significant plundering of the public treasury. The project may also be the swan song of a government agency struggling to carve out a new mission for itself, now that Americans have decided that the costs of a modern dam are too great to be borne.

Meanwhile, the critics keep protesting the project, and many are terrified at the way A-LP will accelerate growth in the region. It makes you wonder why a terrorist, who wants to harm America, would try to sabotage A-LP.

June 7, 2004

Josh Zaffos writes from Fort Collins, Colorado.

As Dams Fall,
a Chance for Redemption

Daniel McCool

I am sitting next to a two hundred-foot-high concrete apparition. Matilija Dam, not far from the California coast, sits astride the narrow canyon of the Ventura River amid the velvet green foothills of the Santa Ynez Mountains. At the entrance to the dam site, razor wire conspicuously adorns the top of a fence, just above a sign that says "DANGER RAZOR WIRE," as though visitors might not have noticed already that the dam looks more like a concentration camp than a public utility. The control tower's windows are smashed, and rusting cables and slashed wires hang from the abutments. Falling boulders have smashed the staircase that ascends to the control tower, and the face of the dam is a filigree of cracks. This area has the geologic stability of a stack of greased bowling balls. One good shake of Mother Earth, and this dam is beach fill.

The current lessee of Matilija Dam, the Casitas Municipal Water District, based in nearby Oak View, California, would prefer that the public not see this concrete disaster. Numerous signs warn: "trespassing loitering prohibited by law." But I decide to loiter anyway, because I am fascinated by doomed dams: they presage the future. Just as surely as dams were once symbols of progress and the "conquest" of nature, some of them are now symbols of the excesses of the past. Nature and a new political dynamic are dismantling some dams. A dam slated for the wrecking ball is a kinetic form of politics—falling concrete that embodies the energy of a whole new concept of river management. As dams fall, hopes rise—a stark exchange of the past with the future.

I sit down beside one of the no-trespassing signs to rest, utterly alone. I see a piece of concrete from the dam, about the size of a fist, and put it in my pack, a souvenir of the world's largest dam to be slated for removal, so far. At my feet are sixteen thousand-pound chunks of concrete that have already been torn from the lip of the structure, some of them during a visit by former Interior Secretary Bruce Babbitt in 2000. Babbitt is no longer secretary, but this dam will continue its demise without him, the inevitable result of changing values and the law of gravity.

Spring rains have raised the shallow pool of water behind the dam (no one would seriously call it a reservoir), and water is spilling over the rim, creating a series of translucent sheets of water that drop gracefully down the face of the dam. The reservoir bed is filled with six million cubic yards of sand, silt and rock, material that once went to build up Ventura Beach. For the last half-century, this beach fill has been trapped in this canyon behind Matilija Dam, and as a result, Ventura Beach is slowly eroding into the sea. Even the surfers' association lobbied to have the dam removed. The Santa Ana winds are gusting forcefully, and the falling water twists into swirls and drifts. The dark, dilapidated face of the dam is marked with large red circles painted at strategic joints; they look vaguely like targets, as though the dam owners are hoping someone will blow this thing to dam heaven and save a lot of time and money. But this is no monkey-wrench target; if the dam failed, the meager amount of water stored behind it would create no more than a spring freshet downstream.

Matilija is a dam that stores no water, generates no electricity, and offers no recreation. It is utterly, irrevocably useless, other than to serve as a reminder of a time when America built dams willy-nilly without considering their long-term impact or utility. It may be hard to imagine, but this is the future facing every dam in the world. Sooner or later, every dam crumbles.

Two months later, I am walking along the top of Elk Creek Dam, which spans a beautiful mountain stream in southern Oregon. I kick up a fine dust of weathered concrete that settles on the weeds growing from cracks. This is a dam so pointless, so obviously irrational, that even the Corps of Engineers—the Dams-R-Us agency—did not want to build it, and when forced to do so, completed only one-third of the job and quit.

Up- and down-stream from the dam, this little valley is a verdant natural paradise. The river courses briskly through dark volcanic rock and dense stands of pine and Douglas fir. But the dam site is an industrial nightmare. It is strewn with giant piles of crushed rock and gravel, placed there by the Corps to complete the last two-thirds of the dam, but never put to use. Rusting rebar juts from the unfinished escarpment, and the rolled concrete fill is spalling badly.

Elk Creek Dam is the perfect example of pork-barrel water politics, born in an age when politicians equated dam building with re-election. The first standard bearer for the dam was Mark Hatfield, senator from Oregon from 1967 to 1997. According to some sources, Hatfield promised his constituents that he would get the funding to build Elk Creek Dam. When the Corps of Engineers recommended against building the dam, which would produce no hydropower or water supply, and provide only a slim margin of flood control, Hatfield put money for it in an appropriations bill anyway.

The Corps, a military unit, dutifully followed orders. It started digging keyways and pouring concrete. When representatives from an environmental group met with Corps personnel to discuss Elk Creek, a Corps staff member expressed his frustration, asking the environmentalists, "Isn't there anything you can do to get Hatfield off our backs?"

There was: environmental groups sued the Corps for failure to complete an adequate environmental impact statement. They were unsuccessful in the district court, but prevailed at the appeals level. That gave the Corps the excuse it needed; the agency turned its back and walked away from the construction site, leaving building materials lying around as though it planned to resume work the next day.

That was in 1987—seventeen years ago. Now, the unfinished dam just sits there, blocking salmon and steelhead migration on the river. The Corps is now operating an expensive trap-and-haul system, catching fish on their way upstream to spawn, dumping them into trucks, and driving them around the dam—a scheme that has Rube Goldberg written all over it. Efforts to remove or "notch" the dam have been stymied by some local politicians and Congressman Greg Walden, who still see dams as the key to future development. They hope that some day the dam will be finished and provide additional water storage for area farmers. Elk Creek Dam is a symbol of how difficult it is to change a mindset and overcome the inertia of a hundred years of pork-barrel water policy.

Later, in the fall, I head to Escalante Canyon in southern Utah. If this canyon was anywhere else in the United States, it would be a national park. But it had the misfortune of running into the Colorado River upstream of Glen Canyon Dam, and thus the most impressive part of the canyon was submerged under Lake Powell. I have come here with members of the Glen Canyon Institute, a group with the unthinkable idea of draining Lake Powell and restoring Glen Canyon. The Bureau of Reclamation will not even discuss draining the lake, but Mother Nature seems to have other ideas: after five years of drought, the reservoir is at less than half capacity.

Most of Glen Canyon's ninety-six side canyons are marked with buoys, like street signs at busy intersections. Our motorboat takes a hard right turn into the Escalante Arm and enters a maze of side streams, dead-end cirques, and spiraling rock buttresses. We pause for traffic to clear, turn left into Davis Gulch, and slow the motor to a crawl. Still, our wake bounces off the narrow rock walls and rolls back and forth across the channel.

We follow this avenue of water, its surface like green polished marble, around innumerable switchbacks and meanders. All the while, the water channel becomes more confining while the surrounding walls remain high and often over-hanging. It's as though we are descending into a cleft in the crust of the earth itself. After a mile or two, we come to a sandy beach that stretches across the canyon—the end of this arm of the reservoir. Perhaps a hundred feet above us, we can make out the high-water mark on the canyon wall. We have come to see some of the revealed landscape that has emerged from the depths of the reservoir.

We beach the boat and begin walking on ground that has not been trod since Mickey Mantle was in his prime. The area closest to the current water line is practically devoid of vegetation, but nascent sprigs of grass, tamarisk, and willow are sprouting a little farther upstream. As we hike up-canyon, the typical array of canyon flora begins to appear in profusion. After half a mile, we are in a part of the canyon that has been above water for perhaps two years. A meadow has formed on both sides of the stream; evening primrose, prickly pear, and globemallow compete for space. Across the creek, a dense copse of young cottonwood trees crowds the bank, some of them six feet tall.

We can guess how long this area has been free of the reservoir because of the graffiti on the rocks above us; boaters spray-painted their names and the year they visited—two years ago—on the cliff above their lakeside fire ring. The fecundity and regenerative power of the canyon are spectacular, especially compared to the dead zone that immediately surrounds the reservoir's edge. The great push and rush of spring floods has fed a rich load of seeds, soil, and moisture into these previously drowned areas, bringing them to life in just a season or two. Canyon country is fragile, but it does have a habit of aggressively reclaiming its own. Davis Gulch is coming alive, recovering its natural green velour and its complex web of desert life.

There are seventy-six thousand dams in this country over six feet in height, and another 2.5 million smaller dams. The United States entered the dam-building era the way it sometimes goes to war—bold and headstrong, with no understanding of the ultimate costs. For the first two hundred years of this country's history, dams were synonymous with prosperity and stability. But dams also destroyed entire ecosystems, and replaced living rivers with stagnant reservoirs. We dismembered rivers and divvied up the component parts without realizing the value of the rivers themselves.

But the canyons and rivers are still there, below the reservoirs. Extinction is forever; dams are not. This provides us with an opportunity to engage in the politics of healing rivers and restoring riverine landscapes. We can always find another source of energy, a more sensible place to grow high-water crops, and a more efficient way to water our cities. But we cannot replicate Glen Canyon; we cannot genetically engineer a massive salmon run; we cannot invent a mountain canyon that funnels sand to the edge of a continent. We have great power to foul our own nest, but we have a commensurate power to mend that nest, and create a future of free-flowing rivers and deeply carved canyons.

In years to come—maybe one or two hundred years from now—when a free-flowing river is no longer as rare as a quiet moment, people will stand on the edge of the Ventura River, or Elk Creek, or the Colorado River running wild again through Glen Canyon, and marvel at the grandeur. They may even give thanks to their ancestors for having the foresight to save America's rivers for them.

June 21, 2004

Dan McCool is a professor of political science and the director of the American West Center at the University of Utah.

Super-sized Dam Could Be Cash Register for California Farmers

Hilary Watts

At a time when some dam engineers are biting the environmental bullet and tearing down the concrete that once defined their existence, the Bureau of Reclamation is trying to figure out how to make the largest dam in California even bigger.

The Bureau is in the process of renewing its twenty-five-year contracts with the more than two hundred water districts that receive water from the twenty dams and reservoirs that make up the Central Valley Project, or CVP.

The Bureau has been able to make full deliveries to the districts in only thirteen of the last seventeen years. But late last year, Reclamation Chief John Keys pledged to deliver full quantities to water districts under the new contracts. At the same time, the Bureau has promised to meet growing urban water demands and restore the San Francisco Bay Delta under the CALFED program.

Doing all this will require expanding dams or developing other water projects, all at taxpayer expense. Ironically, this could give water districts more water than they can actually use, at incredibly cheap prices: $15 for an acre-foot, or 325,851 gallons. Cities can pay between eight and thirty-three times that.

Although most irrigation districts say they just want to make their supplies more reliable, some critics claim that the districts will be able to market their extra water to thirsty cities. The watchdog organization Environmental Working Group speculates in a March report that the new contracts "will set up the districts to reap windfall profits by reselling water at much higher prices."

Essentially, Reclamation has committed to delivering about one million more acre-feet of water than is available in the Central Valley Project today. To capture that water, the agency is considering an array of possibilities: enlarging either Shasta Dam near Redding, Los Vaqueros Dam in the San Francisco Bay area, or Friant Dam near Fresno; or building a brand-new dam northwest of Yuba City. The Bureau is also contemplating storing water on islands in the Bay Delta or in underground aquifers.

The most likely option, because of its comparatively cheap cost, is raising Shasta Dam. Currently, the reservoir can hold more than 4.5 million acre-feet of water. Adding another 6.5 to 18.5 feet to the dam will increase its storage capacity by 6 percent to 14 percent. The environmental impact statement on the dam raising should be finished by 2007.

One of the biggest beneficiaries of a taller Shasta Dam will be Westlands Water District, arguably the largest agricultural district in the United States. With more than six hundred thousand acres and nearly six hundred farms, Westlands receives 14 percent of the water in the CVP.

But to cope with dwindling supplies in dry years, Westlands, like many water districts, has fallowed land and lined ditches with concrete. Farmers in Westlands have already taken 11 percent of their land out of production, and the Bureau of Reclamation is now considering fallowing another 39 percent because it is contaminated with selenium.

Nonetheless, Westlands' new contract will guarantee it the same amount of water it was promised twenty-five years ago. {That's the irony of all this," says Hal Candee, senior attorney with Natural Resources Defense Council. "They're proposing to renew the contract at the full amount, while simultaneously the same agency wants to take half the land out of production."

Representative George Miller, Democrat-California, who has long pushed to reform the CVP, has raised concerns about the districts reselling their water. In a February letter to Interior Secretary Gale Norton, Miller asked whether the government was essentially trying to "outsource the management of the CVP water supply to current CVP contractors—who collect substantial personal profits from sales."

Bureau spokesman Jeff McCracken says the view that water districts will sell any excess water is "probably an illusion." He says, "No one is getting rich selling CVP water."

Will water flow south?

The most likely customer for water is the Metropolitan Water District of Southern California, which supplies water to eighteen million people in Los Angeles and San Diego. After California agreed in 2003 to end its overuse of Colorado River water, the agency has been scouting out replacement supplies within the state. Metropolitan has tried to lease Central Valley Project water several times, though it has never actually completed a deal.

In 2002, Metropolitan signed a $125 per acre-foot deal with one CVP customer, the Glenn-Colusa Irrigation District north of Sacramento. But the agreement only allows Metropolitan to lease water from farmers whose rights pre-date the water project—and only during drought years. Metropolitan is still interested in pursuing actual CVP water.

"We'd consider any seller," says James Roberts, the chief deputy general counsel for Metropolitan. One hurdle that has kept his agency from pursuing CVP water more aggressively is the $50 to $60 per acre-foot fees the Bureau would impose on such transfers. Those, he says, "would put that seller at quite a disadvantage."

That's likely to change, however, as demand for water increases and the market gets tighter during the next twenty-five years. Says Candee, "It's safe to say that heavily subsidized CVP water is an extremely valuable asset for any irrigation district."

August 22, 2005

Hilary Watts is a biologist living in Paonia, Colorado.

Elwha Dams Move Closer to Destruction

Michelle Blank

In early March 2007, the long-anticipated removal of two dams on Washington's Elwha River took a giant step closer to reality when the state Department of Ecology gave the project the go-ahead.

The dams' removal will help floundering salmon populations. Prior to their construction in the early 1900s, all five Pacific salmon species had spawned prolifically in the Elwha. Within twenty years of dam removal, says Amy Kober, Northwest communications director for American Rivers, hundreds of thousands of salmon are expected to once again travel up the river. And those salmon runs should help the endangered Puget Sound orcas that feed on the fish. "Restoring this river," says Kober, "is going to have reverberations … through the entire Puget Sound ecosystem."

Breaching plans have been in the works for years, as we reported in 2001. Responding to growing concerns about vanishing salmon, Congress passed the Elwha River Restoration Act in 1992. It authorized the Interior Department to acquire the dams and remove them. Funding, however, lagged behind. It wasn't until 2000 that the federal government finally purchased the Lower Elwha Dam and Glines Canyon Dam, which sits inside Olympic National Park.

The next stage of work will begin in the coming months, once the Army Corps of Engineers issues the final permit. Before the dams come down, mitigation projects must be completed to protect downstream water-treatment plants and fish hatcheries from sediment released during dam removal. Federal funding has already been appropriated for those projects.

Actual dam deconstruction should begin in 2009. The upper dam, at 210 feet, will be the highest ever breached in the nation.

March 14, 2007

Michelle Blank works as a backcountry ranger at Rocky Mountain National Park.

A Downside to Downing Dams?

Michelle Nijhuis

"In the view of conservationists," author John McPhee once wrote, "there is something special about dams, something—as conservation problems go—that is disproportionately and metaphysically sinister."

For many conservationists, there is also something special about tearing those dams down, something satisfyingly unambiguous about the very phrase "dam removal." If rivers, as McPhee speculated, symbolize life, and dams symbolize their humiliation, it's easy to see dam removal as a victorious restoration—even a glorification—of life itself.

More than two hundred U.S. dams have come down since 1999, and dozens are slated for removal. Most, if not all, are reaching the end of their life expectancy. Many are unsafe, inefficient, or simply no longer needed for their original purpose. Many have harmed fish or river ecosystems in ways not recognized at the time of their birth. Their decline and imminent fall means conservationists can, for once, simply sit back and celebrate. Right?

Yes—and no. In the arid highlands of central Arizona, along a newly liberated spring-fed river known as Fossil Creek, a Northern Arizona University research team is watching what happens as a dam comes down. They're learning that it's much more complicated than one might expect.

"Since some of these dams were built, there's been a hundred years of sediment built up, a hundred years of nutrients, and a hundred years of new opportunities for invasive species to set up shop," says Emily Stanley, a dam-removal researcher at the University of Wisconsin. "So when you remove the dam, you're not necessarily going back to that lovely, pristine ecosystem you had before the dam."

In the late 1800s, visitors to central Arizona described an oasis in the desert. Fossil Creek, a fourteen-mile-long stream, was fed by springs rich in calcium carbonate, which formed a series of travertine barriers and striking blue-green pools along the river reaches. The creek "was constantly building great round basins for itself, and for a long distance flows over bowl after bowl," the naturalist Charles Lummis wrote in 1891.

But as the city of Phoenix grew, it put Fossil Creek to work. The Childs-Irving hydroelectric project was built in the early 1900s; its diversion dam and two associated power plants, intended to serve both Phoenix and the mining town of Jerome, reduced most of Fossil Creek to little more than a trickle.

The federal government granted the project a fifty-year license in 1951. By the time its expiration date neared, newer projects had dwarfed its contribution to the region's power supply, and environmental groups began pushing the Federal Energy Regulatory Commission to decommission the dam.

While environmentalists dreamed of a resurrected desert stream, scientists at Northern Arizona University in Flagstaff saw an unusual research opportunity. Beginning in the late 1990s, ecologist Jane Marks and her colleagues, funded by the National Science Foundation and other sources, formed a research team that included not only biologists, but also a hydrologist, a geologist, an engineer, and a social scientist.

Though Marks had never studied dam decommissioning firsthand, she knew from previous research that it usually had ecological costs as well as benefits. She also knew, as other researchers had discovered, that no two decommissionings were exactly alike. No one was certain how the return of full flows to Fossil Creek and the subsequent lowering of the dam would change the geology and ecology of the stream. Her team's challenge was to observe these changes, untangle their causes, and use that knowledge to help turn a demolition project into a genuine restoration.

The federal government approved the decommissioning of the Childs-Irving project in 2004, ruling that the environmental benefits of river restoration outweighed the benefits of hydropower. The first step would be to shut off the flume that fed water to the hydropower plants, a move that would return full flows to Fossil Creek. Two or three years later, the utility would begin to lower the twenty-five-foot-high dam.

Wildlife managers knew that for native fish above the dam, the $13 million restoration project would be meaningless—even harmful—unless they controlled the swarm of non-native fish, such as bass and sunfish, that flourished below the dam. So a group of state and federal agencies poured $1 million into protecting the native fish of Fossil Creek. They built a barrier near the mouth of the creek, hoping to block the entry of new exotic fish. They netted as many native fish from the creek as they could, keeping more than nineteen hundred fish in storage tanks while they poisoned the exotic fish remaining in the water. They then brought the native fish back to the river via helicopter.

While similar fish barriers exist throughout the country, the Fossil Creek structure is larger than most. No other dam-removal project had undertaken such an elaborate effort to protect native fish. But results were far from guaranteed.

On June 18, 2005, after nearly a century of water diversion from Fossil Creek, Arizona Public Service shut off the flume that fed its power plants, allowing full flows to return to the creek. "Everyone was there, just waiting for the water to move downstream," remembers Marks. "There are a lot of places in a riverbed for water to go, so it came down slowly, filling all the nooks and crannies, all the pools and side channels." By the end of the day, the creek was filled, transformed from a trickle of one to two cubic feet per second to a robust flow of as much as fifty cubic feet per second.

Just weeks after the return of full flows, the travertine formations in Fossil Creek responded. "You can practically stand on the shore and watch the bedrock form," says Marks. Northern Arizona University geologist Rod Parnell, who has studied travertine at Fossil Creek both before and after the decommissioning, says the travertine is not only spreading over a wider area, but also forming at a faster rate than before the return of full flows. "When geologists see extremely rapid responses, they're usually looking at floods or volcanic eruptions—things that don't have a whole lot of benefits," says Parnell. "It's been great to see such a positive response in such a short period of time."

The native fish population also reacted dramatically: in reaches where flows had been restored and exotic fish removed, native fish increased by more than fifty-fold, rivaling the longstanding native fish population above the dam. (In a stretch where flows had been restored but exotic fish remained, the increase in native fish was comparatively meager.) Within six months, the invertebrate population bounced back from the effects of the poison used to eradicate the exotic fish, and the new travertine dams helped feed the invertebrates by trapping leaf litter. "In the short term, at least, this is a huge success," says Marks. "We couldn't ask for better results."

But the real-world experiment is far from complete. The Fossil Creek dam, by pooling water upstream, has actually preserved a stretch of key habitat for the rare lowland leopard frog. Before the restoration began, biologists warned that simultaneously returning full flows and lowering the dam would radically alter this upstream habitat before the habitat downstream had a chance to recover. The utility heeded their advice, and postponed the lowering.

Since the return of full flows, tadpoles and young frogs have reappeared below the dam. "It's crazy how much the habitat has changed," says Forest Service wildlife biologist Janie Agyagos, who has worked closely with the Northern Arizona University researchers on the Fossil Creek project. "Before, we had stagnant pools and very little running water. Now we have deep, deep pools that adult frogs like, and shallow pools with good cover for tadpoles and egg masses, and lots of aquatic vegetation." But because researchers are still awaiting the return of a healthy adult population, the utility has delayed the start of dam lowering for an additional year, until late 2008.

When dam lowering does begin, the utility will remove only a small portion of the estimated twenty-five thousand cubic yards of sediment behind the dam. The remainder will wash downstream, and Marks and her team will be watching closely. They don't expect the sediment to do any lasting damage to the ecosystem—it's comparable to what might come downstream in a "really big storm," says Marks—but it may smother some macroinvertebrate and leopard frog habitat.

Another uncertainty lurks within the beautiful travertine formations in Fossil Creek, which provide a perfect home for crayfish—a voracious species, exotic to Arizona, that Rod Parnell calls "the aquatic equivalent of the cockroach." Crayfish survived the poisoning of the creek—likely because they could burrow into the riverbed or crawl out of the water—and have multiplied since flows returned. Researchers suspect that, ironically, exotic bass helped keep the crayfish at bay. But here again, the story is not yet finished: the travertine now forms with such gusto that it even grows on crayfish shells, threatening to turn the crayfish into miniature statues.

Despite conservationists' fervent hopes, dam removal alone is no panacea. On the Sandy River in Oregon, the Marmot Dam has separated populations of wild fish from hatchery fish. Dam removal will allow hatchery fish to move into wild fish habitat. Likewise, the oft-discussed removal of the two Elwha River dams in Washington state—recently postponed again, this time until approximately 2012—could allow an invasive species of brook trout to move into Olympic National Park, where it would compete with native bull trout.

Science is beginning to inform how and when dams come out, and, at Fossil Creek and elsewhere, it is helping to anticipate and minimize some of the downsides of dam removal. But the field is a young one—"There's still a lot more talk about dam removal than there is study of dam removal," says University of North Carolina researcher Martin Doyle—and frequent delays in dam deconstruction continue to make new knowledge difficult to acquire.

The result is that while dam removal is a powerful restoration tool, it remains an uncertain business, and that uncertainty has both ecological and political consequences. "Everyone knows what a pristine ecosystem looks like, so it's easy for them to embrace it and say, 'We're going to protect this,' " says Andrew Fahlund of American Rivers, who worked on the campaign to decommission the Childs-Irving project. "With restoration, you're asking people to trust that the picture you've painted for them is the picture they're going to get. That's a big leap of faith for the general public, and for the decision-makers who are going to be held accountable." But in dam removal, as in so many other conservation efforts, the unknowns are enduring, and leaps of faith are unavoidable.

October 1, 2007

Michelle Nijhuis is contributing editor to *High Country News.*

Tribal Power

ॐ

Bracing Against the Tide

Rebecca Clarren

The flat disk of abalone shell that adorns Heiltsuk Chief Councillor Pamela Reid's headdress glares angry green beneath an ambivalent gray sky. Squint, and the iridescent shell could be a small topographic map of the mountains that fall seamlessly into the icy waters of this coastal inlet. Abalone, once a Heiltsuk delicacy, was poached to such an extent that the Canadian government banned all harvesting of the shellfish over a decade ago. Reid, twenty-eight, says that many of her peers don't remember what abalone tastes like.

"Within our culture, everything is interconnected. The abalone, the cedar trees, the salmon are all a part of what we call the circle of life," says Reid, one of only two women ever elected to lead the Heiltsuk. "When you take any factor out of the circle, you take away the foundation of our way of life."

Reid stands on the bow of a fishing boat headed across the fjords of this sparsely populated coastline. She and one hundred other Heiltsuk have sailed two and a half hours from their village, Bella Bella, to protest what they call a threat to another critical piece of their culture and livelihood.

Here in Ocean Falls, a Norwegian company is building a hatchery that, when completed next spring, will produce ten million Atlantic salmon smolts each year. While the company, Omega Salmon Group Ltd., a subsidiary of Pan Fish, is coy about its plans for those fish, there is really only one plausible answer: It is planting the seeds for a massive buildup of industrial fish farms.

Fish farms have dotted the coastline south of here, in British Columbia and in Washington State, for the past two decades. Most raise non-native Atlantic salmon in net-lined pens dropped directly into the ocean. These pens have been known to breed disease and spread pollution. But worse than that, according to critics, is the risk of farmed fish escaping into the ocean and migrating into rivers—threatening the native wild salmon.

For the thirteen hundred members of the Heiltsuk Nation, the danger is poignant because they are salmon people. Reid says the Heiltsuk consider salmon to be their brothers. The fish inspire countless dances, songs, and ceremonies. More than that, salmon are literally their lifeblood: the average Heiltsuk family lives on $5,500 a year, and people rely on salmon for most meals. From midsummer through fall, smokehouses and open barbecue pits fill the air with the rich smell of next winter's nourishment.

On the bow of the fishing boat, headed north to Ocean Falls, the wind tears through the layers of Reid's traditional button blanket. She wraps it closer to her pregnant form and dances with her elders to a low and steady song. They want the provincial government and the industry to know that they plan to fight the hatchery construction.

The Heiltsuk are swimming against a powerful current, however. There are now about eighty salmon farms operating in British Columbia, most of them located off the coast of Vancouver Island, and the recent lifting of a moratorium on new farms clears the way for more. Industry boosters say they want to double the number of farms over the next five years. For many small towns and government officials, who are struggling to revive an anemic economy, fish farms represent good jobs and a much-needed steady export.

For indigenous peoples, commercial fishermen, and environ-mentalists in the Northwest, however, the fish farms are an overwhelming threat to communities and the ecosystem.

"We don't want our central coast—our breadbasket—to become a garbage dump for the fish-farm industry," says Edwin Newman, a Heiltsuk elder. "We've been here for ten thousand years, and we aren't going anywhere. Long after they're gone, we will be the ones to clean up their mess."

All that's visible of the Young Pass fish farm is a series of rectangular steel frames, punctuated with yellow buoys, bobbing calmly on the water of Johnstone Strait, a narrow waterway squeezed between the northeastern shore of Vancouver Island and the coast of British Columbia. But beneath the placid surface, the water writhes with life. Nylon nets drop from the steel frames nearly eighty feet to where they are anchored to the ocean bottom by concrete blocks weighing up to ten tons each. The collection of eight pens—a literal tenement house for fish—is home to five hundred sixty thousand salmon.

It's feeding time here, and brown pellets the size of sesame seeds shoot from a metal pipe that sweeps over the surface of the water like a sailboat boom coming about. A few salmon jump through the air, skimming the mesh covering that keeps out the circling gulls. But despite their innate impulse to leap and dive, nothing about these fish is wild. Born in a hatchery and reared for six months in glorified lap pools, they will spend up to eighteen months in these pens, feeding and growing into fat, seven- to eighteen-pound adults.

The Young Pass farm grows chinook, but 80 percent of farmed fish are Atlantic salmon. Industry prefers Atlantic salmon, because they can be handled aggressively without bruising and because the business is dominated by Norwegians, who are accustomed to working with the fish.

Farm workers liken these salmon to cattle—a fitting comparison, since the company that raises these fish is also in the feedlot business. The farm's owner, Marine Harvest Canada, is a subsidiary of the Netherlands-based Nutreco, the world's largest fish-farm company, and one of five multinational corporations that own farms in British Columbia. Nutreco, a $3 billion company, mass-produces pork and poultry at factory farms around the world.

Compared to producing chicken, pork, or beef, raising farm fish is light on the land, says Vivian Krause, Nutreco's aquaculture specialist, as she strolls the grated walkways between the Young Pass pens. It takes over three pounds of feed to grow a pound of pork, she says, vs. 1.2 pounds of feed for a pound of farmed fish. Otherwise, she says, raising fish isn't terribly different from raising cattle, although, she adds, "when a farmed fish escapes, you can't exactly whistle him back home."

As with any corporate farming operation, getting the meat to consumers around the world is no small feat. When the fish are full-grown, boats equipped with giant cranes scoop them from the water and transport them to processing plants on Vancouver Island. En route to towns such as Campbell River and Port McNeill, the fish are stunned with carbon dioxide or a high-pressure "air hammer."

At the Brown's Bay Packing Co. in Campbell River, freshly unloaded fish float in frothy pink water, dying slowly as their blood drains away from their gills in a temperature-controlled tub. Inside the plant, nearly three thousand salmon a day are de-headed, de-tailed, de-boned, and gutted by men and women in aprons and hair nets lined up on both sides of a winding conveyer belt. An automated saw with an electronic eye then cuts each fish into four- to six-ounce portions. The process is sanitary, exact, and efficient.

Shipped overnight in ice to Seattle, roughly one hundred thirty-five thousand of these perfectly standard portions are flown each day to California, the Midwest, and even the East Coast, where they're headlined on restaurant special boards and grocery-store meat counters as "Fresh Atlantic Salmon."

It's a booming business: British Columbia's largest agricultural export, farmed fish contribute $603 million annually to the provincial economy, creating forty-seven hundred full-time jobs. With a coastline and environment ideal for salmon farming, British Columbia could see those figures double in the next five years, says a financial advisor for Omega Salmon Group Ltd.—and double again in the five years after that.

This is terrific news, says Bill Shephard, the chairman of the regional government of the Mount Waddington district, which is based in Port McNeill and encompasses the northern end of Vancouver Island. This region specializes in dismal economies: logging and commercial fishing have declined steadily, and a mine closure several years ago eliminated six hundred jobs. Food banks in coastal communities from Campbell River to Port Hardy report record need.

Fish farms offer a way for a former logging town like Port McNeill to reinvent itself, says Shephard. "These are good jobs in a rural community," he says. Fish-farm jobs start at $14 an hour Canadian—"a far spit from clerking for $7 an hour at the corner market."

But just across the water from Port McNeill, in the village of Sointula, commercial fishermen are singing a gloomier tune. Founded at the turn of the century as a Finnish utopian community, Sointula is not exactly Eden anymore. For decades, fishing for everything from salmon to herring to shrimp provided steady work, if not riches. But fishermen have watched their livelihood spiral into oblivion, as decreasing runs of wild salmon lead to plummeting catches and to fishing quotas. Fish farms just add to the problem, driving down the price of wild fish. Chum salmon, for example, that was worth a dollar a pound (Canadian) to fishermen ten years ago, now only catches 25 cents a pound. (The same is true to the south: Washington tribal members report that sockeye that once sold for $2.50 a pound in American dollars now fetches just $1 a pound.)

Today in Sointula, red "For Sale" signs pepper front lawns. School enrollment has dropped by over half in the past decade; there are only twelve children in the single fifth-grade class. "Fish farms are breaking the backs of the commercial fishermen," says Calvin Siider, a fourth-generation fisherman. "I'd be better off to burn my boat than to sell it."

On a drizzly midwinter morning, Siider sips a cup of coffee and looks out the window of a local bakery onto a bay that gleams like dirty nickels and dimes. Siider's brother, also a fisherman, committed suicide last year, due in part to the dismal economy.

"Our federal bureaucracy seems to be working against us and not for us," he says. "In lots of respects, the government is our enemy."

That's unfair, says Shephard, with the regional government in Port McNeill. "We're trying to do our part for the greatest good, but some people don't have any perspective," he says. "I'm sure there were people in Saskatchewan and the Dakotas a hundred fifty years ago who were opposed to farming because it meant the end of buffalo hunting. But times change."

A growing crowd of critics isn't content to watch the times change without a fight. Their concerns go beyond the economic: they say fish farms aren't worth the cost to the environment, especially to the wild salmon.

"These farms are the equivalent of the mad-cow feedlots in Britain that wiped out every herd of cattle," says Montana writer David James Duncan, author of the novel *The River Why*, and a longtime advocate for wild salmon. "Every place in the world these multinational meat growers have gone, they have caused a major environmental collapse."

The problems start with the tons of food pellets that farmed fish are fed, which are made from shellfish and small fish and laced with antibiotics. This translates into what Duncan delicately refers to as "a shit problem."

The average salmon farm creates as much raw sewage as a town of sixty-five thousand people, says Ian McAllister, a Bella Bella-based environmental activist who works for the Raincoast Conservation Society. The antibiotic-laden sewage overloads the water with nutrients, creating an oxygen-starved "dead zone" that can extend up to five hundred feet around the pens, killing shellfish and even the beneficial bacteria living on the sea floor.

"Imagine if the poultry industry was allowed to dump a million tons of chicken manure onto a national park. People would be outraged," says McAllister. "But the fish-farm industry is allowed to do just that."

Disease and parasites are easily spread in the close quarters of farm pens. Despite regular treatment with pesticides, fish farms are breeding grounds for sea lice, tiny parasites that eat away at, and can eventually kill, young salmon.

Two summers ago, in the Broughton Archipelago, a cluster of islands near the north end of Vancouver Island, fishermen discovered tiny salmon fry covered with as many as twenty-five sea lice. Some scientists now suspect that the wild salmon picked up the lice from the twenty-six fish farms situated along their annual migration routes. McAllister says the consequences have been dire: of the over three million juvenile salmon that migrated to the ocean from eight different river systems in the area, only one hundred forty-seven thousand returned this past summer. It's the worst return ever seen on the British Columbia coast, since the Department of Fisheries and Oceans started keeping record in 1953. At this rate, McAllister says, sea lice spread by fish farms could "be responsible for the extinction of complete races of salmon."

Extinction could become epidemic, critics warn, if farmed fish continue to escape into the oceans and rivers where wild salmon feed and spawn. Over 80 percent of farmed fish are non-native Atlantic salmon, while chinook and coho comprise the remainder. There is little research on how farmed and wild fish interact, but many scientists worry that Atlantic salmon, a more aggressive species than their Pacific cousins, will outcompete native fish for habitat and food. Farmed Chinook may interbreed with wild fish, diluting the genetic purity of wild salmon runs.

Native salmon have evolved with specific rivers. They know how to make use of every pocket of available habitat. After migrating out to the ocean as babies, they make their way by scent back to the river where they were born, returning home to spawn another generation. If Atlantic salmon out-compete the natives for food and habitat, but fail to return to the rivers, sustainable salmon runs—and the ecosystem that depends on them—will become a distant memory, say critics such as Duncan.

"We have all these examples globally of what happens when exotic species are introduced," says Duncan. "All of Montana's native grasses have been totally wiped out by two invasive species of weeds; snapping turtles have consumed all the habitat of the world's wild turtles. I see in Atlantic salmon, a Pacific salmon apocalypse."

The Canadian government is charged with protecting wild salmon, but critics say its track record is inconsistent at best. When salmon farms first set up shop in the mid-1970s, government and industry said that if a few farm salmon managed to break free, they would pose no threat to wild fish. "Atlantic salmon have no home stream to return to in order to spawn," read a brochure distributed in 1987 by the British Columbia Ministry of Agriculture, Food, and Fisheries. "Instead, they would return (if they survived that long) to their home fish farm. Without a freshwater spawning ground, they would be unable to reproduce."

Out of the ten million Atlantic salmon raised in British Columbia annually, the government reports an average of forty thousand runaways. In the history of the industry, only two fish farms have been fined for allowing fish to escape.

That's not exactly good news. On the seas, anecdotal evidence paints a very different picture than the official numbers do. In the summer of 2000, a storm tore a hole in the net pens of a fish farm off the northern tip of Vancouver Island, and fishermen immediately began pulling the dark speckled fish out of the water. Independent whale researcher Alexandra Morton spent the next month interviewing fishermen, and in one month her informal tally reached 10,233 escapees. Yet for the entire year of 2000, the federal Department of Fisheries and Oceans lists only 7,833 escapes along the length of the British Columbia coast.

Part of the reason for this fuzzy math is that although fish farmers are required to report escaped fish, there are no government employees to police the waters, and the Department of Fisheries and Oceans acknowledges that it doesn't know how well companies follow the rules. Currently, there is no way to trace an escapee to its farm of origin.

Concerned that escaped farm fish could jeopardize its $258 million a year wild salmon fishery, the Alaska Department of Fish and Game investigated further. According to the agency's study, released in March 2002, over four hundred fifty thousand Atlantic salmon slip away from salmon farms in British Columbia and Washington annually. Many of these fish are released intentionally; farms set free small or slow-growing fish because it's cheaper than raising them to full size. There are anecdotal reports of Atlantic salmon ascending every major river drainage on Vancouver Island. In 2000 alone, eighty-one Atlantic salmon were found in Alaska's marine waters, and one was caught ascending the state's Doame River.

Despite government assurances to the contrary, these fish are reproducing, according to John Volpe, a biology professor at the University of Alberta. Volpe has spent the past four years snorkeling Vancouver Island's whitewater rivers, stalking Atlantic salmon. His results are chilling: after surveying only 1 percent of potential rearing habitat, he has found wild spawned juvenile Atlantic salmon in three river systems.

Officials with the provincial government continue to deny that there is a problem. Volpe says they're not looking in the right places. "The [Department of Fisheries and Oceans] characters think you can collect data from a desk in Ottawa," he says. "If you want to do fish biology, you've got to get in the water and get wet."

The problem of poor government regulation isn't unique to British Columbia, says Anne Mosness, in the Bellingham, Washington, office of the national Institute for Agriculture and Trade Policy. In the United States, Oregon and California have banned fish farms in response to a powerful commercial fishing lobby—and because their rocky coastlines tend to discourage aquaculture. Alaska has outlawed fish farms, as well. But in Washington, few groups or government agencies are keeping an eye on the industry.

Part of the problem is government bureaucracy, says Mosness. The Washington Department of Fish and Wildlife, the state Department of Ecology, the U.S. Department of Agriculture, and the National Marine Fisheries Service are each charged with different aspects of monitoring and permitting aquaculture. None of these agencies have even one full-time person working on aquaculture, and there is no state or federal budget to enforce regulations.

Compounding the issue, says Mosness, is the fact that "people are in regulatory agencies to promote fish farms; it's clearly a revolving door." She points to Washington State Senator Dan Swecker, Republican, a former fish farmer who currently works as secretary treasurer of the Washington Fish Growers Association. In the nine years Swecker has been in office, he has sponsored legislation to streamline the permit process for fish farms, revised a state law to extend aquaculture leases, and helped to secure funding for a new aquaculture certification center. Swecker freely acknowledges he got into politics to "help solve the regulatory problems faced by aquaculture."

The situation is even more complicated in British Columbia, where the Ministry of Agriculture, Food, and Fisheries plays the paradoxical role of both promoter and regulator. The department's former minister, John van Dongen, was forced to resign in January amid allegations that he passed confidential information to a fish-farm company. A huge booster of fish farms, Van Dongen was responsible for lifting a seven-year moratorium on new fish-farm applications, which the previous administration had imposed in response to concerns about escaped salmon.

Van Dongen's replacement, Stan Hagen, says he plans to move forward with processing the nine permits now pending for new operations. No stranger to environmental controversy, Hagen recently proposed opening up half the province to logging and mining companies. He is also facing conflict-of-interest charges: the single largest contributor to his last political campaign was an aquaculture company.

Hagen says the British Columbia government has a handle on fish farms and their associated impacts. There are fifty-two federal and provincial acts governing a broad range of aquaculture issues, from farm practices to environmental impacts to employment standards. The provincial government also recently spent over $1 million and more than two years to complete an eighteen hundred-page report that found that fish farms pose little threat to either wild salmon or the environment.

Still, in light of rising concerns about sea lice spreading to wild fish, Hagen has closed eleven of the twenty-eight farms in the Broughton Archipelago, and he plans to study the remaining seventeen. Hagen also wants to create a panel of stakeholders to help build public consensus about the future direction of the aquaculture industry.

"The most important fish on the West Coast is wild salmon," says Hagen, who once worked as a deckhand on commercial fishing boats. "We must ensure nothing we do harms them." Wild salmon are also a priority for the aquaculture industry, says Mary Ellen Walling, executive director of the B.C. Salmon Farmers Association. Fish-farm companies spend millions of dollars on environmental research, Pacific salmon hatcheries, and community events and charities. One company, Marine Harvest Canada, recently completed a voluntary $200,000 environmental assessment of all its facilities, and divers check the nets weekly for tears through which fish might escape. All members of the Farmers Association adhere to a "code of practice" that is currently being revised to "reflect industry's commitment to continual improvement," says Walling.

While what happens in British Columbia could have far-reaching implications for its neighbors to the south, most U.S. regulators seem unconcerned. "We certainly don't have any heartburn about fish farms," says Brian Gorman, a spokesman for the National Marine Fisheries Service, the federal agency charged with protecting wild salmon. "While

I suppose there is a potential problem, because you're dealing with an exotic species and there are inevitable escapes, so far there hasn't been a problem, and I don't anticipate one."

In part, that's because the nine fish farms in Washington are peanuts compared to British Columbia, and Gorman doesn't expect the industry to expand along his state's highly populated waterfronts when the British Columbia coastline is still relatively empty.

Asked if he is concerned that Canadian fish farms could spread Atlantic salmon to U.S. rivers, another regulator is nonchalant. "This all boils down to your view of risks," says Andy Appleby, with the Washington Department of Fish and Wildlife, who has sole charge of monitoring the aquaculture industry. "Atlantic salmon are going to escape, we can count on that, but by our estimates and those of the British Columbia government and [the National Marine Fisheries Service], the consequences of those escapes are very low."

Appleby says John Volpe's findings that Atlantic salmon can reproduce in the wild are sound: "No one questions his results." He adds, however, that Volpe's conclusion that Atlantics pose a significant threat to Pacific salmon stocks is "a quantum leap." Despite attempts in thirty different countries, he claims Atlantic salmon haven't colonized—that is, they haven't spawned and returned to the same river.

Even so, in the past year, the Department of Fish and Wildlife has beefed up the state's regulations. Starting in 2004, all Atlantic salmon will be marked or branded like cattle, so that if any escape, managers will be able to tell them from wild fish. Every farm must have a plan for preventing escapes, for reporting them to authorities when they do occur, and for capturing escapees when possible.

While Appleby is confident in the science, which, he says, has been "reviewed to death," he adds, "time will certainly tell."

Not everyone is content to wait and see. In an effort to combat a government that critics claim is deaf to their concerns, fishing, tribal, and environmental groups in both Canada and in the U.S. are trying a new tactic: they're targeting the group driving industry expansion—American consumers. Eighty-five percent of British Columbia farm fish end up on dinner plates in the States.

Last fall, the Coastal Alliance for Aquaculture Reform, a British Columbia-based coalition that is working with one hundred thirty organizations throughout the United States, launched the "Farmed and Dangerous" campaign. The coalition has distributed tens of thousands of postcards and brochures on the potential health effects of eating farmed fish. The campaign wants farmed salmon to be labeled as such in grocery stores, fish farms moved onto land or contained in heavy duty tarps so that feces—and fish—can't leak out, and more science about how wild and farmed salmon interact.

"We cannot afford to see this as a Canadian issue," says Dave Lutz, a former commercial fisherman who now guides ecotours along the coasts of Washington and British Columbia. He organized a group of U.S. fishermen, Native Americans, and environmentalists to travel to Ocean Falls and protest with the Heiltsuk. On the boat ride to the protest, he and McAllister huddle against the wind and joke about how finally Canadians and Americans are "overcoming the language barrier" in order to work together on this issue.

"If these farmed fish move across the border, they could take over our natural ecosystem," says Harlan James, a member of Washington's Lummi Indian Nation, who traveled to Ocean Falls for the protest. "We're trying to heal a wound before it festers into something infectious."

As the boats laden with protesters dock in Ocean Falls, they are greeted by eighty members of the Nuxalk Nation, the Heiltsuk's historic enemy. Standing in a circle on shore, adorned in red button blankets and cedar-carved masks, tribal leaders from both bands speak of working as brothers to fight the hatchery. As the afternoon wears on and rain drizzles from the sky, the First Nations and their supporters march onto the construction site to sing and dance in protest.

Omega Salmon Group Ltd. evacuates employees the day of the protest, but resumes construction the next day and expects to finish this summer.

Protesters acknowledge that as long as there is an American market hungry for farmed fish Canada will continue to throw its doors open to aquaculture. Until consumers in America and Canada are willing to vote with their pocket books, activists are dubious that government or industry will be inspired to reform.

Still, with or without American support, Canadians will continue to fight for change. In February, the Heiltsuk sued the provincial government and Omega Salmon Group Ltd., claiming that the new hatchery violates the tribe's aboriginal rights. The case may be heard by the Supreme Court of British Columbia as soon as May.

"Our cultural survival is at risk; our whole resource base is at risk," says Pamela Reid after the protest, her voice flat with fatigue. "There's a Heiltsuk phrase: *kaxlaya gwilas*. It means we have an obligation to uphold the laws of our ancestors. We have no choice about whether or not to fight fish farms. This is a way of life we are responsible for."

March 17, 2003

Rebecca Clarren lives in Portland, Oregon, and writes about environmental and labor issues for several magazines.

The New Water Czars

Daniel Kraker

Thirty miles south of downtown Phoenix, past the rugged South Mountains rising out of the city's southern edge, past the acres of asphalt and the ten-lane highways, the city stops abruptly at the bone-dry bed of the Gila River. On the other side of the riverbed, where you might expect to find desert saguaro and cholla, emerald green farm fields blur into the horizon: perfectly flat rectangles laid out one after the other, separated by canals and irrigation ditches into a gigantic crossword puzzle-like grid.

Here, on the 375,000-acre Gila River Indian Community, Pima and Maricopa Indians tend fields of alfalfa, cotton, wheat, and vegetables, groves of citrus and olive trees, and even giant ponds full of tilapia and shrimp. The community's sixteen thousand-acre farm, and a handful of smaller farms operated by tribal members, are sustained by more than two hundred thousand acre-feet of water, funneled every year from the Gila, Salt, and Colorado rivers, or pumped from underground aquifers. (An acre-foot is one year's worth of water for a family of four.)

Already, the Gila River Indian Community is one of the largest agricultural operations in southern Arizona. But a deal pending before Congress would more than triple its water share, and turn the tribes' land into what some tribal leaders hope will be the "breadbasket of Arizona." The landmark settlement would provide this community of fewer than twenty thousand with more than six hundred fifty thousand acre-feet of water annually. That's enough to serve the residential needs of almost three million people, nearly the entire Phoenix metropolitan area.

The deal has been nearly eighty years in the making. If approved, it will be the largest Indian water-rights settlement in history, involving literally thousands of parties and hundreds of millions of federal dollars. And it will give the Gila River Indians a huge tap into the massive Central

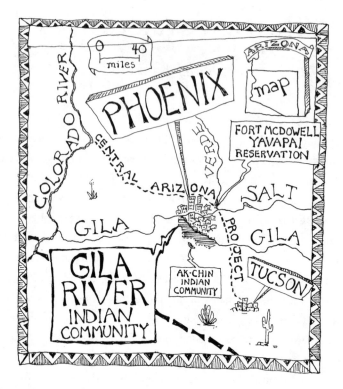

Arizona Project, which funnels water from the Colorado River into the heart of Arizona.

If the Gila River Indian Community scores this huge victory, it will put the Pima and Maricopa people in a position of tremendous power—and at the center of more than a little controversy. Critics complain that the deal will put vast amounts of precious Colorado River water—literally the lifeblood of the Southwest—in the hands of a tiny minority of "Indian water czars." But where some people see a frightening reshuffling of power, others see a bit of long-overdue justice, and even question whether the tribes are getting enough out of the deal.

However you look at it, the Gila River water settlement paradoxically stands to either shape—or strangle—many other tribes' ambitious quests for the West's most valuable resource.

Ramona Button and her husband, Terry, have operated Ramona Farms on the Gila River Indian Community for the past thirty years. Currently, they farm about twenty-five hundred acres, growing cash crops like alfalfa and cotton, as well as heirloom crops like Hopi corn and tepary beans.

Ramona is in her sixties, her skin weathered from hours spent in the desert sun. She grew up in a traditional Pima home, and has vivid memories of her father's ten-acre farm. He dug ditches to bring water from the irrigation laterals, and grew alfalfa to feed the family's horses, as well as a cornucopia of fruits and vegetables, even sugarcane. Ramona would ride with him in their wagon to trade with surrounding tribes and non-Indians in the 1950s.

Ramona's father's farm offered a glimpse of her tribe's unusual agricultural history. Long before Europeans arrived on the scene, the Pimas farmed along the banks of the Salt and Gila rivers, the two main arteries that drain Arizona's eastern mountain country. They're descendants of the Hohokam, who, from about 300 B.C. to 1450 A.D., farmed the rivers' rich floodplains, hand-digging a complex canal system to divert water during spring runoff.

"They were one of the most remarkable agricultural civilizations in the New World," says Gary Nabhan, who directs the Center for Sustainable Environments at Northern Arizona University. The Hohokam eventually dug more than six hundred miles of canals, some as wide as sixty-four feet across, that carried water as far as sixteen miles from the rivers—all using only stone instruments and highly organized labor.

In the eighteenth century, the Pimas banded together with the Maricopas, who migrated into the area from along the Colorado River. As late as the 1870s, the tribes were the largest producers west of the Mississippi of wheat and other crops.

During the Civil War, the community, which was formally established in 1859, supplied both the Yankees and the Rebels with all their wheat flour, sent east by rail. Shortly thereafter, the Army stepped in, laying out its own giant farm amongst the canals. The Army grew thousands of acres of hay to feed the horses it used in the fight to subdue renegade bands of Apaches—and eventually, to capture Geronimo, the leader of the last band of American Indians to formally surrender to the United States.

But the long, lush fields of the Pimas and Maricopas began to wither in the late 1800s, when Mormon farmers upstream began diverting huge amounts of water from the Gila. Partly as repayment for the tribes' cooperation in the Arizona Indian Wars, Congress approved the construction of Coolidge Dam upstream on the Gila in 1924, as well as the San Carlos Irrigation Project, a network of canals to transport enough water to irrigate fifty thousand acres on the reservation.

But the Bureau of Indian Affairs (BIA) only got halfway through construction of the irrigation system before it ran out of money. With the canals that were completed, the tribe and some individuals have managed to farm some twenty thousand acres.

Now that money from the BIA has begun to trickle in again, the community has embarked on a massive rehabilitation and expansion of the irrigation works. But to really make the project work, says Lee Thompson, director of the tribes' Department of Land and Water, the community needs the $200 million in federal money included in the water settlement now before Congress, because its vision is now much grander than the original San Carlos Irrigation Project. When the expansion is completed, Thompson says, there will be a twenty-four hundred-mile spiderweb of canals, pipelines, and laterals that will carry enough water to irrigate 146,000 acres of farmland.

The water settlement will allow the Pimas and Maricopas "to go back to our agricultural heritage," says Thompson, expertly navigating the rutted dirt roads between the canals and fields in a giant Ford Expedition. New canals carry crystal-blue water to vivid green fields of alfalfa and huge citrus groves—oranges, nectarines, grapefruit, lemons, and the tangerine and grapefruit hybrids called tangelos. "The idea is, if there's a lot of water coming into the community, the quickest way to use that water is by putting it into agriculture. We want to use the water to preserve the [agricultural potential of the] land, because that's one of the last things we have left."

The project offers hope for the tribes' approximately twenty thousand members, about two-thirds of whom live on the reservation. Over the years, small-scale farming has largely died out; most tribal people don't have the capital to get into it, and financing on the reservation is next to impossible, because the land, held in trust by the federal government, can't be used as collateral.

The tribes operate two profitable casinos, and the revenues have helped fund new homes, public waterworks, and health-care clinics. But per capita income on the reservation is still a scant $6,000. Half of the adult population suffers from diabetes, brought on by a switch from traditional foods to the sugar-rich foods of Anglo culture—the highest per capita rate of diabetes in the world.

The tribes are already setting up a grant program to help small farmers dig irrigation laterals, and buy seeds and equipment. A seed bank has been established to preserve ancient varieties of drought-resistant corn, squash, and tepary beans, which offer a return to a more traditional, healthier diet. There is also a ready market in high-end restaurants that incorporate Indian staples into their menus. Thompson's staff at the Department of Land and Water helps teach gardening basics to grade-school kids on the reservation.

But Terry and Ramona Button say it will be difficult to re-establish their tribes' small-scale farming tradition. "There are three or four generations of people who haven't been directly involved in agriculture," says Terry Button. He can see a place for small subsistence gardens, but he doubts that the Pimas and Maricopas can ever return completely to the old ways.

The new way is to grow crops for cash, and much of that will happen on Gila River Farms, the mammoth tribally owned operation. Like the casinos, Gila River Farms is under the tribal umbrella, but it has its own general manager who oversees day-to-day operations. Revenues from all tribal enterprises go into the general fund, and are spent on various public-works projects at the discretion of the popularly elected tribal council.

While some tribal members may return to farming, Terry Button says non-Indian corporate farmers are already looking into leasing land on the reservation, drawn by the guaranteed, long-term supply of water.

If the Gila River water settlement is creating a buzz on the reservation, then talk in the broader western water world, where Indian water rights have long been the elephant in the corner, has risen to a roar.

Indian tribes enjoy what are known as "Winters" reserved rights to water, named after a century-old Supreme Court case in which each tribe's water rights were tied to the date its reservation was created. Most western states divvy up water based on "prior appropriation," meaning that whoever first puts the water to use has the rights to it. Typically, that has been non-Indian farmers. But once tribes affirm their rights in court, they take precedence over all other users, even if it means leaving no water for anyone else.

And tribes can potentially claim historic rights to the lion's share of water in the West. In the landmark 1963 case *Arizona vs. California*, the U.S. Supreme Court ruled that tribes were entitled to as much water as necessary to farm all the "practically irrigable acreage" on their reservations. In some instances, that has meant huge tribal claims: the same court case awarded the Colorado River Indian Tribes, whose Arizona reservation sits in the Colorado River's rich floodplain south of Hoover Dam, the rights to more than seven hundred thousand acre-feet of water a year.

In most cases, however, Indian water claims have simply meant endless litigation: of the hundreds of Indian water-rights lawsuits filed since the Winters Doctrine was established near the turn of the last century, only three have been resolved in court. But anyone involved in western water knows that, eventually, Indian water claims will come home to roost. And in the case of the Gila River tribes, the claim—and its consequences— have been massive.

The Gila River Indian Community first went to court in 1925, and has spent millions of dollars in an effort to quantify its water rights. Originally, the tribes made a claim on the Gila and Salt rivers, which form the boundaries of the reservation. In 1974, they sued for nearly the entire annual flow of the Gila, almost two million acre-feet.

If the tribes had pursued that claim, it would have posed a major threat to the water supply of fast-growing Phoenix, according to City Water

Manager Tom Buschatzke. Phoenix took the threat so seriously that, in 1988, it created an adjudication section within its law department, staffed by an attorney, a paralegal, a historian, and a hydrologist, to try to work out a settlement with the Gila River Community and other tribes.

"We believed, and still do believe," says Buschatzke, "that without settlements, [Indian tribes] are threats to our water supply."

It took eight years, but the city, working with the Arizona Department of Water Resources, the Central Arizona Water Conservation District, the Bureau of Indian Affairs, the Bureau of Reclamation, irrigation districts, and other metropolitan cities, finally came to an agreement with the Gila River Community. The proposed settlement makes a trade: the city of Phoenix will hang onto most of the water from the Gila and Salt rivers; the tribes, in return, will get a huge slug of water from the Central Arizona Project (CAP), the $4.7 billion system of canals that pumps 1.5 million acre-feet of water annually from the Colorado River.

The losers in the Gila River settlement—at least on paper—are those non-Indian farmers with junior rights to the Central Arizona Project, who grow mostly cotton, along with some feed grains and vegetables. They will have to give up some two hundred thousand acre-feet of water to the Gila River Community, as well as another sixty-seven thousand acre-feet to an "account" reserved for future Indian settlements. In exchange, they'll receive a waiver of more than $73 million in debt that they owe for the Central Arizona Project.

Tribal attorney Rod Lewis, who has spent thirty-one years working to get water for the Gila River Indians, speaks proudly of the settlement, but he also says it is a "bundle of compromises."

Lewis says the CAP trade-off wasn't easy for some tribal members to swallow. Many elders remember when the Gila River used to flow through the reservation, he says; although the tribe will use some of the settlement water and agricultural runoff to restore wetlands along the river, the Gila will flow no more.

And, he says, some members thought the tribe deserved more than six hundred fifty thousand acre-feet: "Some people thought we should fight it out in court and extract every acre-foot of water that we could." But ultimately, the tribes agreed to the lesser amount to avoid the possibility of losing their case in court, and because the federal government agreed to foot the bill to upgrade the reservation's water-distribution system. That gave Gila River Indians actual "wet water," as opposed to "paper water"—water that a tribe owns rights to, but lacks the means to actually put to use.

That's what Arizona Department of Water Resources attorney Gregg Houtz calls the "Wind River situation." In the 1980s, the Eastern Shoshone and Northern Arapaho tribes on the Wind River Reservation in Wyoming went before the Supreme Court three times. They ultimately won rights to almost the entire annual flow of the Bighorn River. "But they have absolutely no money to develop those resources," says Houtz. "What you get in settlements is the resources to develop water for use on the reservation. That is probably what brings the tribes to the [negotiating] table more than anything else."

The Gila River tribes hit another sticking point on an issue that is one of the most controversial—but lucrative—parts of most modern Indian water settlements: provisions that permit tribes to lease at least some of their water to other users. Under the proposed settlement, the Gila River Indian Community can lease about forty-one thousand acre-feet of its water to cities and it has the option to lease upwards of one hundred thousand acre-feet in the future.

Water marketing is already a big moneymaker for Arizona tribes that have settled their water rights claims. The tiny Ak-Chin Indian Community, which forged the first water-rights settlement with the federal government in 1978, leases water to Anthem, a plush planned community north of Phoenix, with its own four-acre fishing lake and Big Splash Water Park, for $1,200 an acre-foot—compared to the $106 an acre-foot valley cities currently pay for CAP water.

And the Gila River Indian Community will get even more for its water. Tom Buschatzke says the city of Phoenix anticipates leasing fifteen thousand acre-feet for about $1,500 per acre-foot. That's $22.5 million per year for the tribe. If the tribe is able to lease forty-one thousand acre-feet at that price, that equates to annual revenues of $61.5 million.

All this worries critics of Indian water deals. In an editorial in *The Arizona Republic* after the Gila River deal was announced, Arizona water historian Earl Zarbin wrote that if it becomes law, "Indian water czars"— the thirteen tribes with rights to Colorado River water that make up slightly more than 1 percent of the state's population—will control more than half of the state's Colorado River entitlement. Zarbin and others argue that water should just be given to the cities, rather than allotted to Indians and leased to cities at cutthroat prices. "In my mind," Zarbin says, "it's unjust enrichment. Why should anybody in an arid state be given more water than they need so they can turn around and lease it?"

But in reality, even the right to lease the water is one more compromise. The Gila River Indian Community will only be able to lease roughly one-sixth of the water it gets in the settlement. The settlement forbids leases to out-of-state buyers, and the tribe is severely limited in what it can charge for its water.

When it comes to Indian settlements, the price for water isn't set by competing buyers in an open market—it's determined by a complicated formula written into the terms of the settlement. A 1988 water rights settlement with the Salt River Pima-Maricopa Indian Community just east of Phoenix established a lease price of $1,100 an acre-foot. "Subsequent [Indian water] settlements," says Phoenix's Tom Buschatzke, "have used that price as a baseline" and adjusted it based solely on inflation.

The price of Indian water may seem exorbitant now, but a few years down the line, it may look dirt-cheap when increased demand drives open-market prices sky-high. Los Angeles, for example, is already considering buying water at prices of up to $10,000 an acre-foot.

University of Utah professor Daniel McCool, who has written two books on Indian water rights, says the Gila River tribes would be better off with a smaller amount of water that they could lease to other users, anywhere, at any price they wanted.

The real test of Indian water settlements might not come for another hundred years, when prices on the open market are phenomenally high. Tribes will look back, says McCool, "and I think they'll say, 'The albatross around our neck is the inability to freely market water to whomever we want, whenever we want.'"

Whatever angle you take on the Gila River water settlement, it is dripping with irony.

The settlement will slowly wean many non-Indian farmers in central Arizona from Colorado River water, but it will simultaneously subsidize a massive expansion of Indian farming. Some of that farming will be traditional subsistence agriculture, but much of it will be large-scale and water-intensive, even as critics question the economic and ecological wisdom of flood-irrigated desert farming.

Another irony is that, as non-Indian farmers lose access to CAP water, they are likely to turn back to pumping Arizona's limited groundwater—a practice that CAP was explicitly designed to end.

Also, when the Central Arizona Project was initially funded, the federal government saw it as a way to settle the water-rights claims of the state's Indian tribes, many of which were wending their way through the federal courts. While this settlement would give the Gila River Indian Community its due, it could cut out the claims of many other tribes, including those of the much-larger Navajo Nation.

That's because the Gila River deal divides up the Central Arizona Project's annual allotment of 1.5 million acre-feet: the federal government gets 735,000 acre-feet to help settle the state's Indian claims; the state gets the rest. Nearly all of the federal allocation would already be spoken for: Almost half of it has been awarded to a number of tribes in the southern half of the state, and the Gila River tribes would get almost all the rest. The deal would leave the feds with only sixty-seven thousand acre-feet to divide among the Navajo, the Hopi, the White Mountain Apache, and six other tribes that still have unsettled water-rights claims.

The Navajo Nation alone, with a seventeen million-acre reservation that borders the Colorado River, may have a claim to many times that amount of water. And the Navajos arguably are in more dire need of surface water than any other tribe in the state: Nearly a third of the two hundred thousand people living on the reservation still haul water to their remote homesteads for drinking, cooking, and washing. Towns on the western side of the reservation, including Tuba City and Kayenta, are projected to run out of groundwater within the next three decades.

Thousands of ranchers have been forced to sell livestock because wells have dried up.

"The decision to use such a huge quantity of CAP water in the Gila River settlement is being made in a vacuum," says Navajo water-rights attorney Stan Pollack. The government, he says, is "tying its hands."

For this reason, the Gila River settlement will likely only pass Congress if another bill—a complex trade-off that will send water to the Navajo Nation capital in Window Rock—passes as well. New Mexico Senator Pete Domenici, Republican, hopes to have that bill introduced this spring, about the same time Arizona Senator Jon Kyl, Republican, hopes to have the Gila River settlement marked up in the Senate Energy Committee.

Water for the eight other tribes in the state with outstanding water-rights claims will likely have to come from existing users, predominantly non-Indian farmers, as well as from groundwater, and from the Little Colorado River and some smaller mountain streams.

Of course, many see Indian water settlements, including the huge amount of water the Gila River Indian Community is on the cusp of receiving, as reparation for a century-and-a-half of failed federal Indian policies. And therein lies perhaps the deepest irony of all.

Those policies confined Indians to reservations in the mid-1800s, then divvied up the land and tried to turn tribal members into individual landowners and farmers. The federal government for a century did its best to transform Native Americans into an Anglicized ideal—essentially, happy hay farmers. And now that the Indians are finally taking the government up on that offer, it's difficult to argue about it. That's especially true in the case of the Gila River Indians, who have already been farmers for centuries.

And what if, years from now, the tribes push to renegotiate the settlement, and sell more of their irrigation water to cities? "If it's going to be called Indian water," says McCool of the University of Utah, "they should be able to do what they want with it."

March 15, 2004

Daniel Kraker directs the Indian Country News Bureau at KNAU, Arizona Public Radio in Flagstaff, Arizona.

Protecting the Treaties, Saving the Fish

Tim Sullivan

Kat Brigham's daughter once asked if she would be able to fish in the open water of the Columbia River the way she remembered her father doing—or if she would have to simply stand on the bank, and hope for more fish next season.

Brigham has made it her life's work to see that her daughters, her grandchildren, and subsequent generations of Oregon's Confederated Tribes of the Umatilla can fish in the Columbia every year. She is one of her community's strongest advocates for restoring native salmon and trout fisheries, and for maintaining tribal treaty rights to fish in the Columbia and its tributaries.

The 1855 treaty between the Walla Walla, Cayuse, and Umatilla tribes, which make up the Confederated Tribes of the Umatilla, created the tribes' reservation near Pendleton. It also gave their roughly twenty-five hundred members exclusive rights to fish in streams on and bordering the reservation.

Fishing is a tribal tradition, and the Columbia River was only about thirty miles away from Brigham's childhood home on the reservation. But she grew up more familiar with the mountains than the river, becoming better acquainted with the Columbia when she married an Umatilla commercial fisherman in 1965.

Brigham left the reservation for the small downstream town of Cascade Locks, where her husband, Robert, and his family had their operation. Like many Umatilla families, they caught fish for a variety of purposes: tribal ceremonies, commercial profit, and their own use. Although Brigham's parents had taught her that women weren't supposed to hunt or fish, this was more accepted by her husband's family. Soon, she was setting nets with her in-laws, and eventually, she had her own all-female crew.

Meanwhile, Brigham gave her grandfather rides to tribal, state, and federal agency meetings in Portland, and she often asked him questions about the complex web of agencies and rules that govern fishing in the Columbia.

"He taught me that I had a responsibility to watch out for future generations, to protect the treaty," Brigham says.

After joining the Umatilla Fish and Wildlife Committee in 1976, Brigham realized that her simple fishing life had become complicated. She was especially frustrated, she says, by the ongoing over-fishing by non-Indian fishermen. They caught so many fish that the Confederated Tribes believed that if Indian fishermen took any, the salmon would no longer be able to reproduce in healthy numbers. Many years, Brigham winced as she told her neighbors that the tribes had decided they would have to stay off the river.

"I could have been upset, but what does that accomplish?" Brigham says. "There was a realization that we needed to move on and improve things."

So Brigham traveled to southeast Alaska, Canada, and Washington, where she helped to coordinate the harvest of salmon throughout the Northwest—an effort she says helped curb over-fishing. Throughout the 1960s and 1970s, the Umatilla, the Yakama, and other tribes also won court decisions that allotted them rights to 50 percent of all harvestable fish in the Columbia Basin. More recently, Brigham helped lead the reintroduction of chinook salmon in the Umatilla River, which had lost its fishery to irrigation and a dam some seventy years earlier.

In 1995, after being elected to the tribal Board of Trustees, Brigham moved back to the reservation with her husband. Following in her grandfather's footsteps, Brigham has begun to teach her grandchildren about tribal traditions, and she has given them Indian names. Her three daughters, meanwhile, are coming to understand why she spent all those years traveling to distant meetings. Having worked with five generations of her family and community, Brigham might be on her way to a truly long-term management plan for salmon.

May 16, 2005

Tim Sullivan writes from Portland, Oregon.

Tribal Victory

Terri C. Hansen

On maps it is called Lyle Point, but to tribal fishing people it has always been Nanainmi Waki Uulktt, "the place where the wind blows from two directions."

The rocky promontory overlooks the confluence of the Klickitat and Columbia rivers, providing spectacular views of the Columbia River Gorge as it cuts through the Cascade Range. To the west, Oregon's Mount Hood stands sentinel over magnificent canyon walls rising to four thousand feet above the river.

The gorge was the center of trade for tribes from the Plains to the Pacific. Lyle Point was home to a Cascade and Klickitat village, and provided an important fishery and meeting place for over ten thousand years. But like many tribal lands in the Northwest, it was lost when white immigrants moved to the area in the mid-1800s. The drowning of Celilo Falls, another traditional tribal fishing place, under the waters of The Dalles Dam fifty years ago was a further blow. Now, at least one of those lost fishing grounds will be restored to the tribes that once depended on it. On May 8, the Yakama Nation announced the $2.4 million acquisition of Lyle Point from the Trust for Public Land, ending a long-simmering battle with would-be developers.

"This is a great day for the Yakamas—to get the land returned back for access to our fishing right areas," announced Yakama Tribal Council Chairwoman Lavina Washines. "The younger generation will continue to exercise their Creator-given right to our very important salmon."

The same winds that made Lyle Point a primary salmon-drying area for thousands of years also made it a world-class windsurfing mecca in the late 1980s. Klickitat County approved a thirty-three-lot subdivision in 1992, threatening to turn the area into a gated community.

Yakama Margaret Saluskin was the first to raise the alarm about the subdivision plans. One day while she was drying salmon that her husband, Douglas, had caught at Lyle Point, she noticed bulldozers carving the first roads into the promontory. Protests by tribal members and environmentalists swiftly ensued. When vandals destroyed a fishing scaffold at the point, the protesters began a nine-month encampment on the site. The tribe's access to traditional scaffold fishing, protected by the treaty of 1855, was at stake, Saluskin said.

Conservation groups joined the protest, saying Lyle Point was a resting place for bald eagles. The Trust for Public Land, a nonprofit specializing in conservation of real estate, began negotiations to purchase Lyle Point and held discussions with tribal members about ways to protect and manage the sacred site.

By 2002, the trust had purchased most of the lots, paving the way for conveyance to the Yakama. But tribal councils could not reach a consensus until the current administration, led by Washines, accomplished the acquisition.

Word spread like wildfire among Columbia River tribal peoples when the land deal finally became official. Nearly two hundred tribal members and their supporters gathered at the point on May 15 to celebrate their long-awaited victory.

"Today marks the return and protection of sacred land," said Charles F. Sams III, director of the trust's Tribal and Native Lands Program and a member of the Cocopah, Payuse, and Assinoboine Sioux tribes. "My grandfather took me up and down the river and showed me what we had lost. He told me I had a responsibility to the People, and to the salmon, to ensure their existence so they would continue to feed the People."

Some visibly struggled to maintain composure as memories were brought to life. "We fought for this," Cascade Chief Wilbur Slockish said. "It almost came to actual blows! So they can recreate? Make money, and windsurf? It was because we were standing in the way of economic progress. Progress."

He brought out a chuckle when he told the crowd, "Progress always involves our homes, our cemeteries, our fishing grounds. There would have been coffee shops, cheese shops, wine tasting here."

In 1945, Nisqually Billy Frank Jr. was arrested at age fourtreen for illegal fishing, starting a fight with the state of Washington that culminated in the 1974 Boldt Decision affirming tribal fishing rights as reserved in treaties with the United States. "When I started singing today, I started thinking about all my partners," he said. "All the good times here. All the bad times." He paused in reflection. "I'm happy to be here to witness this great occasion. It feels good."

Even as the tribes and the Trust for Public Land celebrate, the nearby town remains divided. There are those who still hope to see Lyle Point developed. "We need the tax basis for schools and fire departments and so forth," resident Don Smith said. Others, like Pam Essling, support the return of the land to the Yakama. "We honor the historical, cultural, and spiritual significance of this place," she said. "We're here to congratulate the Yakama people for reacquiring their land to preserve, protect, and enhance their cultural and natural resources for all people. It can be a place for healing old wounds and misunderstanding."

The purchase of Lyle Point ensures that thousands of years of tradition will continue along the river. Supporters from nearby communities will continue to be invited to tribal gatherings and feasts, Yakama leaders say, aiding cultural understanding and reconciliation.

After those who'd gathered finished a dinner of salmon and dried venison, Margaret Saluskin, who had fought so long and so hard, said with a peaceful smile, "Whatever you had in your hearts and minds for saving this land where the wind blows two ways, I want to thank you."

June 11, 2007

Terri C. Hansen writes from Portland, Oregon, and is a member of the Winnebago Tribe of Nebraska.

Turning the Tide

Eve Rickert

One hundred and fifty years ago, the Indian tribes of Washington State signed treaties that were supposed to guarantee, forever, their right to collect shellfish from the beaches of Puget Sound. Not long after, the government started selling off the region's most productive tidelands to commercial shellfish growers, who were never notified of the Indians' harvest rights. The bitter struggle over how to divvy up the bounty from those lands finally came to an end earlier this month, when seventeen tribes signed a settlement agreement with growers and the government that ends the tribes' right to take shellfish from private, commercial beaches.

In exchange, the tribes will get $33 million from the government to buy, lease, or improve other tidelands for their own harvest. For their part, the growers will spend $500,000 over ten years to improve habitat or seed shellfish beds on public tidelands. The settlement restricts Indian harvest only on land owned by commercial growers who had an "aquatic farm registration" prior to 1995; the tribes can still take shellfish from public tidelands and from noncommercial, private tidelands, such as those owned by residents of beachfront homes.

Though it was more than a century in the making, the dispute finally reached its breaking point in the last twenty years, in the wake of the historic 1974 Boldt Decision. That ruling, which affirmed the tribes' treaty rights to half of the state's salmon harvest, set the stage for a 1994 decision hailed as "Boldt II." In that case, U.S. District Court Judge Rafeedie ruled that the Indians had the same rights to shellfish as they did to salmon, and on both private and public land.

But there was a catch: on lands owned by commercial growers, the tribes could take half of only the naturally occurring shellfish. If a grower did anything to improve shellfish production, the tribes couldn't share the extra catch. To harvest on any enhanced commercial beach, they'd have to get a court to agree on how much of the harvest was "natural"—and the growers promised to fight them every step of the way.

It was an unworkable proposition, and in the meantime, the tribes and the growers needed to work together on the shared concerns of water quality and habitat protection so they could all keep harvesting clean, tasty oysters and clams. So in 1998, just as a new case was on its way to trial, everyone involved decided to do something that seemed remarkable after the years of litigation and resentment: they sat down to talk.

The growers wanted the Indians off land they considered exclusively theirs, but that meant the tribes would have to give up historical rights and a potential harvest worth more than $2 million a year. Still, "everyone realized it made more sense for tribes not to have to go onto growers' property, if the tribes could replace the take," says Phil Katzen of Kanji & Katzen, who has represented half of the tribes in the case for over twenty years.

Once the tribes and growers reached an agreement, Washington Gov. Chris Gregoire and Commissioner of Public Lands Doug Sutherland helped secure $11 million for the settlement from state coffers, and U.S. Rep. Norm Dicks, Democrat-Washington, got the other $22 million into the federal budget. The money, which was allocated to each tribe based on how much of the harvest it's giving up, will be used for habitat projects, seeding shellfish beds, and acquiring tidelands for the tribes' exclusive use.

Though the settlement ends a decades-long stalemate and clears the way for cooperation between tribes and growers, the idea of sacrificing any treaty rights at all was painful for many of the tribes. Tony Forsman, shellfish coordinator for the Northwest Indian Fisheries Commission and member of the Suquamish Tribe, says he spent a lot of time convincing people they weren't selling out. He sees the agreement as an improvement for the tribal harvest. "The money can go really far if they use it right," he says.

July 16, 2007

Eve Rickert is a freelance writer based in Vancouver, British Columbia.

Seeking the Water Jackpot

Matt Jenkins

In early February, a series of fierce storms racked the Navajo Nation, which sprawls across more than twenty-seven thousand square miles of Arizona, New Mexico, and Utah. At dawn, the highways were burnished to an icy sheen that sent cars pinballing into ditches. As each day warmed, the misery took on a new quality: the dirt roads that crisscross the reservation melted into *hash glish di'tsidi liba'*, a goopy gray gumbo that sucked pickup trucks into a death grip. By late afternoon, on the cusp of the next storm, many Navajos, still stuck up to their axles in mud, were simultaneously sandblasted with wind-driven grit.

The tribe's woes don't end with the weather. Half the Navajos on the reservation are unemployed, and that number may actually be as high as 67 percent—no one can say for sure. More than 70 percent of those who do have jobs work for government agencies. The closure of a coal mine later this year, on top of another mine shutdown two years ago, will likely reduce tribal revenues by a third. Per capita income on the reservation is a little more than $8,000 a year.

Navajos often speak of the cosmic geography of the Four Sacred Mountains, which mark the boundaries of their ancestral homeland. But the lives of many people here are shaped by a more pragmatic geography, centered on a coin-op water dispenser in a muddy turnaround behind a city maintenance building in downtown Gallup, N.M. A water pipe with a piece of yellow fire hose hanging off the end sticks out the back of the building. Navajos load water tanks and blue plastic fifty-five-gallon drums into the beds of their pickups and come here for drinking water. On weekends, the line can stretch around the block.

But on a bitter-cold Friday afternoon, the whole operation was seriously dorked. Ernest Leslie, who had driven twenty-two miles from Tohatchi, couldn't get any water because a quarter was jammed in the coin slot. He tried to coax another coin into the machine with the tip of his pocketknife, but it popped back out like a bad joke and landed in the mud at his feet. "Huh," Leslie said. He looked down at the quarter. "Sometimes we have problems like this."

Even as the Southwest's cities have flourished with water from the Colorado River, the Navajo Tribe has stood on the sidelines, holding an empty bucket—and waiting. For decades, it seems, the tribe has been just one good plan away from prosperity. Now, however, the Navajo Nation is beginning to assert its right to claim water from the river. Many Navajos feel that the tribe could soon transform water from something that eats up their quarters at fifty gallons a pop to a virtual jackpot. But as tantalizing as the prospect of river water is, it is also opening painful rifts on the reservation.

The capital of the Navajo Nation is a town called Window Rock, on the eastern edge of the reservation in Arizona. It is a slow-paced place with a couple of gas stations, a supermarket, and a clutch of mom-and-pop storefronts that serve up squash soup and roast mutton.

Lena Fowler lives on the other side of the reservation, but came to town in February for a tribal council meeting. A member of the tribe's water-rights commission, she has a cool intensity and a vaguely sexy set of crow's-feet at the corners of her eyes. Fowler began by explaining how the language of white-dominated water law, saddled with abstruse notions like *qui prior est in tempore, potior est in jure*—Latin for "first in time, first in right"—often defies translation into Navajo. Then she conceded that water may, in fact, be a language unto itself.

"And when you speak water," she said, "people get real emotional.

"For us, for most of our Navajo people, they wake up in the morning [and] they go out and they pray. And once they're done," she said, "they turn around and have to figure out how much water they have: Is it safe to drink the water at the windmill? Or do I have to go buy Clorox to treat it with? That's where we are today."

The Navajo Nation sits almost exactly in the center of the 244,000-square-mile Colorado River Basin, and it occupies fully one-tenth of the basin's area. Yet when the seven Colorado River states met to divide the river's water between themselves in 1922, they neglected to invite either the Navajo or any of the other Indian tribes with reservations in the basin.

"Agreements were being made before we even knew how to speak English," Fowler said. Indians weren't recognized as United States citizens until two years after the Colorado River Compact was signed in 1922. It wasn't until almost three decades after the Indian Citizenship Act was passed that Navajos were finally allowed to vote.

When they excluded tribes from the Compact negotiations, however, the seven states disregarded an important fact. In 1908, the U.S. Supreme Court had—paradoxically—dealt Indians a powerful trump card. In what is known as the Winters decision, the court granted Indian tribes the right to retroactively claim water sufficient to create what would later be termed a "permanent homeland."

Water rights are ranked by chronological priority, and the priority date of a tribal claim is tied to the year that a particular tribe's reservation was established. In the Navajos' case, that was 1868. If the Navajos received so-called Winters rights, their water rights during times of drought would take priority over those of the West's more recently established urban centers.

Qui prior est in tempore, as the saying goes, *potior est in jure*.

The seven states' negotiators acknowledged the Indians' dormant power in one small way: they added the "wild Indian article" to the water Compact. The article—whose name came from then-Secretary of Commerce Herbert Hoover, the facilitator of the negotiations—reads: "Nothing in this compact shall be construed as affecting the obligations of the United States of America to Indian tribes."

With those twenty words, the negotiators punted all their gnarly Indian problems sometime into the future. "The states have basically ignored that there are Native claims to the river," Fowler said. In the eighty-six years since the Compact was signed, the downstream cities of Los Angeles, San Diego, Phoenix, and Las Vegas have boomed, while the Navajo have been left parked in a dusty time warp high on the Colorado Plateau.

"Even today, it's like there's a curtain," she said. "[The seven states] are over there, making decisions, knowing full well that we're here. They can see our silhouette."

Hoover's wild Indian clause put off the Indian water-rights question for as long as possible. But the costs of that delay, compounded over time, are now coming due. The Navajo Nation is moving to claim its water rights in New Mexico, and may soon do so in Arizona and Utah as well.

Indian tribes can sue for water rights—or they can negotiate settlements with individual states, and then take them to Congress for approval. That's the path that the Navajo Nation has taken in New Mexico. In 2004, the tribe and the state announced a settlement agreement that would award the Navajo 326,000 acre-feet of water from the San Juan River, a major tributary of the Colorado. (An acre-foot is enough for about two families in Phoenix or Las Vegas for a year.) The settlement also authorizes more than $800 million in federal and state money to build a pipeline that will take the water to the east side of the reservation and to the city of Gallup. The Navajo Nation is now seeking congressional approval of the deal, the tribe's first step toward asserting its rightful claims on the Colorado.

"We have learned the language. We have learned the laws. We learned the court system," Fowler said. "Now we're saying, 'Hey! We're back. We're here to reclaim our water rights.' "

In Window Rock, the tribal government operates out of a cluster of rustic-looking buildings a stone's throw from the towering sandstone arch after which the town is named. There's a BEWARE OF FALLING ROCKS sign next to the stone-and-timber hogan where the tribal council meets.

Stanley Pollack, an assistant attorney general for the Navajo Nation's Department of Justice, works out of an unprepossessing, barracks-style building nearby. Pollack exhibits definite left-leaning sensibilities, but he also observes the staid rituals of water lawyering. He keeps a turquoise bolo tie and a gray tweed jacket ready for tribal council briefings. He is also a *bilagaana*—a white—and, as a result, occupies a very complicated place in the Navajo water cosmology.

Pollack, who is fifty-four, arrived here in 1985. Four years later, he suddenly found himself preparing legal briefs for the prosecution of the tribal chairman, Peter MacDonald, on corruption charges that would eventually land MacDonald in federal prison. It was a turbulent time: at one point, MacDonald's supporters rioted in Window Rock and tribal police shot two of them dead.

Pollack is reticent about the experience, but it was obviously a bracing one for him. He worked around the clock, protected by bodyguards from the American Indian Movement, better known for its 1973 standoff at Wounded Knee on the Pine Ridge Reservation. At night as they stood watch outside, the guards warmed themselves by setting fires in empty oil drums. Whenever Pollack took a break, he says, "I'd go out and talk to them and look at the stars. It was really cool."

Compared to the MacDonald drama, you'd think the process of defending the tribal water rights, which now absorbs all of Pollack's time, would be a pretty humdrum affair. But it's not. He's had rocks thrown through his office window, and been called the Navajos' Number One Enemy. And, in 2001, a flier appeared in chapter houses—the reservation's equivalent of town halls—with Pollack's likeness X-ed out and "Osama bin Pollack" written underneath.

Pollack keeps a lot of this stuff in a ring-bound binder in his office. One flier calls him—with more vehemence than orthographical precision—a "water rights sabbotager" and "one of the lawyer oppressors of the Navajo people who's helped cheat us out of hundreds of millions of water rights that is rightfully ours." Another reads: "Pollack infiltrated our government and has us on the path to a form of water rights holocaust."

After I read that one aloud, Pollack—who is Jewish—looked a little chagrined and said, "Oh yeah, genocide."

Pollack would really rather not talk about any of this. "It was just 100 percent libelous crap," he says. "Just totally reckless." But the homegrown opposition he has faced attests to the depth of emotion that water inspires—and to local unhappiness with Pollack's role as a compromiser and, to a large extent, a realist.

One wall of Pollack's office is lined with mean-looking filing cabinets, and the rest of the room is filled with steel bookshelves packed with court documents and all manner of hydrologic divination. It is from this mass of paper that Pollack is slowly assembling a Colorado River claim.

A year and a half ago, as the water settlement with New Mexico was working its way toward Congress, Pollack put the federal government and the seven states on notice that the tribe could also justifiably use 336,856 acre-feet in Arizona. When we talked, Pollack indicated that the tribe might claim eighty to one hundred thousand acre-feet in Utah, as well. If you throw in the water from tributaries, that would put the total size of the Navajo Colorado River water right at somewhere around eight hundred thousand acre-feet.

That is a lot of water—one-and-a-half times more than Las Vegas has rights to. And, because much of the Navajo water would have an 1868 priority date, several big, powerful water users would be booted to the back of the line behind the tribe during a drought. The city of Las Vegas and the Central Arizona Project, or CAP, whose massive canal supplies water to Phoenix and Tucson, already have the worst water-rights priorities on the river. With the Navajo ahead of them in the hierarchy, they'd face an even more serious risk of being cut off.

Pollack has been steadily making it harder for the seven states to continue ignoring the tribe. In 2003, the Navajo Nation filed a lawsuit against the states and the U.S. Secretary of the Interior to prevent any further water allocations until the Navajo claims are resolved. Pollack and a team of Navajo negotiators have been in ongoing talks with representatives from Arizona, Las Vegas, and Southern California over that lawsuit.

But Arizona, in particular, has been pushing back. Because the CAP is so vulnerable to water shortage, the state has been pressuring the Navajo Nation to reduce the size of its water claims. Last fall, the director of the state's water-resources department appeared before Congress to testify against the Navajo-New Mexico settlement, saying it shouldn't be approved unless the tribe also settles its claims with Arizona.

"Arizona's playing the leverage game," Pollack said—seeking to get a deal that the tribe might not otherwise make "on the assumption that because Navajo wants this New Mexico settlement, they'll make concessions to benefit Arizona."

The Navajo Nation's decision to seek water through a settlement, rather than by going to court, reflects a broader trend in Indian Country. Over the past decade and a half, tribes have increasingly turned to settlements, in part because the U.S. Supreme Court has become increasingly hostile to Indian rights. Still, the Navajo are keeping their options open. Last summer, Navajo President Joe Shirley traveled to Washington, D.C., to warn Congress that "if the [New Mexico] settlement were to fail, and the Navajo Nation were forced to pursue the litigation of its claims, the United States would still be exposed to horrific liabilities even if the Navajo Nation were to obtain only modest water rights."

Back on the reservation, however, Pollack was being dogged by critics who accused him of selling out the tribe. Some insisted that the Navajo Nation should settle for nothing less than every last drop of water in the Colorado River.

Peter MacDonald was released from prison and returned to the reservation in 2001. Many Navajos see him as a folk hero, a sort of leader-in-exile, and he seems to be constantly on the road. When we talked by phone, he was headed to Phoenix for the dedication of a Navajo veterans' memorial there.

In the late 1970s, when MacDonald was tribal chairman, he commissioned a study that, he hoped, would form the backbone of a Navajo water claim. Water-rights studies tend to be pretty tedious things, but this one conjured up a vision that was positively messianic.

Rather than focus on the eighteen-million-acre Navajo reservation to determine what water the tribe might claim, MacDonald directed his engineers to consider the entirety of what he calls "the Navajo holy land": an area roughly twice the size of the reservation itself that lies between the Four Sacred Mountains, which stretch from Flagstaff, Ariz., to the San Luis Valley in Colorado. That territory includes not only the Colorado River and two of its main tributaries—the San Juan and Little Colorado—but the Rio Grande as well.

"Navajos were there even before the states were created," MacDonald said. "So by the Winters Doctrine, Navajo has first and primary right to all that water within the Four Sacred Mountains." (He neglected to mention that the area also includes the ancestral territory of the Hopi, Utes, Zuni, Jicarilla Apache, and the nineteen Indian pueblos on the Rio Grande.)

MacDonald's engineers began figuring out exactly how much water the tribe could claim, by calculating its "practicably irrigable acreage," or PIA. In 1964, the U.S. Supreme Court had endorsed PIA as a way to determine the size of water-rights claims made under the Winters Doctrine. A PIA determination evaluates how much of a tribe's land can be "practicably"—meaning economically—irrigated, and then uses a formula to derive a total water right for the reservation.

There can be a big difference between what's irrigable and what's practicably irrigable, but the engineers didn't get too hung up on observing that distinction. They ultimately determined that, as MacDonald put it, "Navajo has claim to every drop of the water that's presently being used by New Mexico, Arizona, California, Nevada, Utah, Colorado and Wyoming." As he said this, I suddenly had a vision of the world turning upside down: the *bilagaanas* forced to drive to the watering point with fifty-five-gallon drums in the backs of their Volvos and Range Rovers, a roll of quarters in their pockets to fill up their backyard swimming pools and keep their lawns lush.

On a roll, MacDonald instructed the engineers to draw up plans for a Navajo version of the Central Arizona Project. But for all the talk about creating an irrigated agrarian utopia in the desert, the real idea, he allowed, was this: for decades, all the thirsty cities downstream had been using water—Navajo water—for free. Once the tribe won its water-rights claim, the cities could keep using the water—but only if they finally started paying the Indians for the use of what was rightfully theirs.

"We were ready to go to court" to win that water, MacDonald said. But the dream faded with his arraignment, and the blueprints for the project apparently vanished into thin air. And now that he was out of prison, all this business about a settlement with New Mexico was pissing him off. "It's like you had a hundred head of sheep, and somebody stole them from you," MacDonald said. "Finally, you find your sheep in somebody else's corral. So you go and say, 'Hey, these are my sheep! Look at the brands, look at the earmarks: they're all mine.' And the guy who stole them says, 'Let's have a settlement here. I'll give you three of these sheep back.' "

But even though the blueprints for an Indian CAP have gone missing, the idea still casts an enthralling spell over more than a few Navajos.

The rumors first came roaring up eight years ago with the appearance of a mimeographed pamphlet, an open letter entitled "Lawyers, Water Rights, Betrayals and the Fate of the Navajo Nation." It was written in the name of a group called the Dine Sovereignty Defense Association, or DSDA. (Dine is the Navajo word for Navajo, and the group's acronym is pronounced "DEZ-duh.") Thanks to the fury of its leafleting campaign, I came to think of DSDA as a sort of Irish Republican Army, minus the bombs and kneecapping.

The letter, which did not mention Pollack by name, alleged that "one or more of the Nation's lawyers are secretly working for outsiders." The water-rights issue "amounts to a national emergency for the Navajo people," it said. It asserted—with a phrase that recurred like the come-on in a Nigerian Internet scam—that a Navajo water claim "has a potential value of 100s of $millions and more."

The author of the letter was a guy named Jack Utter, another *bilagaana* who is a hydrologist for the Navajo Nation's Water Resources Department in Fort Defiance, a couple miles north of Window Rock. Utter works out of a cramped office in the back of a mobile unit parked behind the water resources building—a forbidding spot that feels a little like Antarctica's McMurdo Station. Utter is animated by the thrill of conspiracy, and he keeps a copy of Paulo Freire's anti-imperialist screed *Pedagogy of the Oppressed*—which largely draws its inspiration from the British colonization of India—close at hand.

In the years since he wrote the letter, Utter has become circumspect to the point of silence, but his theme of colonial victimization resonates deeply on the reservation. During the 1960s and 1970s—call it the high era of western natural resources treachery—the tribe was cheated in a massive royalty deal with a company called Peabody Coal. Indian Country has also long grappled with the federal government's failure to honor its trust responsibility to the tribes. Elouise Cobell, a Blackfeet Indian woman, has doggedly fought for years to prove that the federal government mismanaged as much as $176 billion in oil-and-gas royalties owed to Indians across the country.

But there was an added dimension here. Navajo grassroots groups like DSDA were also fighting against what they saw as a breach of trust at home. In 2003, Norman Brown, who was then president of a group called Dine Nationalists, told me that "when we talk about breach of trust, we talk about breach of trust within our own tribal organizations"—by which he meant the tribal government.

Not long after the Lawyers-and-Betrayal letter appeared in 2000, DSDA—as part of a broader grassroots coalition called Dine Bidziil, or Navajo Strength—called for major reform in the Navajo government. The groups weren't going after anyone with AK-47s, but they did seem to constitute a genuine insurgency.

Much of their wrath focused on the tribal council, but DSDA also targeted four white lawyers, including Pollack. The group placed an ad in the *Navajo Times* that called the tribal government "a colonial government that is run by WHITE POWER"—this one did mention Pollack by name—and bumper stickers began to appear that read "Four Lawyers Out / Dine Freedom In."

People on both sides of the fight reported having their tires slashed and the lug nuts on their wheels loosened. There was an allegation that someone had slipped poisoned cough drops into a tribal council member's desk drawer. There were dark rumors that the *'adlaaniis*—the notorious Navajo drunks—had been recruited into the fight. Several people made mention of witchcraft and "evil way" ceremonies secretively held in the remotest reaches of the reservation.

Finally, when the votes were counted in the 2000 tribal election, more than half of the council's eighty-eight delegates were unseated. Pollack survived: after weathering subpoenas to appear before two tribal council subcommittees, he was exonerated from the charges in the Lawyers-and-Betrayals letter. The three other white lawyers left, however. Then DSDA and Dine Bidziil melted back into the shadows.

The annual tribal fair, held each September in Window Rock, is one of the few times when Navajos from across the reservation come together in one place. Last year, some of the old DSDA hands ran into each other there and shared concerns that their government had again grown complacent. Not long afterward, a tribal member named Ron Milford resurrected the fight with a letter to the *Navajo Times* that insisted, "We must maximize Navajo water rights now."

A low-level war in the local newspapers followed, and I'm pretty sure Lena Fowler rolled her eyes when I happened to mention it. "They give an open mic to people like Ron Milford, and somehow he becomes credible enough for you to interview him," she said. "I'm tired of these one-sided stories where it's all about"—she switched to the Navajo word for "rumor" and repeated it like an incantation—"*jini, jini, jini.*"

On a sloppy, miserable day, I went looking for Milford. He was in Tuba City, three hours from Window Rock, on the reservation's west side. I had just reached the ramshackle houses on the edge of town when another storm hit, and the world went *leezh lichii go' bilni'yo*—a bloody maelstrom of red dust.

Half an hour later, I sat with Milford and another DSDA organizer named Max Goldtooth at a table in the back of a restaurant called The Hogan. Outside, the weather had turned again. Now it was *chiil bilni'yol*: blowing snow like a mother. Forty minutes into our conversation, all the lights went out.

The three of us sat huddled in the back of the restaurant as the storm raged outside. "Our starting point should be five million acre-feet of water," Milford said. That was considerably less than Peter MacDonald's idea of a winning number, but it was still more water than the entire state of California is entitled to, and nearly twice as much as Arizona gets.

As Milford and Goldtooth talked, I could appreciate their resentment about water getting sucked away to fuel prosperity everywhere but on the Navajo Nation. Fifty-five miles north of us was the Navajo Generating Station, which burns Navajo coal and provides royalties for the tribe. But, Milford said, "All that power goes right to those big pumps [on the Colorado River] that pump water into the canals"—the Central Arizona Project's mainline—"and down to Phoenix and Tucson."

The tribe's quest to build its economy has been fitful, at best. Last year, the tribal council approved the Navajo Nation's first casino and began negotiating a $100 million loan from JPMorgan Chase to finance the project. But the deal became controversial when the bank asked the tribe to pledge $125 million worth of its assets as collateral.

"They have money here if they assert their water rights," Goldtooth said. "There's money flowing all around us. We're sittin' on a national treasure here."

When he said that, I could pretty well imagine the sound of a slot machine pumping out streams of quarters. "If we had receipts from leasing water and stuff like that, we would be investing in our infrastructure," Milford continued. "We could pump a lot of money into different things."

But instead, they watched as more and more of the river's water rolled away downstream. Just last year, the seven Colorado River states negotiated a new round of drought-protection agreements for themselves. "Now that global warming and everything has spanked them in the butt, they're over here divvying up what's left," Milford said. "I bet they're just smiling from ear to ear because Navajo is not gonna file this big ol' claim for the water that we said we were entitled to."

Milford had, however, thought his way forward through the bitter paradoxes of the situation to a position of strategic advantage. Water demand from the seven states has been growing steadily since 1922. If the Navajo ever did get the water, that mounting demand would make it even more valuable for the tribe.

There was a certain Red Power strain to Milford's argument, but he was also starting to sound an awful lot like a water broker. In fact, by this point he had thought his way pretty well into a supply-and-demand graph. "Two factors will raise the price of that water," Milford said. "Global warming. And drought."

His eyes lit up, and the slot machine in my head went nuts.

But after we paid for the meal, we went outside to discover that the world had turned to ice. Neither Milford nor Goldtooth had an ice-scraper in his truck, and Goldtooth snapped his I.D. card in half trying to scrape the frozen spackle off his windshield.

There is an aphorism that occasionally bobs up in water circles and goes like this: the Navajos would rather have 100 percent of nothing than 50 percent of something.

It is an uncomfortable thing to hear, but it may hold some truth.

Back in the 1980s, after Peter MacDonald's engineers drew up the plans for an Indian Central Arizona Project, he spent several years trying to persuade the federal government to fund it. The Bureau of Reclamation repeatedly lowballed the cost estimate and, finally, Sen. Pete Domenici, Republican-New Jersey, who is now co-sponsoring the Navajo-New Mexico settlement legislation, asked MacDonald to accept the lowball figure. MacDonald refused: "I said, 'If that's the case, we may have to do it ourselves.' "

That was roughly two decades ago, before MacDonald's trip to prison and everything that followed. When MacDonald and I talked in February, I asked how him how, exactly, he had planned to finance the project without federal help.

He answered that the tribe could take the seven Colorado River states to court for illegally using Navajo water. The tribe, he said, would fine the states—"we'll charge them maybe one or two or three cents a gallon and add [that] all up." It wouldn't matter if it took twenty or even thirty years to resolve the case, he said: the Navajo Nation could request that the court require the states to put money in escrow until it was decided. MacDonald had deployed the strategy once already, when he sued Peabody Coal for lost royalties, and the tribe wound up with about a billion dollars.

Yet that strategy was not a sure-fire thing, and Lena Fowler's words echoed inside my head: "Some Navajos out there say, 'This is 100 percent ours,' " she'd said. "Let's say we claim all of that 100 percent. Now where are we going to get the money to put our water to use?"—to build the pipelines it would take to actually get water to people's homes.

"That's what a settlement does," Fowler said. "When you negotiate, that's what you're negotiating for."

In 2002, MacDonald's daughter, Hope MacDonald Lone Tree, was elected to the Navajo tribal council. Since then, she has shouldered her father's cause. Still, I couldn't help but think that the pair was marching their tribe down a cruel, hard trail: toward a vision of water in the distance, without a pipe in sight.

When Pollack and I talked in Window Rock, he had just returned from another negotiating session with water bosses from Arizona, Las Vegas, and Southern California. "Nobody seemed to be happy," he said. "And when nobody's happy, it's usually a good sign. It means you're coming to 'yes.' "

But Pollack had also been thinking about the opposition he faces on the reservation. "People hear 'Winters,' " he said, "and [they] say: 'Well, Winters stands for the proposition that the tribes get all the water.' That's not what Winters says. It says that water was reserved to create a permanent homeland for tribes."

We talked about how the idea of practicably irrigable acreage lay at the heart of the whopping claims that Peter MacDonald and Ron Milford were calling for. "PIA has been sort of guiding doctrine in terms of trying to put together the basics for [previous Indian] claims," Pollack said. "But PIA isn't necessarily always consistent with a permanent homeland."

In fact, PIA looked more and more like an anachronism, a perverse insistence on turning Indians into farmers at exactly the same time that, in much of the West, agriculture is losing ground to cities. Relying on the principle to claim water—even if that water might ultimately be leased to cities downstream—seemed a problematic tactic.

That irony appeared to have been lost on Milford when we'd met at The Hogan, where he had conjured up the same sort of agro-utopian vision that Peter MacDonald had. In the 1960s, the Navajo had won Congressional approval of a big irrigation project near Farmington, New Mexico. Despite having been heavily subsidized by the federal government, the project only managed to squeak out a profit during the past couple of years. Maybe. Nobody could say that for sure, either. Still, Milford felt the project could be cloned all over the reservation. "There's a lot of open space out here," he'd said. "Down toward Leupp and all of that area? There's tons of flat property down there, you know? You can imagine fields running clear down to Winslow."

But I had talked with white farmers along the San Juan River who were losing money and had to work in the local oil-and-gas supply business to make ends meet. It was a little weird to hear Milford argue that his people's water claim should be calculated according to a standard that would give them enough water to farm their huge reservation. It struck me as an insistence on the Navajos' right to go broke.

Pollack suggested one practical alternative to PIA. In the Pacific Northwest, for instance, the "salmon tribes" such as the Nez Perce and the Yakama have used their treaties to argue for water rights sufficient to protect the salmon runs on which they'd long depended. "What we've said is, 'Look at the fishing cases. Look at what the courts have done there. They've said the real key isn't PIA. The real key is the water necessary to create the permanent homeland.' "

In Navajo's case, Pollack said, mining was a far more realistic moneymaker than agriculture. But, he added, there was a more pressing issue. "In a settlement, you have to put the rhetoric aside and figure out what your goals and objectives are," he said. "And if your goal and objective is to get drinking water to people, claiming millions and millions of acre-feet of water doesn't get drinking water to the hogans."

Pollack regularly works extremely long hours, a habit that I couldn't help but think was a carryover from his days on the Peter MacDonald case. He keeps one of the "Four Lawyers Out" bumper stickers pinned up in his office, like a trophy. And it was clear that, despite Pollack's reluctance to talk about the attacks he'd weathered, they were something that was never far from his mind.

As I gathered my things to go, Pollack shifted into closing-arguments mode. "These are people that have had a lot stolen from them. And they've come up on the short end of the stick all the time," he said. MacDonald and his followers were, he conceded, hawking a pretty alluring vision. "It's this casino mentality of getting free money. If somebody comes along and says, 'Water is your casino' ... you know: 'Your water's worth billions of dollars, and if you just get rid of Pollack, you, too, can be a millionaire!'

"You know? They're like, 'Well, shit. Why do we have this guy here? I want to be a millionaire.' "

March 17, 2008

Matt Jenkins is a *High Country News* contributing editor.

Tribes Make a Controversial Deal on Salmon

Rocky Barker

After three Columbia River tribes decided to stop pushing for the breaching of four federal dams on the Snake River, many critics spoke the ugly word "sellout." The tribes will receive $900 million in new salmon projects in exchange for halting their court battle for the next decade.

However, the Warm Springs, Yakama, and Umatilla tribes—joined later in the day on April 7 by the Colville tribe—are following in the footsteps of the region's leaders, even though many scientists say that the dam breaching is necessary to save thirteen stocks of endangered salmon. The tribes gave up their fight to breach the dams because they read the current political tea leaves: not one political leader in the Pacific Northwest in either party supports breaching dams.

Both of Washington's Democratic senators, Patty Murray and Maria Cantwell, campaigned to keep the four dams, and not one of the three presidential candidates is in favor of breaching dams. There is no surprise in any of this.

And the deal the tribes negotiated with federal dam regulators is better than their critics charge. They got federal dam managers to agree not to challenge a tribal agreement with Oregon and Washington that will let the tribes catch more salmon in years when hatchery fish are more abundant. For the Columbia River tribes, protecting treaty rights is a top priority. In the 1970s and '80s, the tribes won battles in Washington and Oregon that recognize their right to half of the fish harvested in the Columbia and its tributaries. Ever since then, they have resolutely defended those rights.

Meanwhile, those still in favor of restoring salmon runs through dam breaching—including the Nez Perce tribe, which shares its treaty rights with the other tribes—continue to fight. The dam-breaching strategy is to convince U.S. District Judge James Redden that the Bush administration's current salmon and dam plan remains inadequate both scientifically and legally. If Redden is so convinced, he has promised to consider ordering harsh and costly measures, such as spilling more water around hydroelectric turbines, drawing down reservoirs behind dams, or requiring the draining of upstream reservoirs for water to help salmon migration.

Many advocates believe these measures would prove even more costly than breaching the four dams. This will force the region's political leaders—and the next president—to take the painful steps necessary to resolve the issue. The tribe's recent deal could sidestep this outcome only if Judge Redden is convinced that the two hundred hatchery and habitat projects promised to the tribes, along with projects offered in a separate $65 million deal with Idaho, would help the Bush administration's plan meet the law and enable salmon to survive.

The Bush plan might have a chance before Redden if the Bonneville Power Administration, the agency that markets hydroelectricity from the dams, can get Oregon on board with a separate deal. But Oregon is currently aligned with environmentalists, fishermen, and sporting businesses in challenging the Bush administration plan. Oregon has made it clear that it wants a truly aggressive non-breach option on the table.

The two hundred hatchery and harvest-restoration projects are mostly to help fish in the Columbia River and not in the Snake River. With the Nez Perce tribe unwilling to back off from breaching, the projects in Idaho that BPA offered the tribe weren't a part of the deal. Instead, the Bonneville Power Administration went to the state of Idaho offering $65 million for similar projects. Like Oregon, the Nez Perce could still make a deal that would help dam managers convince Redden they have done enough for now.

So unless the things change dramatically in the next two years, dam breaching isn't going to Congress for approval anytime soon. Under this new deal, the tribes will get some money, get even tougher measures through further negotiations, and still have another shot at the dams in ten years.

That's assuming, of course, that there's still time to save the salmon.

April 21, 2008

Rocky Barker is a veteran reporter in the Northwest, and a fellow at the Andrus Center for Public Policy in Boise, Idaho.

Underground Tension

Grand Canyon Oases Face Faraway Threats

Anne Minard

A hike into the Grand Canyon in mid-August is a journey into a world dominated by dust and dryness. Even if you start at 7 a.m. from Hermit's Rest, on the west end of the South Rim, the heat soon becomes stifling. Each step stirs the fine red dirt on the trail, and shadows shrink to become tiny sanctuaries under spindly trees. Beyond the narrow trail, vast white and red rock walls stand in stark contrast to a cloudless blue sky.

But three miles below the rim of the Grand Canyon lies the secret world of Dripping Springs. A miniature garden of moist green and brown plants clings to an overhanging ledge in the canyon wall. Three separate trickles of water, backlit by the sun, fall silently for ten feet before splashing into a shaded, rock-rimmed pool. Birds dart in to quench mid-morning thirst, and even during the worst drought in northern Arizona in a century, scarlet monkeyflowers are in full bloom, enticing monarch butterflies.

This oasis is one of hundreds of such islands in the midst of this Southwest desert. Scientists now believe that places like Dripping Springs are part of an interconnected system of springs that trickles from the aquifer underlying all of northern Arizona—one that humans have used for centuries.

If proven true, this theory could have startling implications. While the impacts on springs from livestock and exotic plants have been widely known, scientists are now realizing that the springs may be threatened by development as far as seventy miles away, in cities such as Tusayan and Flagstaff. Protecting Southwestern springs could take sweeping changes in the way humans use not just the springs, but water in general.

The first step toward protecting springs is understanding them. The Flagstaff-based Grand Canyon Wildlands Council is working to document springs ecosystems on the Arizona Strip—the eight thousand-square-mile area between the Grand Canyon and Utah's border, mostly administered by the Bureau of Land Management—as well as in Grand Canyon National Park and at the San Francisco Peaks, north of Flagstaff.

"Springs take up a tiny, tiny area on the Arizona Strip, but support a huge amount of life," says Bianca Perla, a biologist with the Council. The group has found that 11 percent of the plant species on the Strip occur only at springs. Seventy-five percent of the butterflies in the area rely on the springs, along with a third of the bird species and more than half the land snails.

Larry Stevens, another Wildlands Council biologist, says the springs are "absolute hotspots for biodiversity." Their biological diversity is a hundred to five hundred times that of surrounding landscapes, he says: "Saving a spring might be equal to saving ten square miles of land."

For the species that have adapted to live exclusively at springs, these cloistered oases are worlds unto themselves. The endangered Kanab ambersnail, for example, is a relic of more widespread populations that existed before the last ice age. As glaciers receded and former swamps turned to deserts, the snails' habitat became increasingly restricted.

Now, they live at only two places in the Southwest, one of them a well-known spring at Vaseys Paradise in the Grand Canyon . Ambersnails are called "extreme cases of endemism," meaning they exist at only a small number of isolated places.

But a brightly colored, parasitic flatworm so rare it doesn't even have a common name is even more specialized. Kanab ambersnails eat the eggs of *Leucochloridium cyanocittae* off leaves, where they're deposited in bird droppings; a single worm can then grow to fill half a snail's body cavity. When the worm is ready to move on, it pushes neon pink and green projections out through the snail's eye sockets and ejects itself to form a ready meal for birds—and continue its life cycle.

"This is a rare parasite, on a rare snail," says Perla. "That's extreme endemism."

Safeguarding and restoring degraded springs will be a challenge. In Stevens' words, it "remains a rather large sociological experiment."

On private, state, and BLM land, he says, many springs are altered by pipes and long-forgotten stock tanks, where some species hang on by using water that drips from the tank sides. There, Stevens and Perla are advocating a mantra of "leave a little"—20 percent of the original water source is often enough to protect aquatic species.

Even springs protected within national parks and monuments aren't completely safe. "Overall, the biggest problems facing these springs are human visitation and the invasion of exotics," says National Park Service biologist John Spence. The problems go hand in hand: human visitors inadvertently introduce tamarisk, Russian olive, and exotic thistles, all of which can draw down spring water and outcompete native plants.

Efforts are under way to reduce these threats. At Grand Canyon National Park, a full-time biologist and a couple of volunteers are working to attack the most damaging of 156 species of non-native plants in the park. And at the new Grand Canyon-Parashant National Monument, the nonprofit Conservation Fund recently purchased Pakoon Spring—and another exotic resident, a nine-foot pet alligator—as part of a buyout of a two hundred-acre ranch.

But the greatest threat may be more difficult to address. Scientists have long believed that the water pouring from the springs comes from a huge aquifer deep underneath northern Arizona. Now, researchers at Grand Canyon National Park and Northern Arizona University in Flagstaff are documenting the chemical composition of springs along the South Rim to determine whether they're impacted by groundwater pumping in Tusayan, Valle, Williams, and Flagstaff.

Preliminary results from the chemical composition study should be available by December, but it will still be years before scientists truly understand the springs' relationship with the broader world that overlies the aquifer.

Says Cole Crocker-Bedford, Grand Canyon National Park's chief of natural resources, "Whether it's environmentalists who sound the alarm, or developers who will say we're trying to take away their rights, we owe it to all of them to get the science right."

November 11, 2002

Anne Minard writes from Flagstaff, Arizona.

Pipe Dreams

Matt Jenkins

Out here in a rock-strewn, desolate sweep of creosote bush and blackbrush called the Tule Desert, there's a patch of land bulldozed clear of vegetation. Standing in the middle of it is a well called PW-1. It doesn't look like much; just a thirty-two-inch-diameter steel pipe, painted black and sticking out of the desert. But in heartbreak country like Lincoln County, Nevada, it's a beacon of hope.

Over a century ago, the county's mining towns—places with names like Hiko and Pioche—boomed with the discovery of gold and silver. Now, they're dirt-poor. The county sprawls across 10,634 square miles, and has just forty-five hundred residents. Economically, they're in a straitjacket: ninety-eight percent of the land is federally owned, so opportunities for private development are limited and tax revenues are woefully small. But PW-1 taps the magical—and most elusive—ingredient in the recipe for economic success in the West: water.

"Water's one of the last natural resources we have that we can do anything with," says Spencer Hafen, the chairman of the Lincoln County Commission, who owns a land-surveying business and splits his time between Panaca, in Lincoln County, and Mesquite, just over the Clark County line to the south.

Lincoln County sits on a water gold mine, but until PW-1, it had no way to get at the water; wells and pumps and pipelines cost millions of dollars. And while the county thought of the water as its own, in reality, it belonged to no one: Western water law says that you can only lay claim to water if you can convince the state that you have the ability to put it to "beneficial use."

This left Lincoln County's water vulnerable: the county line is only forty-five miles north of one of the fastest-growing cities in the country, Las Vegas, which has been eyeing the water in Lincoln and other rural counties for more than a decade. In all likelihood, Vegas would have snatched Lincoln County's water before the locals could do anything about it. Many Lincoln County residents feared a possible repeat of Los Angeles' infamous early-1900s water grab from the rural Owens Valley—a grab that turned that valley into a dustbowl, and later inspired the movie *Chinatown*.

But in 1998, Lincoln County found a way to beat Vegas to the punch. County commissioners teamed up with Vidler Water Company, a path-breaking private water developer. Vidler had the money to drill wells like PW-1 into the desert and to start pulling the water out. The company agreed to provide the initial investment in return for a cut of the county's profits, once the water was sold to developers, power plants, or whoever needed it. At stake were thousands of acre-feet of water—and millions of dollars in revenue.

For Lincoln County—whose major employers are the county government, a treatment center for troubled youth, and a minimum-security prison— the water deal is one of what Hafen calls "the many could-bes" that might lead the county out of its economic slump.

But the water deal has touched off a scuffle across Nevada, the driest state in the nation. Critics accuse Vidler of water speculation, or acquiring water rights in the hope of reselling them and turning a profit. The practice is anathema in the western water world, where the "use-it-or-lose-it" paradigm reigns supreme. They see Vidler's deal with Lincoln County as a major step toward privatizing water, which has long been viewed as an essential public resource.

But water has always existed on murky legal ground, and even the West's water wizards don't really know what to make of Vidler. It's by no means the first private water-development company, but experts are at a loss to name any other outfit that's so artfully blurred the lines between the private and public realms.

Are private companies like Vidler the future of water development in the West? Or will Vidler be swept away as the water flows uphill—as water tends to do in these parts—toward the money in the fastest-growing

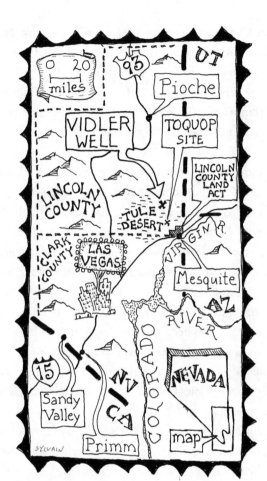

cities? Answers to these questions are being fought over in the statehouse and the courts. In the meantime, PW-1 sits silently in the desert.

In one telling of the story, Vidler is a visionary company. While multinational companies like Vivendi Universal, Suez, and Bechtel are taking over municipal water-supply systems in places like Bolivia, South Africa, and Atlanta, Georgia, Vidler has a much simpler *modus operandi*. "We're not a utility, and we're not a water marketer," says Dorothy Timian-Palmer, the company's president, who cut her teeth as the manager of the water department in Carson City, Nevada's capital. "We're a water developer."

Not so long ago, Vidler—named after its founder, Rees Vidler, a turn-of-the-twentieth-century Colorado real estate developer—was an unpretentious Colorado company with one asset: a tunnel carrying water from western Colorado under the Continental Divide to the city of Golden. Things changed in 1995, when La Jolla, California-based PICO Holdings bought Vidler and began pumping in money from its other ventures to finance water projects.

PICO moved Vidler to Carson City, where the water company shares a staff of twelve—including lawyers, water engineers, and mapping specialists—with its sister, a real estate company called the Nevada Land and Resource Company. Nevada Land's 1.2 million acres, originally granted to the Central Pacific railroad in the mid-1800s during the building of the transcontinental railroad, make it the largest private landowner in Nevada.

Vidler has quickly turned the West's water problems into business opportunities. Need water that's tied up in agriculture? Vidler is there to act as a middleman. Need a place to store water for use during dry years? Vidler's got space in underground "water banks." Looking for a new water source? Vidler knows where to find it—and has the money to bring it to market.

It's a model that even attracted the interest of Marc Reisner, the author of *Cadillac Desert: The American West and its Disappearing Water,* who served on Vidler's board of directors for about a year until his death in 2000. To Reisner, Vidler was enlisting economics to move scarce western water toward its "highest and best use."

But Vidler is up against tough odds: a raft of other water companies have self-destructed spectacularly in recent years. The Enron water subsidiary Azurix has gone the way of its parent company, and the stock prices of Cadiz Inc. dropped through the floor last fall, after the collapse of its water-storage deal with Southern California's Metropolitan Water District.

Debra Coy, a Washington, D.C.-based water analyst with the investment firm Schwab Capital Markets, says that as water supplies become ever scarcer—and more valuable—the lure of profit will draw investors to the field. "Water seems inherently valuable, and if you can put deals together to sell water, there's got to be money to be made." But so far, she says, efforts to make this work have "all been disasters."

Still, Vidler has insulated itself from some of the risk. PICO is a "closely held" company; its majority shareholders are insurance companies and investment funds that can ride out short-term economic turbulence. It has also tried to keep itself out of the limelight. The company's key to success, says Timian-Palmer, lies in maintaining a lower profile than companies like Cadiz and Azurix, which blundered into public-opinion minefields with their swashbuckling deal making.

"We're going to crack the nut," she says.

Before it came to Lincoln County, the company's record had been mixed. Its greatest success came in Arizona's Harquahala Valley, seventy-five miles west of Phoenix. In 1996, the company began buying farms that carried rights to the groundwater below them. Then, it leased the land back to the farmers and waited for water buyers. In 2001, Vidler clinched a $9.4 million deal with Allegheny Energy for land and water for a power plant in the valley.

A project near Bakersfield, California, didn't turn out so well. In 1998, the company bought into the Semitropic groundwater-banking project, which would store water underground during wet years and then sell it to thirsty cities during dry ones. Hamstrung by a welter of regulations and overlapping jurisdictions, Vidler has since sold off most of its stake in Semitropic. It's now developing its own groundwater-banking project below the Harquahala Valley.

Its experience in Nevada had also been troubled. In 2000, the company moved into Sandy Valley, thirty-five miles southwest of Las Vegas, with plans to develop groundwater and sell it to nearby Primm, a glorified truck stop on the California line with a couple of casinos, a fashion outlet, and a new power plant. But Vidler's application inspired a folksy self-defense movement among the valley's retirees and hermits, who have tied up the company's water application in court.

Overall, however, Vidler's bottom line looked good. Last year, its parent company, PICO Holdings, generated $29 million of revenue for an impressive 20 percent profit margin. Half of those revenues came from Vidler.

Water transfers and water banking are standard fare for private water companies. But in Lincoln County, Vidler is playing a different game.

In Pioche, the county seat—a busted mining town perched on a rocky piñon- and juniper-covered hillside—county commission chairman Hafen and county manager Doug Carriger are looking for an economic jumpstart. "We've been in decline here for about a hundred years, ever since mining petered out," says Carriger.

Nothing could happen without water, which was in abundant supply in the ground, but completely inaccessible without the money to drill wells and build pipelines.

Then Vidler showed up, and changed all that. Under the company's deal with the county, Vidler would tap groundwater with wells, file joint applications for water rights, and scout out customers. Once Vidler recoups its infrastructure investments (which total $4 million so far), half the profits will go to Lincoln County. Vidler will walk away with the other half.

Vidler and Lincoln County applied to the state engineer—who decides whether or not to grant water-rights applications—for rights to almost one hundred thousand acre-feet of water across the county (an acre-foot is enough water for a family of four for a year). And when Vidler drilled PW-1 in the summer of 2001, it hit paydirt: the well pumped up to seventeen hundred gallons per minute. Suddenly, the many economic "could-bes" that Hafen talks about seemed like they might, someday, bear fruit.

There were a couple of hopeful prospects. Down south, just over the line in Clark County, beckoned a vision of what Lincoln County might become: the gambling oasis of Mesquite, growing like crazy and running north toward the county line. In 2000, a bill sponsored by Senator Harry Reid, Democrat, directed the BLM to sell off thirteen thousand acres of land in Lincoln County, land that could soak up growth sprawling across the county line from Mesquite (and would take plenty of water to do so). The developers of the massive, fifty-thousand-home Coyote Springs development, straddling the Lincoln-Clark county line, might need more water. And Lincoln/Vidler did manage to land one firm contract, for water to cool a North Carolina company's proposed Toquop power project, also at the southern end of the county.

But while Vidler's private money might empower a poor rural county, critics say the company had an ulterior motive—one that ultimately shook up a nine-year-old standoff between Nevada's rural counties and Las Vegas.

In 1989, Las Vegas had filed applications for three hundred thousand acre-feet of groundwater—equal to southern Nevada's entire cut of the Colorado River—across four counties. Because it is a city, Vegas could file for water rights that it claimed were necessary for future growth, but didn't immediately need.

"It unleashed quite a hullabaloo," says Patricia Mulroy, the German-born, famously hard-nosed head of the Southern Nevada Water Authority, which provides the water that fuels Las Vegas' white-hot growth and sizzling economy. The move drew a flurry of protests from the rural counties.

When the smoke finally cleared, Vegas got rights to water from the Virgin River instead. The city agreed to hold off on its claims in Lincoln, Nye, and White Pine counties, and even relinquished claims to water that the rural counties would need for near-term growth. Legally, Vegas still had first crack at the water. But if Lincoln County could develop it, it had a chance to get some first—and Vidler saw this.

Acting alone, Vidler would have to step to the back of the line for water rights; but by partnering with the Lincoln County government to develop groundwater in the county, the company could jump to the front. But there was a huge bomb tucked inside Vidler's 1998 agreement with Lincoln County: it contained provisions to sell the water outside the county—which most observers read as plans to sell to Vegas.

Pat Mulroy was livid. She said Vidler had "imploded" the truce between Las Vegas and Lincoln County: "They're sandwiching themselves in the middle to make money."

Vidler and Lincoln later backpedaled and said that the water would only be used within Lincoln County. But they had already incurred Mulroy's wrath: in November 2001, Vegas launched a legal counterattack, asking the state attorney general's office to issue an opinion on the legality of the Lincoln-Vidler partnership.

In March 2002, the deputy attorney general declared that the agreement was illegal after finding "no provision of Nevada law that … permits the County to form a partnership with a private corporation and to share in a for-profit enterprise of this nature." Vidler promptly took the opinion to state court, where it still lingers.

Meanwhile, Las Vegas was only getting thirstier. The city's population had more than doubled since 1989, when Mulroy made her big claim to rural water. At the same time, a massive drought had hit the seven-state Colorado River Basin, which supplies 90 percent of the city's water.

The rural counties' water was looking more attractive all the time, and Mulroy began making noises about asking the state engineer to start processing the city's 1989 applications.

Then, she went to Lincoln County to negotiate a so-called "stand down": in March, the city and county signed a deal dividing up contested groundwater throughout the county. Vegas agreed to leave some water to the county (including that tapped by PW-1), while Lincoln County agreed not to contest the city's water-right applications elsewhere in the county.

For Vegas, the "stand-down" deal was a way to get some rural water quickly. For Lincoln County, it was a way to hang on to at least some of its water. Otherwise, says County Commissioner Hafen, "We'd have a lot of dust and an uphill battle in court, and in the end we'd run out of money, and Clark County"—the home of Las Vegas—"would still be fat and sassy and wet."

And Vidler? There was one small provision in the deal that had enormous significance: Mulroy agreed to abandon her opposition to Vidler's partnership with Lincoln County. With Mulroy and Las Vegas out of the way, Vidler set out to legalize the partnership. To do that, however, the company would have to change Nevada state law.

Vidler was well positioned to get its way: its office is three miles from the state legislature's doorstep in Carson City; Stephen Hartman, Vidler's corporate counsel, once worked for a prominent Carson City law firm, where his former law partner was Mark Amodei, who is now a state senator; and Vidler's sixteen-person lobbying force in the state legislature is a third again as big as the company's staff.

One week after the Lincoln-Las Vegas "stand-down" agreement took effect, state Senator Dean Rhoads, Republican, who represents Lincoln County, introduced a bill that would legalize public-private partnerships in any county with a population of less than four hundred thousand. That's every county in the state, except for Clark.

Vidler's opponents read that as opening up practically the entire state to the company. "[Vidler is] half-owner in all these water rights in Lincoln County," says Mike Winters, general manager of Mesquite's Virgin Valley Water District, who believes that pumping in the Tule Desert—where the PW-1 well is located—would suck up Mesquite's groundwater. "Well, now, let's go up to Douglas County, Churchill County. Let's go over to Nye County, all these places that are struggling. Pretty soon, you've got a private company owning half your water rights. And it's purely for speculation."

On April 21, Sen. Rhoads' bill passed the Senate, fifteen to six, and headed to the Assembly, Nevada's version of a House of Representatives. During the Senate debate, however, Sen. Warren Hardy, Republican, sounded an impassioned warning that the deal "makes our most important natural resource an instrument of commerce." And suddenly, Vidler wasn't flying under the radar screen anymore.

Hardy caught people's attention and thrust Vidler uncomfortably into the spotlight. As the legislature neared its June 2 end of session, opponents, including Nevada's environmental community, rallied in determined opposition.

"It was really unprecedented. We generated more phone calls on this issue than any other one in this legislative session," says Grace Potorti, director of the Nevada Conservation League. "We packed the hearing, and we did it in like forty-eight hours."

Critics said Vidler was pushing Nevada into a brave new world, a hazy conflation of the public and private realms, where economic development in a poor rural county would have to generate good-looking numbers on the company's quarterly profit-and-loss statement. From the sidelines, Pat Mulroy went so far as to say the deal put Lincoln County under a "corporate dictatorship."

In spite of the rally, the bill passed the assembly's Government Affairs Committee. But insiders say that an informal poll by the leadership of the Democrat-dominated Assembly revealed that its members had little stomach for a floor vote on such a controversial bill, and committee chairman Mark Manendo, Democrat-Las Vegas, kept the bill from ever making it to the full Assembly.

"We had the votes," says Vidler president Timian-Palmer, "but they wouldn't let it go to the floor."

Two days before the session ended, legislators from Lincoln County introduced an amendment to another bill that created a "Lincoln County Water District," run by the county commission, with powers to issue bonds, secure loans, and apply for federal grants. That gave Vidler a chance to redo its contracts with the county on less contentious ground, but it meant the end of the company's statewide push.

As the dust settles yet again, some say Vidler is stuck with a dry hole, as its prospects in Lincoln County may be evaporating. Cogentrix bailed out of the Toquop power project last year, and although Vidler bought the project, it's still nothing more than paper; the massive Lincoln County Land Act, meanwhile, is tied up in the U.S. Department of the Interior's Board of Land Appeals.

Vidler hasn't given up, however. "Some people say the Lincoln County Land Act is pie-in-the-sky, but that's what they used to say about Mesquite," says Hartman, Vidler's corporate counsel. "Development in southern Nevada has gone weird places in incredibly short periods of time."

Whatever the fate of Vidler, its activities in Nevada have raised an important debate about the future of the West's most precious resource.

"These issues are becoming more and more visible to the public," says Hugh Jackson, a Las Vegas-based policy analyst for the watchdog group Public Citizen. "The more the public thinks about it, the more they think, 'Gosh, water is a human right, water's a necessity of life, and not everything has to be privatized and profited from.' Nevada was a little microcosm of that awakening."

And at a time when the conservation ethic is finally gaining steam in the West, many argue that private water development works in precisely the opposite direction. "Wall Street works on selling more," says Pat Mulroy. "You can't do that [with water]. You have to find ways to use less, not more."

She points to the 2001 energy crisis in California as a classic example of what can go wrong in a deregulated market. "Financially, [the power companies] couldn't promote conservation, because they needed to sell more to dig themselves out," she says.

But for Mulroy, there's something viscerally disturbing about Vidler's foray into Lincoln County. "Peel away all the layers, and it's really Owens Valley in a different form," she says, referring to the notorious L.A. water grab. In Mulroy's mind, Vidler plays the role of L.A., robbing rural water.

But behind the high-minded talk—the kind of talk that rallied opponents to pack the public hearing—Mulroy also has a cold bottom line: she needs to provide water for Las Vegas. And there's the great irony: strip away Vidler, strip away questions about commodifying a public resource, strip this story down to its most basic elements, and you are left with a story that parallels Owens Valley. In the end, though, it's Las Vegas, not Vidler, that may ultimately walk away with the water.

Warren Hardy—the state senator who so eloquently warned of privatizing a public resource—is a former lobbyist for the Virgin Valley Water District, which, once Mulroy agreed not to challenge the Lincoln/Vidler agreement, became Vegas' proxy in the fight against Vidler. Hardy is also president of the Associated Builders and Contractors of Southern Nevada, which clearly has an interest in quashing water-development deals that could threaten Vegas' growth.

Mulroy herself concedes that lining up water to meet Las Vegas' plans for the future means severely limiting Lincoln County's hopes for its future. In fact, that's a fate that Vegas itself narrowly avoided. Back in 1922, Las Vegas got stuck with a relatively paltry three hundred thousand acre-foot cut of the Colorado because it was just a podunk railroad depot.

"That's what's wrong with a lot of the water law," she says. "[If] we need it now [and] you have no use for it, the assumption comes along that you'll never have a use for it. Well, that's not true. We're living proof of that, or we'd have gotten more out of the Colorado River. So I feel kind of like a hypocrite, singing out of both sides of my mouth."

Mulroy is careful to say that "we don't ever want that Owens aura," and that the rural counties' water is a "shared resource" for both them and Las Vegas.

But up in Lincoln County, County Commissioner Hafen is scratching his head about the "could-bes." Maybe the deal with Vidler will work out, and maybe the power plant or the Lincoln County Land Act will come through, or the Coyote Springs development will need more water. But if they don't, the water under Lincoln County will be fair game for Vegas, smacking its lips to the south.

"No matter what we'd like to do, or how much we'd like to call it our own, it's the state's water," says Hafen. "They can do whatever the state feels is in the best interest of the people. And if Vegas has a need for it, it would be shipped south."

And stacked against Hafen's "could-bes," there's one stark certainty. Last year, the population in Clark County hit 1.6 million, four hundred times larger than Lincoln County's. Even in the middle of the fourth year of drought on the Colorado, Vegas' growth boom seems to be unstoppable: the population is forecast to nearly double by 2035.

In the end, perhaps it doesn't matter whether water is privatized or not—it's going to move. And, as the old saying goes, it's going to move uphill, toward the big money in the cities.

August 4, 2003

Matt Jenkins is a *High Country News* contributing editor.

Idaho Gets Smart
about Water

Rocky Barker

It might seem like the wrong time to be optimistic about Idaho's water. Five years of drought have set an all-time record for dryness. Despite the increasing water needs of cities, recreation, and native fish, farmers still account for nearly 90 percent of the state's total water use. Farm irrigation routinely causes some streams to go dry and aquifers to shrink.

Thousands of farmers are now arguing over who gets what from the state's biggest pool of water, the Lake-Erie-sized Eastern Snake River Plain Aquifer, which stretches underground from Twin Falls to Yellowstone National Park. The farmers are divided into two camps—the surface-water users and the groundwater pumpers—and Lynn Tominaga, director of Idaho's Groundwater Appropriators Association, says, "This [water struggle] is either going to bring us together, or drive us further apart."

Ironically, the farmer-versus-farmer struggle may actually be a sign of progress. A flurry of recent actions by the state's water powers shows that Idaho, which began shaking off a long adolescence ten years ago, may finally be reaching maturity when it comes to water management.

Farmers began tapping surface water above the Eastern Snake River Plain Aquifer in the early 1900s, especially from the huge springs that gush from the Snake River Canyon walls at the aquifer's western edge. Then, from the 1950s to the early 1990s, other farmers began drilling thousands of wells to pump groundwater.

The groundwater pumpers put more than a million acres into irrigation for potatoes, beets, and grain, but caused declines in the flows of springs, streams, and rivers.

Finally, the Idaho Department of Water Resources, which had basically ignored the connection between groundwater pumping and surface-water declines for decades, started acting like a grown-up. In the mid-1990s, it instituted "conjunctive" management, which treats the state's farmers as part of a single, interconnected water system. The department formed groundwater districts to manage the well pumpers. It also set up a leasing system, so that water needed for farmers or for salmon migration could be leased from farmers who aren't using all of their allotted water.

But the surface-water users continued to complain about shortages. Those holding senior water rights began to make "calls"—legal maneuvers demanding that the groundwater pumpers either cut back or compensate them with leased water.

In response, the legislature and Governor Dirk Kempthorne, Republican, took several more steps this year. According to Tominaga, they approved spending about $60 million over the next fifteen years, to help launch the federal Conservation Reserve Enhancement Program in Idaho. That program is expected to match state money with $180 million of federal money, paying farmers to idle fields and hence reduce the demand for water.

The political leaders also agreed to an expensive settlement of the Nez Perce tribe's claims on the Snake River. And they arranged to bill groundwater users for some of the costs of the reforms.

Idaho is looking realistically at water systems in a way not seen in some other western states; for instance, Arizona does not acknowledge the interdependence of surface and groundwater. And Barbara Cosens, a law professor at the University of Idaho who has worked on water issues in Nevada and California, says, "In comparison to those states, Idaho is way ahead in recognizing the connection between surface water and groundwater, and acting accordingly." Idaho's reforms and its newfound enlightenment about water systems are helping the state weather the severe drought.

Idaho's water management is increasingly based on science. University of Idaho researchers, working with a range of hydrologists, have spent eight years developing a sophisticated computer model. It predicts how water moves through the aquifer, and shows the effects of shutting down specific wells.

Karl Dreher, who has run the water department since the mid-1990s, uses this model to decide which specific groundwater pumpers should be held responsible for surface-water shortages. It also helps him determine how to respond to the recent water calls.

Both this year and last year, for example, trout farmers and big canal companies issued massive calls that threatened to shut down 40 percent of the aquifer's wells. Those calls could have devastated southern Idaho's economy. One was settled with a temporary compromise, but several others are yet to be decided.

Evaluating one of the biggest calls, Dreher concluded that about thirteen hundred groundwater pumpers owe two canal companies and five irrigation districts a total of 27,700 acre-feet of water this summer. They may owe up to 101,000 additional acre-feet later, depending on rainfall and other variables.

The groundwater pumpers will have to spend more than $2 million this year to lease water for the callers, Tominaga says. Much of that water will be leased from "high-lift" pumpers, who draw water hundreds of feet uphill from the bottom of the Snake River Canyon. And they are generally eager to lease or sell their rights: sharp increases in electricity costs have made their operations marginal.

The groundwater pumpers are also figuring out ways to use less groundwater, in some cases by leasing surface water instead. And they're anticipating buyout offers from the federal Conservation Reserve Enhancement program. With that money, Tominaga says, more than sixty thousand acres could be disconnected from groundwater, to answer the current calls. Down the line, the total could reach a hundred thousand acres.

In all the recent activity, salmon have not been forgotten: In April, the state paid $24.5 million to high-lift pumpers, so seventy-five thousand acre-feet per year can go down the river to aid salmon migration. That's the first time the state has bought out farmers' water rights.

Idaho's water management still needs tweaking, especially to help the fish. Recent progress shows that the state is at least headed in the right direction, according to John Tracy, director of the Idaho Water

Resources Research Institute. However, he cautions that translating scientific understanding into sound water policy may prove arduous: "It's one thing to understand the physical system; it's another to change water management to meet all these goals."

June 13, 2005

Rocky Barker is a veteran reporter in the Northwest, and a fellow at the Andrus Center for Public Policy in Boise, Idaho.

Getting Fresh with the West's Groundwater

Morgan Heim

That shot of hot air coming from the bottom of the refrigerator may soon serve a greater purpose than just warming your feet. A new saltwater distillation technique that uses solar energy and waste heat from appliances could provide remote Southwestern communities with clean drinking water.

Researchers Nirmala Khandan and Veera Gude of New Mexico State University in Las Cruces have created a desalination system that could provide almost a million gallons of fresh water annually—enough to supply twenty-five homes with up to a hundred gallons of water each per day.

Salty water has long plagued states like New Mexico, Arizona, and Nevada, where high levels of naturally occurring minerals, as well as industrial waste and agricultural runoff, have made most groundwater too salty for drinking or agriculture. The U.S. Geological Survey estimates that 75 percent of New Mexico's groundwater has salt levels above one thousand micrograms per liter, the point at which water becomes saline.

But that briny reserve has a lot of potential, if technology can convert it to freshwater. "We live in a pretty dry area, and more people are looking to live here every year," says Thomas Mayer, project manager for Sandia National Laboratories' geochemical department. "We're just plain out of [fresh]water. But desalination is relatively drought-proof."

So far, a major challenge of desalination has been the enormous amount of energy it requires, something this new method addresses.

Traditional distillation technologies, which require boiling salt-water, take as much as 11,000 kilowatt-hours of electricity to produce 36,500 gallons of freshwater (the amount of water per house per year produced by Khandan and Gude's project). Their prototype creates a natural vacuum, which makes water boil at lower temperatures. The new technology saves about half of the energy used by traditional methods; it's roughly equivalent to running a household water heater.

Unlike other desalination methods, the prototype runs almost entirely on renewable energy: solar power and waste heat, like that emitted by air conditioners. Other desalination methods—such as reverse osmosis, a method that filters water through special membranes—use even less energy, but that efficiency is offset by their reliance on fossil fuels.

The prototype uses a more sophisticated version of a three-thousand-year-old method. A vacuum sucks water from a saltwater tank into a depressurized container. This evaporation tank acts much like a glass jar left out in the sun, turning water into steam and leaving a more concentrated salt solution behind. Those salty leftovers collect in a waste bin, while the freshwater steam travels through tubes and condenses in a final tank. From there, pure water can then be pumped away to fill empty glasses in nearby communities. Because it produces water more slowly than other methods, solar desalination works best for small communities.

Regardless of the desalination method used, researchers must contend with the waste that's left behind. "There's salts left over, and there are not very good options for disposing of them," says Mayer. One technique for treating waste is to evaporate leftover water in ponds, package the salts left behind, and ship them to industrial waste facilities. However, doing this exposes wildlife and the public to potential environmental hazards.

Another uncertainty is the cost of building a solar desalinator. "Even if [a solar desalinator] was cheap to run, the capital cost of building it would be astronomical," says Mayer. But Gude contends that "desalination is like it's almost free" because the energy is free, and Khandan estimates that building one of the plants would cost about $50,000.

Meanwhile, Khandan and Gude are testing their prototype, have already applied for a patent license, and are fielding offers from water utilities and private contractors interested in their invention. They hope to have a final design available next year.

Despite some skepticism, competing researchers admire the possibilities. Mayer says, "The New Mexico prototype is a very ingenious device."

July 19, 2007

Morgan Heim is a freelance journalist and photographer.

Facing the Yuck Factor

Peter Freiderici

Sometime this fall, Mike Nivison plans to take a healthy swig of water that exemplifies everything you'd expect from a small resort town set high in a western mountain range. The water will be cool, clear, refreshing. But it won't be pristine spring water pouring from some mossy crevice.

Nivison is Cloudcroft's village administrator, and what he anticipates savoring will come from the village's drinking-water treatment plant— and, not too long before that, from its sewage treatment facility.

Cloudcroft's will be one of the first wastewater systems in the nation to allow—or require, depending on your perspective—residents to drink treated wastewater that hasn't been naturally cleansed in a river or aquifer. It will be built entirely as a matter of necessity. At an elevation of more than eighty-five hundred feet in southern New Mexico's Sacramento Mountains, Cloudcroft is high and, thanks to recent years of drought, dry.

"A city like San Diego can go buy more water," says Bruce Thomson, a University of New Mexico civil engineer who has been helping Cloudcroft develop its new water system. "It's expensive, but they can. But Cloudcroft is simply out of water. Because they're at the top of the mountain, there's no new place to drill wells. They're at the top of the watershed. They don't have any other alternatives."

Cloudcroft has only about seven hundred fifty residents, but its population swells to a few thousand on summer weekends. All those people escaping the lowland heat—and drinking, showering, and flushing—can use more than a third of a million gallons of water on a single hot Saturday. But the village's major wells produce only about one hundred fifty thousand gallons a day. To make up the shortfall, village officials have resorted in recent years to hauling water, which is expensive, inconvenient, and energy-intensive.

Nivison figured that Cloudcroft's only sure source of what he calls "wet water"—that is, usable liquid, rather than theoretical legal rights or hard-to-reach water that might be buried somewhere deep underground—was right at his feet, in the stream of effluent pouring from the village's wastewater-treatment plant. With several million dollars in state funding and the help of engineers from two universities and a private firm, the village has been building a plant to purify that water. After conventional treatments that settle solids and utilize microbes to degrade or remove pathogens, the plant will use multiple filtration methods, including reverse osmosis, to remove chemical contaminants. Then the water will be sent to covered tanks and mixed with groundwater pumped from the village wells.

After three or four weeks, the blend will be sent back through drinking-water treatment and distributed for use. The wastes squeezed out during the reverse-osmosis process, meanwhile, will be concentrated in briny effluent, which the village will store for use in dust control on roads, fighting fires, and, possibly, for making artificial snow at the local ski area.

And then the toilets will flush, and the sinks and tubs will drain, and the cycle will repeat again—and if Nivison and his collaborators are lucky, no one will think much about it.

"By any parameter you can measure—suspended particles, salts, bacteria, pharmaceuticals—the water from this process is going to be extraordinarily clean," Thomson says. "But you have to overcome the 'yuck factor.' It's not measurable, it's not quantifiable, but it's every bit as important as the particles you can measure."

"All we've done is recycle the same water on this earth since the beginning of time," Mike Nivison says. "This is just a more controlled environment for doing the same thing. I do believe this will be our salvation."

He's right, of course: using water is fundamentally a matter of recycling. Mathematically, you can show that the liquid pouring from your faucet today probably contains some of the same water molecules that George Washington drank in 1776. Remember the water cycle diagram you saw in grade school: two hydrogen atoms bound to one of oxygen precipitate from clouds as rain or snow, seep into the soil, transpire from leaves, get lapped up by animals, course through streams and rivers, and finally settle, temporarily, in the ocean, only to evaporate once again to start the cycle anew. The idea of reuse is central to our understanding of water— perhaps even a bit compelling, when it comes to sharing molecules with George Washington.

It's a good deal less so when you're talking about wastewater of newer vintage, such as the stuff they're going to be cleaning up and drinking in Cloudcroft. As the West grows in population, though, and as climate change seems to be decreasing the reliability of some water supplies, some of the region's residents are reconsidering the notion that effluent is something to get rid of as efficiently as possible. Only a few are willing to go quite as far, yet, as Mike Nivison, but many are at least embracing the idea that wastewater is a valuable resource. What's happening in Cloudcroft, then, is a portent of what is happening, and what likely will happen, in other arid places.

But the prospect of brewing your morning coffee with water that was recently washing greasy dishes or flushing a neighbor's toilet has many people uneasy, and not just because of what psychologists and water engineers alike call the "yuck factor." The water to be recycled may carry a host of pollutants, some recognized only recently. Among the most worrisome are endocrine disruptors, which pose potentially large but as yet incompletely proven health threats that are making some scientists very nervous.

Twice in the last ten years, San Diego city officials have proposed augmenting the city's drinking water supply with water reclaimed from the city's sewers—and twice, in 1999 and again last year, those plans have been shot down.

It is a telling comment on the disjointed nature of much water management in the United States that San Diego has both a water-supply and a water-disposal problem. On the supply side, the city imports between 85 and 95 percent of its water from distant sources, specifically, from the Colorado River and the California State Water Project, which conveys water from Northern California to the state's dry southern half. Those sources have historically been reliable, but only up to a point. In 1991, during a severe drought, water-project deliveries were on the verge of being drastically cut when the rains finally came; this year, water planners are asking users to make voluntary cutbacks. And current climate projections suggest that the flow of the already over-allocated Colorado River may decline significantly in the future.

For wastewater disposal, San Diego relies on a water-treatment plant at Point Loma whose technology is antiquated. It discharges effluent that does not meet Clean Water Act standards into the Pacific. San Diego has a waiver from the federal Environmental Protection Agency allowing it to dump that effluent, but the waiver expires in 2008. The cost of upgrading the Point Loma facility to meet EPA standards has been estimated at $1 billion, and the city has yet to make plans to raise that money.

As part of a settlement agreement stemming from a lawsuit by the EPA and environmental groups, San Diego agreed to reduce its effluent discharge into the ocean by building two plants to treat water for reuse in the city and its surroundings. Those plants are now capable of putting out 37.5 million gallons of reclaimed, non-potable water a day.

Like many other municipalities in the West, San Diego sells some of its reclaimed water to buyers who use it to water golf courses, feed industrial processes, and flush toilets. It's distributed in a network of purple pipes to distinguish it from the potable water supply, and it's currently available at about a third the cost of potable water. The trouble is that the purple-pipe network amounts to an entirely new, parallel water system, and San Diego, like many other cities, hasn't extended it very far.

"It's expensive to pay for the distribution of recycled water," says Maria Mariscal, senior water-resources specialist for the San Diego County Water Authority. "Installing purple pipe in new developments is OK, but retrofitting in established areas can be expensive."

As a result, the city is able to sell only about a third of its recycled water capacity and is unlikely to meet its target, developed as part of the lawsuit settlement, of selling at least 50 percent by 2010.

To figure out how to use more of the reclaimed water, the city Water Department conducted a study that recommended treating it intensively and returning it to the potable water system. The system would be like Cloudcroft's on steroids: sixteen million gallons a day rather than a hundred thousand. Using the treated water to supplement San Diego's drinking-water system at a single point would be much more cost-effective than piping the treated water to an entire network of dispersed users of non-potable water.

Turning treated effluent into drinking water is a widespread practice. It's most commonly done when communities dump their effluent into streams and rivers, knowing that other users downstream will use the same water. But an increasing number of communities are reusing their own water. In Orange County, El Paso, Tucson, and many other western communities, water agencies recycle by dumping treated effluent on the ground so that it can soak in and recharge aquifers. After that water's been underground for a while, it is then pumped up for drinking water use.

San Diego's topography, though, doesn't lend itself to recharging water from the treatment plants into local aquifers. So planners proposed pumping the treated effluent into a reservoir that feeds the city's drinking-water system. The city council's Natural Resources and Culture Committee agreed and forwarded the proposal to the full council. A wide range of stakeholders on a community panel agreed, too.

"To me, this is a win-win," says Bruce Reznik, executive director of San Diego Coastkeeper, an environmental group that monitors coastal pollution. "You're discharging less into the ocean, and you're creating a local water supply that you otherwise wouldn't have."

But opponents exploded, labeling the idea with a visceral and unforgettable moniker of the sort no politician can afford to ignore. "Your golden retriever may drink out of the toilet with no ill effects," editorialized the San Diego *Union-Tribune* under the headline "Yuck!". "But that doesn't mean humans should do the same. San Diego's infamous 'toilet to tap' plan is back once again, courtesy of Water Department bureaucrats who are prodding the City Council to adopt this very costly boondoggle."

Mayor Jerry Sanders came to much the same conclusion, announcing in July of last year that he would not support the reservoir augmentation plan. A year later, the City Council has yet to decide on any new wastewater-reuse strategies.

"It was certainly disappointing," says Jim Crook, a consultant who helped draft California's water-reuse guidelines in the 1970s and served on an independent task force evaluating the city's proposal. "It was a good project from a technical standpoint. We were very comfortable with what they were going to do. The reclaimed water would be of a higher quality than some of the raw water sources that are used now."

That, indeed, is one of the principal ironies here: before it could even be used for reservoir augmentation, the water would be treated to a higher standard than what San Diegans are drinking now. Water discharged from the North City facility has already been shown to be at least as clean as water in some of the city's reservoirs. If it were to be dedicated to potable reuse, it would be subjected to further intensive treatment, such as reverse osmosis, before being pumped to the reservoir.

Reverse osmosis uses pressure to force water through a membrane that allows water, but not most other molecules, to pass through. It's expensive and energy-intensive, but it is better than almost any other technology at taking almost all contaminants out of water. Using it would bring San Diego's erstwhile wastewater up to a much better quality than, say, the Colorado River, which receives the waste from hundreds of municipalities and industrial users by the time it reaches Southern California. Las Vegas alone discharges roughly sixty billion gallons of wastewater a year some miles upstream of its own water intake—a feat of urban engineering that would seem to prove that most of what happens in Vegas really does stay there. What happens in Sin City is fueled by prescription and over-the-counter pharmaceuticals, caffeine, sunscreen, synthetic compounds used in plastics and detergents, and even methamphetamines, say researchers who have found all that in Lake Mead's water.

Las Vegas' effluent is diluted as it flows downstream, and some of the compounds in it are degraded by sunlight, destroyed by microbes, or bound up in sediment. Still, monitoring in 2006 showed that water entering San Diego's municipal system contained, before drinking-water treatment, small but measurable quantities of ibuprofen, the insect repellent DEET, and the anti-anxiety drug meprobamate.

"We can have a lot more monitoring and control if we oversee our own reclamation than if we're relying on a river with a billion gallons of recharge from other sources every day," says Bruce Reznik. "It's better to be drinking our own 'toilet to tap' water than someone else's. I'm pretty confident that this would be a whole lot safer than what we're getting now."

In Windhoek, Namibia, water from a wastewater-treatment plant is piped right back into the drinking-water system. NASA is developing advanced recycling technology that will directly convert astronauts' urine into clean drinking water. Such reuse systems are what a South African pioneer in water reclamation, Lucas van Vuuren, was thinking of when he said, "Water should be judged not by its history, but by its quality." Sufficient treatment, he meant, assures that any water can be reused. Windhoek is achingly dry and almost five hundred miles from the nearest perennial river. It costs NASA about $40,000 to send a gallon of clean water up to the International Space Station. In those situations it makes a lot of sense to clean—carefully—and reuse wastewater.

Van Vuuren's is a technocrat's line, though, because in fact most people's tools for judging water quality aren't up to the task. Conventional wastewater treatment is very good at removing the kind of contaminants people can detect without laboratory equipment, such as odors, suspended particles, and the sorts of bacteria that can cause illness. But most people are relatively helpless when it comes to making more detailed assessments of their water supply's safety. The lower Colorado River looks clean enough; it's more likely to meet most people's standards than cleaner water in a pipe outside a complex-looking treatment plant.

As a result of that perceptual shortfall, people are left with nothing but water's history as a guideline, according to Brent Haddad of the University of California at Santa Cruz, an environmental studies professor who directs the university's new Center for Integrated Water Research. When he began studying water policy, he says, "I kept going to meetings with water managers, and they kept saying, 'How do we deal with these irrational people?'—meaning their customers. I didn't think they were irrational. I thought they were just using a different sort of logic than the water managers and engineers. People as they are generate feelings and opinions about some things that are really based on intuition and not a technical analysis of risk. They're based on what you might call ancient rules of thumb about what's safe and what isn't."

A visceral aversion to unclean water, Haddad says, is an understandable and useful tool that served the human species well through most of its evolution. But it may not be particularly helpful today, when it's necessary to make a decision between two sources of water that are both clear and odorless—but from very different sources.

"When people are aware of the history of their water, it matters a lot to them," he says. "If there's an unavoidable link to prior urban use, that's troubling to people. It's extremely hard to convince people then that the treatment will be good enough to override that history. But people are willing to take Colorado River water or groundwater that's clearly been used by other cities because it's easy to abstract away that use and begin the water's history with its taking from the natural system."

Rivers and soils do, in fact, clean water. But the psychological cleansing they do may be equally important. As a result, even the Colorado River—however thoroughly dammed, diverted, and delivered through aqueducts it may be—appears more natural, and cleaner, to many people than what's produced by San Diego's wastewater-treatment plants. The river takes the yuck out.

The largely unwelcome prospect of drinking treated effluent, though, forces people to ask what's in the water they're already getting, whatever its source. Something long taken for granted—what could be more American than good, drinkable tap water?—becomes a public issue. And as people debate where their future water supplies are going to come from, an increasing number of experts and nonexperts alike are growing increasingly alarmed about the chemicals flowing not only from Las Vegas, but from every community.

Wastewater engineers are rightly proud of what their industry achieved in the twentieth century, bringing safe drinking water to virtually every community in the United States. But most wastewater-treatment plants were not designed to remove the sorts of complex organic chemicals that show up in Lake Mead or, to cite a more pristine-looking example, Boulder Creek, which tumbles out of the Rocky Mountains and through Boulder, Colo., before joining the South Platte River.

Back in 2000, David Norris thought Boulder Creek an unlikely place to look for unhealthy fish. Even below the city's wastewater-treatment plant, the creek looked clean, and fish and other aquatic organisms lived throughout it. There was none of the stench, the brown murk, or the belly-up fish associated with the bad old days of piecemeal sewage treatment before the Clean Water Act was passed in 1972.

Norris, an endocrinologist at the University of Colorado—and an avid fisherman—had read studies in the scientific literature documenting the environmental effects of a poorly understood class of pollutants known as endocrine disruptors. Unlike many toxins, they didn't appear to be killing their victims outright. But in Lake Apopka, Fla., a pesticide spill had caused lingering reproductive failures and sexual abnormalities in alligators. In Britain, odd-looking fish that were not readily identifiable as males or females, but had sexual characteristics of both, were turning up in anglers' creels, especially in waterways below sewage outlets.

Norris and his colleagues, Alan Vajda and John Woodling, figured that Boulder Creek's best indicators of environmental quality were likely to be white suckers, a native fish that's widespread and not terribly finicky about water quality. "A good healthy freshwater stream has a good healthy sucker population," he says. "If you really disturb this species, you've really disturbed the ecosystem."

Norris had no trouble finding white suckers both upstream and downstream of Boulder's treatment plant. Upstream, everything seemed normal. Downstream, it was not. "Much to our surprise," he says, "we were appalled to see the extent of feminization in the fish population." He found five female suckers for every male; further, 20 percent of the fish were "intersex" individuals showing characteristics of both sexes.

Alarmed, Norris looked for similar effects elsewhere, and found them. Fish below wastewater-treatment plants in Denver and Colorado Springs showed some of the same symptoms. In the South Platte River, where Denver releases its waste, he couldn't find a single male sucker below the effluent outlet. Something in the effluent, it appeared, wasn't killing fish, but rather causing hormonal changes in them and producing female traits in male fish.

The evidence was circumstantial, though. Norris knew he had to more closely link cause and effect, which is hard to do in a natural setting, where fish in different reaches of the same stream might be feeding on different food, facing different temperatures, and otherwise dealing with widely variable conditions. So he and his colleagues have since built two "Fish Exposure Mobiles," which are basically mobile laboratories, built inside trailers, with fish-holding tanks. By pumping combinations of river water and wastewater effluent into the tanks on site, they're able to replicate the pollution concentrations fish face at various distances below treatment plants.

When they experimentally exposed fathead minnows—widely used as a test fish—to water like that below the Boulder treatment plant, Norris and his colleagues were able to feminize male fish within fourteen days. They have since tested fish in other Colorado waterways below wastewater-treatment plants in the Rocky Mountains and on the Western Slope. Data from those tests aren't available yet, but Norris will say that he is awfully worried in general about the presence of endocrine-disrupting chemicals in the environment, and in water specifically.

"It's fairly obvious that living populations are being subjected to far more chemicals in the last thirty years than when biological systems evolved, and so we wonder what effect that has on the genetic machinery," he says. "If we want to increase the use of wastewater, unless we're going to remove these compounds from the water, we're going to increase their concentration in the human population, since we're just going to be adding more of these compounds. We keep concentrating our population in cities, and as a result we're concentrating our effluent."

Most of the organic compounds that can disrupt the endocrine system are neither regulated by EPA standards nor often monitored in waterways or the drinking-water system. Few thought they were a problem until recently. But in a national survey published by the U.S. Geological Survey in 2002, researchers found such substances in 80 percent of the waterways they sampled.

The endocrine system is essentially a complex signaling mechanism that tells genes and cells when to do what. It operates by means of chemical messengers, or hormones, that bind to certain receptors in cells. Unfortunately, many of those receptors aren't particularly picky. Receptors designed to react to the natural hormone estrogen, for example, can also be set off by a wide range of other compounds, from complex molecules that naturally occur in vegetables to synthetic chemicals found in soaps, plastics, pesticides, cleaning products, and many of the other manufactured goods of modern civilization. They get into sewage when people urinate, or shower, or flush leftover pharmaceuticals down the toilet.

As in Boulder Creek, waterborne endocrine disruptors have in many places been shown to have harmful effects on aquatic organisms, especially fish. For example, male carp with unusually high levels of female hormones have been found in Lake Mead, where estrogen—the kind naturally produced in human bodies as well as the synthetic variety in birth-control pills—ends up when Las Vegans flush their toilets. Recently, a team of Canadian biologists dosed an entire small lake with synthetic estrogen at levels equivalent to those often found in treated wastewater. They were able to wipe out almost the entire minnow population in only a few years—again, not by killing the fish, but by causing sexual changes in males and females that made it impossible for those fish to reproduce.

Hormones naturally work at very low levels; a human estrogen concentration as low as one part per trillion—so dilute that it's near the lower limit of what monitoring equipment can detect—has been shown to affect fish. The effluent dumped into Boulder Creek typically contains from one to ten parts per trillion of human estrogen.

"People ask why such tiny levels have such a devastating effect," says Norris. "But that's the level at which hormones work. Parts per trillion is common stuff for an endocrinologist."

Consumers are used to thinking of drugs as having precisely tailored effects. But endocrine disruptors don't work that way. Because many different chemicals can activate a given set of hormone receptors, low doses of quite different substances can combine into a higher dose. That's one of the primary reasons a growing number of researchers worry about possible implications for human health.

"What happens when you have a summing-up of the effects of these different chemicals?" asks Theo Colborn, a longtime pollution researcher who runs the nonprofit Endocrine Disruption Exchange in Colorado and coauthored the 1996 book *Our Stolen Future*, one of the first popular publications to raise an alarm about such compounds. "Sometimes there's even a synergistic effect between them. It's like adding two and two and getting five."

Wastewater treatment lowers concentrations of most trace organic compounds—often by an order of magnitude or more—but it can't remove them all. As a result, effluent often contains a stew of complex chemicals. A recent U.S. Geological Survey study found that St. Vrain Creek, into which Boulder Creek drains, carries measurable loads of at least thirty-six different compounds, including artificial fragrances, fire retardants, antibacterial substances used in soaps, and substances used to manufacture plastics. The extent to which those chemicals work together to cause effects on the endocrine system—itself not well understood—is a big unknown.

"The endocrine system is much more than estrogens," says Catherine Propper, an endocrinologist at Northern Arizona University who has studied the effects of trace organics on amphibians. "We have this complicated endocrine system, and every time we find new aspects of it, we find they can be disrupted by some of these environmental contaminants."

It's difficult to draw lines of cause and effect between exposure to endocrine disruptors and human disease or disorder because people are exposed to so many chemicals from so many sources over many years, and because some effects may take years or decades to manifest themselves. But an increasing number of researchers are finding strong correlations between the massive increase in synthetic environmental contaminants produced since World War Two and such health problems as cancer, declining sperm counts in male humans of all ages, increases in birth defects and diabetes, and flawed fetal development.

Of course, humans aren't exposed to the chemicals in effluent in the same way that Boulder Creek's white suckers are; we aren't swimming in the water twenty-four/seven. And by the time a creek, or the Colorado River, enters our faucets, the loads of trace organics poured into it from treatment plants upstream have been significantly reduced. Natural processes, such as degradation by ultraviolet light and the action of microbes, do remove some chemicals from stream water, while others chemically bind to sediment particles. But the intensity of water use in the West means that, in many river systems, water is taken in for further municipal use before natural cleansing mechanisms can do their full work.

"Our rivers and lakes do clean water, especially if they have long stretches between communities using it," says Colborn. "But we've exceeded their carrying and assimilation capacity."

That's especially true, Colborn says, because so many sources contribute to the loads of trace organic compounds carried by streams and rivers. While wastewater-treatment plants are perhaps the largest single sources, leaching from septic systems, runoff from car washes and feedlots, leakage from sewage pipes, and overflows from water-intensive natural-gas drilling all contribute doses.

When surface water is taken in for municipal use, it is treated with filtration and disinfection treatments that significantly reduce contaminant concentrations. But low concentrations of some compounds—often in the parts-per-trillion range—do remain to make their way into drinking water.

Some water experts argue that the amounts of endocrine disruptors people ingest in water are insignificant compared to those we get from other sources—plastic containers, foods, soaps, cosmetics, and many other products.

"In terms of relative risk, the risk from drinking water is minuscule," says Kim Linton, senior account manager at the Denver-based American Water Works Association Research Foundation. "For example, DEET is one of the most persistent of these trace compounds. Are people more likely to get sick from West Nile virus or from trace levels in the water? Are they going to stop spraying themselves?"

No, most probably won't. But some biologists argue that the cumulative effects of endocrine disruptors make it imperative to reduce their concentrations anywhere possible.

"You would have to drink incredible amounts of the water to amount to an effect that these chemicals naturally have," says David Norris. "But adult humans are getting estrogenic compounds from an incredible number of sources. So any amount we get from water will add to that, since these chemicals have additive effects.

"If wastewater is my only source of estrogenic compounds, I'm not going to worry about it. But if I'm also getting them from my water bottles, from my personal-care products, etc., then maybe that's just enough to push me over the edge into prostate cancer or breast cancer. There's a lot of circumstantial evidence in humans that is supported by experimental work in mice and rats that suggests that this may be a much bigger problem than a few intersex fish below a wastewater-treatment plant."

The water-processing system has to balance needs and costs. People may choose to lower the quantities of trace organic compounds they ingest with their water, but they're going to have to pay to do so. And that means they'll have to consider how the risk represented by these chemicals stacks up against others.

"What's more risky, bridges falling or the water you drink?" asks Linton. "The utility folks are out there prioritizing what to spend money on. They may need to focus resources on putting a new pipe in rather than on removing a minuscule level of contaminants. There's a cost associated with all these things."

If consumers do decide they want to lower their exposure to trace organics, though, then water-reuse projects of the sort San Diegans have rejected, for now, may be a good way to go. Such projects are expensive, but they have the virtue of providing dual benefits: concentrations of contaminants that will probably be as low as feasible, and a reliable flow.

Still, there are going to be cases where no amount of investment and public outreach will suffice to assuage public concerns, where the arguments about what's healthy and appropriate touch on realms even more abstract than parts per trillion, and less quantifiable than the yuck factor. One of the flashpoints in proposed reuse projects, for example, is the San Francisco Peaks, a small mountain range in northern Arizona. The owners of the Arizona Snowbowl want to make artificial snow using treated municipal wastewater purchased from the city of Flagstaff. The Snowbowl's skiing seasons have been abbreviated in recent dry winters, and artificial snow would instill an element of predictability in what has been a highly unpredictable business.

But the idea provoked outrage from environmentalists and from members of Southwestern tribes, many of which consider the San Francisco Peaks sacred. The Hopi, for example, see the Peaks as the home of the Kachinas, deities who bring water; to traditional Hopis, making artificial precipitation there is profoundly sacrilegious.

It is offensive to many Navajos, too. Klee Benally, the son of a traditional healer, has become a leading activist in the Flagstaff-based Save the Peaks Coalition. Benally argues that the source of the water—its history, in other words—renders it incompatible with traditional spiritual uses of the San Francisco Peaks, from the gathering of medicinal plants to a holistic view of the entire mountain range as a sacred site.

"We have standards that the EPA could never match," he says. "To have the water coming from hospitals, from morgues, from industry— no matter the process of reclamation, it could never be clean enough to meet those standards from the Navajo perspective. Wastewater would contaminate the entire ecosystem, the entire spiritual purity of the mountain. It's like getting a shot of something: The needle affects only a tiny, tiny area, but the medicine affects your whole system. We couldn't restore it back to its natural state after that contamination occurred."

The Forest Service, which leases use of the ski area to the Snowbowl, approved the artificial-snow proposal; a coalition of tribes and environmental groups sued and lost in U.S. District Court. But in March, a three-judge panel of the Ninth Circuit Court of Appeals agreed with the coalition and denied the snowmaking request, writing that the Forest Service had inadequately assessed how the use of reclaimed wastewater might affect both tribal religious practice and the health of skiers exposed to artificial snow. The U.S. Department of Justice, on behalf of the Forest Service, and the owners of the Snowbowl have asked the Court of Appeals to reconsider that ruling.

There may not be many places where the potential use of reclaimed water arouses quite as much passion as on the San Francisco Peaks. But the yuck factor will surely continue to be an issue water managers have to contend with. It seems to have deep roots in human history and perception, after all, and perhaps will be overcome on a wide scale only when it collides head-on with another deep-rooted but not always accurate western perception—namely, that the water will always be there.

Already, as the West's drought continues, California is looking for new means of conserving water. This summer, the San Diego County Water Authority, citing concerns about the reliability of future deliveries from the State Water Project, began a campaign that urges each of its customers to use twenty fewer gallons of water a day.

The campaign is voluntary, but it may help drive home the message that external water supplies aren't assured, and that recycling may be a reliable way of ensuring that at least some water remains available. After all, people do keep showering, and flushing, and drinking their coffee, no matter how little runoff the Rockies or Sierra Nevada produce in a given year.

"Now that we're going into a dry-year cycle, we're seeing the acceptance of water recycling go up," says the water authority's Maria Mariscal. "Nothing gets the public's attention like a drought."

September 17, 2007

Peter Friederici writes, gardens, and collects rainwater in Flagstaff, Arizona.

Toxic Terrain

❧

Colorado Community Battles a Toxic Shipment

Gail Binkly

Last winter, when Deyon Boughton read in her local newspaper that four hundred seventy thousand tons of 'mildly contaminated soil' might be coming to rest at the uranium mill near her home, she winced. Her husband, Lynn, had been a chemist at the mill from 1958 to 1979, and died of lymphoma that doctors linked to uranium exposure. Learning that the Cotter Corp. mill, which has been in and out of production for years, was now in the business of storing radioactive waste hit Boughton hard.

She wasn't alone. The Canon City suburb of Lincoln Park, home to thirty-nine hundred residents, is just a few miles from the mill and its tailings ponds. The community, about forty miles southwest of Colorado Springs, is also close to the Arkansas River and the Royal Gorge, and enjoys a sunny desert climate that has lured hundreds of retirees, some of whom have built $500,000 homes near the mill in the last few years.

The proposal may not seem surprising, considering that the West has become the destination of choice for storing the nation's toxic waste; dumps planned for Nevada's Yucca Mountain and the Skull Valley Goshute Indian Reservation in Utah have been vehemently, and publicly, debated. But the deal in Canon City, which would have been Colorado's first major waste shipment, nearly slipped by, unnoticed not just by the locals, but by the state as well.

Soon after the Canon City *Daily Record* published the story, a group of citizens formed Colorado Citizens Against Toxic Waste (CCAT), and tried to prevent the Cotter Corp. from accepting low-level radioactive soil from a Superfund site in New Jersey. At the time, there were no laws requiring Cotter to inform residents of its plans. Most locals learned about the shipment as Boughton did in the local paper.

The coalition began to hold public meetings, demanding that local officials refuse the company's request for a new license that would allow it to take the New Jersey waste. The coalition also contacted state-level officials, and last April, Gov. Bill Owens quickly signed a bill requiring tighter controls on businesses storing radioactive waste, ultimately stalling the shipment until Cotter can meet the law's new requirements.

"If Cotter gets by with this, someone might think, 'Hey, this is a good business to get into,'" says Sharyn Cunningham, co-chair of CCAT. "The people of Colorado haven't fully realized the danger."

For longtime residents in Canon City, controversy surrounding the mill is familiar.

Beginning in 1958, the Cotter mill processed ore into uranium oxide or 'yellowcake,' the fuel of nuclear reactors. In those early production years, the mill discharged contaminated waste into unlined tailings ponds—standard practice at the time. Heavy metals and radioactive material leached into the soil and groundwater, contaminating wells, and tailings dust blew off dried ponds. In 1983, the Environmental Protection Agency designated Lincoln Park a Superfund site.

By the late eighties, uranium prices had plunged, Cotter shut down most of its operation, and new homes sprouted near the mill. "It was dormant then," explains Cunningham, who moved to Lincoln Park nine years ago. "People thought it was out of business."

Cotter has since moved the tailings to new lined ponds, paid for residents to hook up to city water, and agreed to monitor about forty wells in the area for uranium and molybdenum. But the company is not out of business. Cotter now wants to begin producing zirconium, a heavy-minerals sand used mainly in the ceramics industry, says Rich Ziegler, Cotter executive vice president. Accepting the soil shipments from Maywood Chemical Co. in New Jersey would provide needed capital.

In addition, Cotter plans to use the soil to cover "beaches" of dry tailings that release radon and must be sprayed to contain the dust, Ziegler says. But in September, the EPA came back to inspect the mill and found leaky tanks, spills, and more than three thousand drums of calcium fluoride that Cotter had been paid to dispose of nearly two years ago.

The EPA wrote to the Colorado Department of Public Health and Environment, which regulates the state's radioactive materials in an agreement with the Nuclear Regulatory Agency, that it had "serious questions" about the company's capacity to handle more radioactive waste.

Regardless of Cotter's poor record, the state health department has allowed the mill to continue to process tailings for residual uranium. The company also plans to resubmit an environmental assessment it hopes will qualify it to accept the New Jersey waste. The study is required under the new state law signed by Gov. Owens, but the health department rejected Cotter's initial assessment for "inadequacies."

"The New Jersey waste's radioactivity is very low," says David Butcher, with the health department. "You could make a case that the natural soils around the Canon City area are more radioactive than the material in Maywood."

But residents don't trust the Cotter Corp. They cite two private tests in the last decade taken after Cotter's "cleanup" that showed high levels of radioactive material in town and at the local elementary school. And they point to years of health problems: just last year, a federal judgment forced Cotter to pay more than $41 million to twenty-six landowners who said they had suffered waste-linked problems ranging from cancer to gout.

Nonetheless, the issue has divided the community, where half of the one hundred fifteen employees who work at Cotter already have been let go.

Some locals contend that those who chose to live near the mill have no right to complain. "It reminds us of people who buy land next to an airport and then whine about the noise," wrote George Turner, director of the city's Chamber of Commerce, in a *Record* guest column. The board of the Fremont Economic Development Corporation passed a resolution supporting Cotter for the economic benefits it provides, including a payroll of $3.5 million.

But Cunningham and Boughton are hopeful they can block the shipment permanently. "We can't undo what happened to Lynn," Boughton says, speaking of her husband. "But can't we stop it from happening in the future?"

November 25, 2002

Gail Binkly writes from Cortez, Colorado. This story was funded with a grant from the McCune Charitable Foundation.

Hispanic Community Takes on Polluters

Enrique Gili

Several blocks from the gilded office towers that grace the downtown skyline of San Diego, the towering superstructure of the Coronado Bridge casts a long shadow over barricaded houses. Here, Latino families live side-by-side with businesses like recycling plants, factory workshops, and auto-body shops—the kinds of businesses you'd expect to find in an industrial park. The wind often carries a metallic tang from the waterfront's processing plants and Navy shipyards.

Perched on the edge of downtown San Diego, the working-class community of Barrio Logan has about twenty-nine thousand residents, 85 percent of whom are of Mexican origin. The median household income here is less than half that of San Diego as a whole, and the community is plagued by high unemployment, a lack of social services, and overcrowded schools. Mixed-use zoning laws allow polluting industries to be located near, and even beside, homes.

Barrio Logan's mishmash of homes and industry dates back to the 1920s, when the bay-front area was marked for industrial development. By the 1930s, the neighborhood had become a largely black and Latino enclave, as restrictive real estate covenants barred people of color from owning property elsewhere in San Diego. Logan also became the dumping ground for businesses that would not be tolerated in more affluent neighborhoods.

Today, two hundred and ten industries with regulated hazardous materials are located within a three-square-mile area in Barrio Logan. Although the community takes up just .07 percent of San Diego's total land area, it's home to 7 percent of the county's toxic hot spots. Residents run the risk of exposure to a haze of diesel exhaust, carbon monoxide, benzene, hexavalent chromium (chromium 6), and lead particulates.

For Michael Martinez, a youth counselor who has lived here for twenty-six years, the impacts hit close to home: His six-and-a-half-year-old son, Robert, has been rushed to the emergency room numerous times during asthma attacks. Martinez points to homes nearby, and says, "There are ten kids his age with the same respiratory problems.

"We're the oldest, largest, and poorest barrio in Southern California," he says. "We never had clout."

That is changing, however.

Residents' efforts to clean up Barrio Logan were at first largely symbolic. They painted the ramparts of the Coronado Bridge with murals depicting the neighborhood's struggle against institutional racism. But in the mid-nineties, says Martinez, "We started picketing, marching, anything to get the city's attention."

Those efforts garnered the help of the local nonprofit Environmental Health Coalition (EHC), which discovered that the children of Barrio Logan suffer from asthma at twice the national average. Armed with reams of testimony and medical evidence, EHC lobbied state regulators to intervene. In 1999, the California Air Resources Board designated Barrio Logan as one of six sites statewide for the Children's Environmental Health Protection program.

After a year of initial surveys, investigators began focusing on the area's chrome-plating businesses, including Master Plating, a small-scale operation that plates auto bumpers and grilles, along with smaller decorative items, such as watches and pendants. When state technicians monitored air quality near two metal-plating operations from November 2001 to March 2002, they found that twenty-nine of the eighty-seven air samples taken violated state health standards for hexavalent chromium, a compound used in the chrome-plating process that causes cancer and can exacerbate asthma.

"We were shocked by the level of chromium, both inside and outside the plant," says Jerry Martin of the state Air Resources Board.

On March 7, County Supervisor Greg Cox announced that the county would pursue an injunction to shut down Master Plating for violating environmental regulations. Eight months later, faced with mounting legal costs and an uncertain future, Master Plating closed its doors.

Allan Beauloye, another local chrome plater, says that after spending eighteen months and $1.2 million to track pollution, the Air Resources Board wasn't going to leave empty-handed: "No one could have withstood the scrutiny Master Plating was subjected to."

But Martin of the Air Resources Board says the state is scrambling to regulate a chemical whose health risks scientists still don't fully understand. "Prior to 1988, there were no environmental controls [on chromium 6] at all," Martin says. "Since Barrio Logan, we're seriously reviewing and updating our emission and control standards." In Southern California alone, there are one hundred fifty such chrome-plating plants, 40 percent of which operate in close proximity to homes.

In Barrio Logan, community activists are now focusing on the area's outdated zoning regulations. At the neighborhood's once-a-month mini town hall meetings, "the level of outrage runs pretty high," says Ben Hueso, the city's project manager for the Barrio Logan Redevelopment Area.

On December 10, the City Council passed an emergency ordinance banning another chrome-plating shop from moving into the building vacated by Master Plating. Another ordinance is pending to update Barrio Logan's twenty-three-year-old Community Development Plan to prevent other polluting industries from moving in.

"The people and the businesses are entrenched. Neither side is going away," Hueso says. Barrio Logan's victory against Master Plating won't be the end of the community's pollution problems, but it may at least open the door to a less lopsided distribution of toxic industry. Says Hueso: "Every community should bear a fair share of the burden."

February 3, 2003

Enrique Gili writes from San Diego, California.

Cold War Toxin Seeps into Western Water

Lin Alder

Thirty miles south of the glittering Las Vegas Strip, the soot-covered Kerr-McGee chemical plant stands quietly behind an impenetrable row of tall evergreen shrubs. The plant sits on the edge of the tamarisk-choked Las Vegas Wash, a desert waterway that drains into Lake Mead.

Built during World War Two to produce magnesium for artillery, airplanes, and ships, the drab-colored factory was converted in 1952 to produce ammonium perchlorate, a component of rocket fuel. Kerr-McGee, an energy and chemical manufacturer based in Oklahoma City, hasn't made perchlorate at the plant since 1998, but downstream water users are now grappling with the fallout from the plant's production years. In 1997, water officials discovered that the factory was releasing a plume of perchlorate into the wash, which then seeps into Lake Mead and the Colorado River—the drinking-water source for Las Vegas and twenty-one million people downstream in California and Arizona.

When the leak was first discovered, perchlorate concentrations were as high as sixty times what the U.S. Environmental Protection Agency now considers safe. Some researchers believe that even small doses of the pollutant can cause thyroid imbalances that lead to developmental problems in fetuses and young children.

It's a bad time to deal with tainted water: drought is stretching water supplies in the West, and Southern California is grappling with a federally imposed 15 percent reduction in its use of the Colorado River. But as officials work to clean up the problem at Kerr-McGee, perchlorate, which is also used in road flares, dry cleaning, airbag inflators, and medication for thyroid disorders, is turning up in more and more places—and may even be showing up in salads across the country.

"It is really one of the most massive pollution problems the water industry has ever seen," says Timothy Brick with the giant Metropolitan Water District of Southern California.

Although the health effects of perchlorate in drinking water are still largely unknown, there's plenty of cause for concern. Ammonium perchlorate is used to treat people whose bodies produce too much thyroid hormone. But Renee Sharp, an analyst with the Washington, D.C.-based scientific-research organization Environmental Working Group, says that fetuses and young children who receive trace exposures of perchlorate are susceptible to disrupted brain development and decreased IQ. "More significant exposures can lead to mental retardation, deafism, and mutism," she says.

The EPA acknowledges perchlorate is a potential health problem, but says "uncertainties in the toxicological database" stand in the way of knowing how great a threat it actually poses. The agency currently has a nonenforceable "provisional reference dose" of four to eighteen parts per billion (ppb). A single part per billion is roughly equivalent to one drop of water in an Olympic-size swimming pool. But according to Kevin Mayer, the EPA's regional perchlorate coordinator, the current definition is not "clear-cut." The agency has twice delayed a comprehensive study and has now asked the National Academy of Sciences to step in as an external review committee.

Perchlorate concentrations in Lake Mead are currently eight to fifteen ppb. In the Colorado River below Hoover Dam, they range from five to fifteen ppb.

Mark Beuhler, Metropolitan's associate vice president, says that his agency is protecting its customers by blending Colorado River water with perchlorate-free water from Northern California. This dilutes the pollutant to below four ppb, the "action level" set by the California Department of Health Services.

Gina Solomon, a Natural Resources Defense Council health expert, argues that the EPA's target should be lower. "The more we know about perchlorate, the more concerned we get," says Solomon. "The science suggests that very low doses can affect the thyroid, which then interferes with brain development."

The problem isn't limited to the Colorado River: perchlorate is popping up in hundreds of groundwater wells throughout the West. In 2000, New Mexico officials detected traces of the chemical in wells near the U.S. Department of Energy's Los Alamos National Laboratory.

John Kemmerer, the deputy director of the EPA's Superfund program in San Francisco, says that perchlorate has contaminated almost two hundred drinking-water supplies throughout California. His office is overseeing a $111 million effort to clean up a contaminated aquifer beneath the Aerojet Superfund Site near Sacramento, an effort that may take two hundred and forty years. Perchlorate contamination below California's San Gabriel Valley has spurred one of the largest groundwater cleanup projects ever proposed under the Superfund program, projected to cost $320 million.

But the perchlorate threat may reach far beyond drinking water, turning up in vegetables irrigated with Colorado River water.

"Between November and March, as much as 90 percent of the nation's lettuce is grown in California's Imperial Valley," says the Environmental Working Group's Sharp. "Perchlorate contamination could potentially become a widespread health problem throughout the nation."

Studies indicate that plants can accumulate perchlorate in their cells at much higher levels than appear in the water used to irrigate them. A 1997 study of vegetables grown with perchlorate-laced water in San Bernardino found perchlorate concentrations thousands of times higher than what the EPA considers to be safe.

In Las Vegas, Kerr-McGee is working to clean up the contamination. In 1998, the company began building a system of thirty-four extraction wells and two "ion exchange" devices to remove perchlorate from the water, and it now trucks dozens of giant bags filled with the sand-like byproduct of ion exchange to an incinerator in Utah each week.

But the cleanup hasn't been cheap: so far, Kerr-McGee has spent over $61 million. In 2000, Kerr-McGee filed a lawsuit against the Navy, which owned and oversaw the plant for nearly ten years, claiming that the military should share the expense. Now, however, the Pentagon is pushing for nationwide exemptions from cleanup liability.

April 28, 2003

Lin Alder writes from Springdale, Utah.

Former Employees Blow the Whistle on Nevada Mine

Rosemary Winters

In Nevada, a mammoth multinational mining company is polluting the air and water, and state regulators are doing little to stop it, according to former mine employees and mining watchdogs. Two whistleblowers are suing Newmont Mining Corporation—the largest gold producer in the world—for firing them after they repeatedly told their supervisors that the mine was violating state and federal environmental laws.

Sandra Ainsworth and Rebecca Sawyer, former environmental specialists at Newmont, say, in order to save money, mine managers ignored their complaints about chemical leaks into the Humboldt River, groundwater contamination, air pollution, and other problems at the Lone Tree mine near Winnemucca.

"The company wants to pay lip service to compliance with environmental regulations and permits," says Henry Egghart, the whistleblowers' attorney. "But when it comes to the bottom line, they want to do as little as they can get away with."

Newmont says Ainsworth and Sawyer were laid off in April 2002 because of "restructuring" after a corporate merger. One week after Ainsworth lost her job, Newmont also fired her husband, a geologist, for forwarding a company e-mail to her. Newmont spokesman Lou Schack says Jack Ainsworth was terminated "for violating company policy with regard to handling internal information." But Jack Ainsworth, who has joined his wife's lawsuit, charges that he was terminated because of his connection with her, and to intimidate other employees.

The Nevada Division of Environmental Protection began investigating the whistleblowers' complaints last fall, but was unable to corroborate many of the claims, because Newmont initially blocked investigators from talking to mine employees. After two months of stonewalling, the state attorney general intervened, but the division "lost the element of surprise, which is oftentimes critical in an investigation," according to its report. The state did verify a few permit violations, including the illegal release of chemicals into the Humboldt River. Deputy Administrator Leo Drozdoff says the Division of Environmental Protection is now working with Newmont to correct the water-pollution problem. In June, the agency slapped Newmont with a $5,000 fine and an order to comply with the Clean Water Act, or face additional fines of up to $27,000 a day.

But the $5,000 fine—the minimum allowed by law—"is not even a tap on the wrist," says Tom Myers, director of Great Basin Mine Watch in Reno. The nonprofit watchdog group is challenging the Lone Tree mine's water-pollution control permit in court. The state renewed the permit in November 2002, despite its ongoing investigation into the whistleblowers' complaints. Dave Gaskin, supervisor of the Bureau of Mining Regulations at the division, says, "We don't use renewal as an enforcement device."

The permit renewal authorized an expansion of the mine's tailings impoundment, which holds waste rock containing acids and heavy metals, even though the impoundment is leaking acidic material in violation of the permit. "Everything suggests that there are some serious problems at Lone Tree that the Nevada Division of Environmental Protection is not addressing adequately," says Nicole Rinke, Great Basin Mine Watch's attorney. "I think they have been taking a very laissez-faire approach to regulating."

August 18, 2003

Rosemary Winters writes from Salt Lake City, Utah.

A Chemical Cocktail Pollutes Western Water

Michelle Nijhuis

Colorado is famous for clear-running streams, but a recent study from the U.S. Geological Survey shows that even the state's most calendar-worthy creeks aren't as pure as they appear.

In January, researchers at the agency's Colorado office announced the results of a study that tested the state's streams and groundwater for dozens of chemical compounds, including caffeine, steroids, and pesticides. Researchers took samples from fifteen urban streams and one forested stream, along with nearly ninety domestic and municipal wells.

Urban streams carried the greatest number and concentration of substances: fifty-seven chemicals were detected, with concentrations of non-prescription drugs, flame retardants, and detergent breakdown products exceeding ten parts per billion. But researchers were surprised to find that samples from the forested stream also contained low levels of eleven chemicals, including disinfectants, artificial fragrances, and insect repellents.

"Most of these chemicals originate with people, so we weren't expecting so many in forested areas," says Lori Sprague, the study's lead author. She speculates that campers, recreational boaters, or nearby septic systems are responsible for the traces of pollution.

Though few of these substances are regulated by federal agencies, especially at such low levels, even infinitesimally small amounts may have a big impact on wildlife and plants—and possibly on human health. Water-quality researchers and regulators usually focus on better-known pollutants like perchlorate and arsenic, but a growing number of scientists are turning their attention to this more subtle set of aquatic contaminants.

Until the 1990s, studies of low levels of pharmaceuticals and personal-care products, or PPCPs, in streams and groundwater were almost unknown: lab equipment just wasn't sensitive enough to pick up tiny concentrations of the substances. Researchers in Europe carried out the first large-scale PPCP studies, and the U.S. Geological Survey (USGS) followed suit in the late 1990s.

The agency's first "nationwide reconnaissance," published in 2002, measured concentrations of ninety-five compounds, ranging from hormones to acetaminophen to codeine to caffeine, in 139 streams throughout the United States, most of which were downstream of cities or intensive agricultural operations. Low levels of PPCPs showed up in about 80 percent of the streams sampled.

The next step—understanding the effects of these small concentrations of PPCPs on the environment, and on human health—is a very tricky business. Environmental Protection Agency researcher Christian Daughton emphasizes that each type of compound behaves differently in nature. "Every single class has a mechanism that's unique," he says. "There are a wide array of possibilities, and aquatic toxicologists are just starting to develop a body of work."

The Department of Energy's Pacific Northwest National Laboratory in Washington state found that captive male trout exposed to low levels of synthetic estrogen (such as that used in birth-control pills) were half as fertile as trout kept in estrogen-free water. At Baylor University in Texas, Professor Bryan Brooks discovered that fish exposed to concentrations of the active ingredient in Prozac approximating those found in streams showed significant differences in levels of certain brain chemicals—chemicals known to affect basic functions such as eating and reproduction.

And in Colorado, University of Colorado physiologist David Norris and his colleagues have been studying sex ratios of white suckers in Boulder Creek and the South Platte River. Unlike the fish upstream of wastewater-treatment plants, he says, the fish downstream are overwhelmingly female. Norris has also observed high numbers of "intersex" fish, with both ovarian and testicular tissue, below treatment plants. For most fish, says Norris, "intersexes are unusual—they've been described in nature, but at very, very low frequencies. So when we find two out of ten, or three out of ten, we think it's of major concern."

Worries about the environmental effects of PPCPs are particularly acute in the Southwest, where some streams are 100 percent treated wastewater. In Tucson, USGS researcher Gail Cordy and her colleagues have been collecting baseline information on the persistence of pharmaceuticals, detergents, fire retardants, and other substances in the Santa Cruz River. "The thing with effluent-dependent streams," she says, "is that you're going to see more compound, and no dilution."

Regulation of low concentrations of PPCPs in the environment isn't likely to happen soon. But the mounting evidence of environmental impacts could eventually spur action by the Environmental Protection Agency or the federal Food and Drug Administration. For its part, the USGS plans to continue studying the presence and persistence of these substances in streams and other water sources. "We're hoping to understand what's in the environment, so that we can help toxicologists and other researchers focus their studies," says Colorado USGS researcher Sprague.

Current wastewater-treatment processes allow most, if not all, PPCPs to slip through, and even state-of-the-art systems are not believed to be entirely effective. And improvements to treatment facilities may soon become more difficult. The Bush administration's proposed 2006 budget cuts funding for the Clean Water State Revolving Fund—which provides states with loans for sewage-treatment plant improvements—by one-third, according to Democratic staff on the House Budget Committee.

Chris Rudkin, water quality coordinator for the City of Boulder, says new scientific findings, or federal rules, could drive the search for solutions. "There might be a new treatment process, or there might be a way to go back to the source," he says. "For instance, can we improve [pharmaceutical] use so that we don't have to put as much material down the drain?"

Awareness of the problem is increasing in the scientific community, but it's just starting to trickle into the wider world. "Most people figure that when they flush the toilet, the water goes into a treatment plant, and that it comes out at the other end and everything's fine," says Tucson researcher Cordy. "This is [the] breaking edge of understanding some of these compounds in the environment."

April 18, 2005

Michelle Nijhuis is contributing editor to *High Country News*.

The Great Salt Lake's Dirty Little Secret

Patrick Farrell

Early this year, scientists made a startling discovery about Utah's Great Salt Lake. The lake, it seems, isn't just salty. It's also loaded with mercury.

"We were all taken aback by the results," says David Naftz, the U.S. Geological Survey hydrologist who headed the survey. Water samples exceeded federal mercury thresholds, and methylmercury—the element's most toxic form—was found in some of the highest concentrations ever measured by the Geological Survey. The lake's brine shrimp tested above mercury thresholds, as did the eared grebes that feed on the shrimp.

Because it lacks a sport fishery, the lake had previously escaped the scrutiny that's led to fish-consumption warnings at places like Idaho's Lake Coeur d'Alene. Were it a freshwater lake, Naftz says, "You can bet that the Great Salt Lake would have been studied for mercury."

The lake's brackish nature could make it a "methylmercury factory," he says. Its deep saltwater supports bacteria that convert mercury's metallic form into methylmercury, which damages the central nervous system. That has some hunters worried about the health risks of eating ducks and geese that nosh on the mercury-laden brine shrimp.

But before it gets into the food chain, the mercury has to get into the lake. While scientists search for the mercury's source, environmental groups are already pointing their fingers at a surprising suspect in north-central Nevada. There, they say, gold mines spew thousands of pounds of mercury into the wild.

In 1997, the Environmental Protection Agency inventoried the nation's mercury sources, from coal-fired power plants all the way down to dental fillings from funeral home crematoriums. Gold mines weren't included, though, says David Jones, associate director of waste management for the EPA's southwest region: "We didn't know they had mercury emissions."

But since the mid-1990s, the mining industry has used cyanide leaching and ore roasting to strip trace amounts of gold from ore. And those methods release large amounts of mercury into the atmosphere.

In 1998, the EPA started requiring mines to report mercury emissions. That year, Nevada gold mines accounted for 8 percent to 10 percent of the nation's airborne mercury emissions, pumping an estimated twenty-one thousand pounds into the air.

In 2001, the EPA and the Nevada Division of Environmental Protection implemented a voluntary mercury-reduction program. They worked with the state's five biggest gold mines, which account for almost all of its mining mercury: Barrick's Goldstrike, Placer Dome's Cortez, Queenstake's Jerritt Canyon, and Newmont's Twin Creeks and Carlin South mines.

Rich Haddock, Barrick's vice president of environment, says, "Our position was pretty clear: we shouldn't have uncontrolled mercury sources." The mines installed air scrubbers, and used venting technology and chemical methods to further curb emissions.

The voluntary program, Jones says, has been as effective as a mandatory program, and faster to implement. Today, Nevada mines account for about 3.5 percent of the nation's total mercury.

Those reductions have not satisfied conservation and mining watchdog groups. They believe that west winds blow mercury across the region and into the Great Salt Lake's twenty-two-thousand-square-mile watershed, where it falls in rain and snow, and eventually collects in the lake, which has no outlet. Earlier this year, they readied a lawsuit to force the EPA to regulate emissions.

But scientists say there's still no easy explanation for the Great Salt Lake's contamination. Scant evidence links emissions from Nevada's mines to mercury deposits in neighboring states. The element also occurs naturally, and gold mining historically relied on large amounts of imported mercury. Further confounding research is the "global mercury pool" ever-present in the earth's atmosphere, which deposits the element indiscriminately.

Mae Gustin, an associate professor of Natural Resources and Environmental Science at the University of Nevada, Reno, says more questions about area mercury need to be answered before blaming one industry. She is beginning a yearlong analysis of atmospheric mercury depositions in Nevada, setting up two sophisticated air-sampling sites to determine just where the state's mercury goes.

To get a better picture of historic mercury deposits, Naftz, with the U.S. Geological Survey, plans to take lake-core samples in locations ranging from Elko, Nevada, to the Great Salt Lake.

Meanwhile, environmentalists have shelved their lawsuit, choosing instead to work with government agencies and mine operators to expand and bolster the voluntary program.

And gold mines seem willing to cooperate: "The net can be thrown wider," says Nevada Mining Association President Russ Fields.

Tentative plans for the voluntary program, which should be hammered out by this fall, include looking at how other industries, such as coal-fired power plants, have reduced emissions, getting more mines on board and, perhaps most critical, conducting more research on mercury pathways.

No matter what happens, it may already be too late for the lake, says Naftz: "If [the mines] are a few hundred miles upwind of the Great Salt Lake and the Great Salt Lake is a major accumulator [of mercury], some of the damage is already done."

August 8, 2005

Patrick Farrell recently graduated from the University of California Berkeley's Graduate School of Journalism.

Smoke Alarm

Kat Leitzell

As October wildfires blazed over much of Southern California, few people realized that a toxic metal was crackling out of the burning grass and trees, billowing up into the sky to travel the world on stratospheric air currents.

Forest fires in the United States may release about as much mercury into the atmosphere as coal-burning power plants—around forty-four tons a year, with roughly eighteen of those in the Western states—say scientists at the National Center for Atmospheric Research in Boulder, Colorado. Their just-published research is now pushing regulatory agencies to include fire-emitted mercury in their annual mercury inventories—numbers that the researchers say have been substantially underestimated for years.

When NCAR scientists Hans Friedli and Christine Wiedinmyer began looking into mercury emitted from wildfires several years ago, they were surprised at how much of the volatile metal—which can cause brain damage and severe birth defects when it reaches humans through the aquatic food chain—was going up in smoke. Their current study, published October 17 on the Environmental Science & Technology Web site, was the first attempt to estimate the emissions on a national basis. "We knew that mercury was being released by fires," says Wiedinmyer. "The big question was how much, and where, and when." Although the mercury levels in wildfire smoke are not high enough to directly harm people, says Wiedinmyer, the increased mercury in the air raises the likelihood that it will end up in waterways, where it can be converted to methyl mercury, the toxic form that accumulates in fish and other aquatic animals.

Wiedinmyer emphasizes the fact that forest fires don't create mercury. Rather, they release the mercury that was already there, previously spewed into the atmosphere by both humans and the earth. The heat of wildfires converts carbon-bound mercury in both plants and soil into its gaseous elemental form. Carl Lamborg, a mercury expert at the Woods Hole Oceanographic Institute, estimates that two-thirds of mercury in surface soils is deposited by human activities such as fossil-fuel burning, power plants, and factories, while the other third comes from natural sources including volcanic explosions and ocean vents. As particulate mercury lands in the forests, it is taken up by plants and tied up in the soil, essentially locking it away in a relatively harmless form.

"Forests, particularly those with thick organic soils, do a really good job of storing the mercury we've been pumping out into the environment," says Merritt Turetsky, an ecologist at Michigan State University.

But as climate change and years of fire suppression lead to more frequent and intense fires, Turetsky and others are concerned that more mercury will be released, particularly from boreal forests that store large amounts of the metal in their thick soils. In the NCAR study, Friedli and Wiedinmyer found that wildfires in Alaska released an average of twelve tons of mercury a year, more than a third as much as wildfires in the lower forty-eight states combined. Over the years, Turetsky says, northerly air currents have blanketed the Arctic with the chemical byproducts of industry, and deep, ancient soils such as peat and permafrost store more than their fair share of the metal. Until recently, Alaskan forests rarely went up in flames. "There's a lot there to burn," says Turetsky. "[If fires keep increasing], wildfire in Northern ecosystems could contribute a lot of mercury into the atmosphere."

And the toxic element will not necessarily stay in one place. "It's an extremely moveable metal," explains Friedli. "If a fire is intense, it may go all the way up into the stratosphere, and once it's up there, it may go all the way around the globe."

The link between wildfires and mercury is adding to the perception of mercury pollution as a global rather than local issue. In 2005, the Environmental Protection Agency implemented the Clean Air Mercury Rule, which was the first federal attempt to regulate interstate mercury emissions, but the agency is only now revising its protocol to include mercury from wildfires. Meanwhile, Friedli is working with the United Nations' Mercury Programme to add the wildfire data to its 2009 assessment. Because including mercury from fires will increase the EPA's annual mercury-emissions estimate by about 30 percent, reducing those emissions to acceptable levels might mean requiring even sharper cuts for industry.

The flow of mercury through the air, water and land is a vicious cycle, Friedli says. "It doesn't go away. The only way mercury gets out of the biogeochemical cycle is when it sediments at the bottom of the ocean—and that's rare." As long as forests harbor the metal, fires will continue to release it, and there's not much that anyone can do about it, says Turetsky: "The only way to reduce emissions is to reduce industrial emissions."

November 9, 2007

Katherine Lietzell is a science writer in Louisville, Colorado.

Toxic Legacy

Stephanie Hiller

Just south of Albuquerque on Kirtland Air Force Base lie thirty years' worth of canisters, boxes, and even plastic bags, summarily dumped into unlined trenches by Sandia National Laboratories during nuclear weapons research.

This mixed waste landfill, loaded with one hundred thousand cubic feet of "low-level" radioactive and hazardous waste, was once out in the middle of nowhere, but now the city of Albuquerque is growing rapidly in its direction. A new ninety-thousand-resident development, Mesa del Sol, is going in west of the Air Force base.

Even as the city creeps toward the dump, some of the toxic substances in the dump may be creeping toward the Albuquerque Aquifer, currently the city's sole source of drinking water. Sandia and the state regulatory agency have struggled to figure out a safe and legal way to keep that from happening.

The area's burgeoning growth has depleted the aquifer, sinking it one hundred eighty feet. By next year a new water project, the San Juan-Chama diversion, should supply 90 percent of Albuquerque's water, but the aquifer will continue to be an important source for the growing city.

The toxic wastes in the landfill, closed in 1988, include tritium, plutonium, and other transuranics, volatile solvents, and some two hundred seventy thousand gallons of nuclear reactor water. Tritium (radioactive hydrogen) has been detected less than one hundred feet below the landfill; it's the most mobile form of waste, and Sandia officials believe the other contaminants have not gone as deep.

Removing the containers of waste, many of which are broken and leaking, would cost about three-quarters of a billion dollars and endanger workers, according to the lab. And no approved "disposal pathway" exists for some of the waste. Sandia has proposed simply covering the

195

dump with three feet of soil, seeded with shallow-rooted plants to take up rainfall and prevent leaching. But critics say that won't be enough to keep contaminants from reaching the groundwater, four hundred sixty feet below.

"The landfill will be a whole lot safer with the cover than it is now," says David Miller, the Sandia engineer who manages the landfill. "But because of litigation from one citizens' group, we've had to put these plans on hold."

For the past decade, Citizen Action has demanded the excavation and removal of the wastes, and in 2005, it sued the New Mexico Environment Department and the U.S. Department of Energy over their approval of the soil cover. In turn, the environment department recently sued Citizen Action, trying to avoid making public a report on the risk of leaks at the dump.

On such legacy waste sites, soil covers are inadequate, according to a 2003 report from the National Academy of Sciences: "[T]he hazards will persist for centuries ... millennia ... or essentially forever." Another NAS report, from 2000, notes that at such sites, subsurface contaminants often travel farther than expected and future risks cannot be accurately predicted.

Even if the soil cover does its job, no one will be able to tell, according to geologist Robert H. Gilkeson, because the wells installed to monitor contamination don't work correctly. Gilkeson was lead consultant for a monitoring project at Los Alamos, but resigned when the state rejected his design in favor of a less expensive, quicker approach. Describing himself as a whistleblower, he now works independently—and for free—evaluating how the two New Mexico labs are affecting groundwater.

"The installation of the wells started in the late 1980s with a belief—a belief—that the flow of water was to the north," Gilkeson says. By 1990, however, data clearly showed that the groundwater was moving southwest instead. Despite this, the wells were not moved.

Gilkeson notes that the aquifer has two layers: a slow-moving sandy layer at the water table, and the actual drinking-water source beneath.

To accurately track wastes, both layers must be sampled. Only one monitoring well reaches the drinking-water layer, but its screens cross both layers, mixing the waters.

Some of the stainless-steel well screens are also corroded and clogged. Sandia engineers say that corrosion is responsible for the chromium and nickel that have been found in water samples at higher levels than drinking-water standards allow. Gilkeson suspects that these levels are too high to be accounted for by corroded screens alone. Bentonite clay from the drilling process clogs many screens, "hiding the contaminants [the wells] are intended to detect, especially radionuclides," he says. The same drilling process was used in Los Alamos, and those wells failed to detect groundwater contamination. Now, plutonium is showing up in Santa Fe's drinking water.

The final montoring plan now being reviewed by New Mexico's environmental department corrects some of these problems, but not all. Three new wells will be dug through the landfill cover, with plastic screens instead of stainless steel. They'll be located on the west side of the dump, closer to the potential contaminants. But there are still no wells on the landfill's south side, and none directly over the "hot spots" where tritium was dumped and where tetracholoroethane (PCE), a probable carcinogen, has been found.

"The landfill is being monitored by very competent staff at present," says Jerry Peace, a Sandia geophysical engineer, "and will continue to be monitored in the future." Sandia officials say the soils appear to slow the transport of wastes, and given the short half-life (12.5 years) of tritium, it may not reach groundwater until it has become relatively harmless.

For the city's half-million residents, though, the implications are unsettling. Sandia and the Department of Energy appear to be taking a calculated risk, banking on the probability that contaminants will not reach groundwater. But in water-sparse New Mexico, Albuquerque's aquifer may well be priceless, and any risk too great.

December 10, 2007

Stephanie Hiller is a freelance writer who researches nuclear issues in Albuquerque.

Urban Pressures

Dust Settles in Owens Valley

Jane Braxton Little

Owens Lake lies barren and dry between the Sierra Nevada and the Inyo Mountains. For nearly a century, the winds sweeping down from twelve-thousand-foot peaks have stirred up the parched lakebed, sending clouds of caustic dust across the eastern California valley from Bishop to Ridgecrest. A single windstorm can kick up an eleven-ton swirl of particles laden with arsenic, cadmium, and other toxins. The people who breathe that air regularly have suffered from asthma, bronchitis, and other, often deadly, respiratory problems.

"When it's blowing real bad, you have to go inside. That dust collects on your hair, your clothes, everything," says Sam Wasson, a retiree who has lived in Owens Valley most of his life. He's now the unofficial mayor of Keeler, a town of one hundred residents on the eastern edge of the dry lake. "It's enough to make your eyes and nose sting until you get out of it."

This year, however, a promise of change is in the particle-filled air. Under an agreement between Los Angeles and Owens Valley officials, the lake will get some of its water back—enough to dampen its salty crust and decrease the dust. The agreement is too little, too late for many of the forty thousand people who have been breathing the arsenic-tainted dust, but it is a start, says Wasson. He's unabashedly optimistic about the future.

"This town will grow once the dust settles. It's going to be the garden spot of Owens Valley," he says.

The Owens Lake agreement represents an uneasy truce in one of the West's most notorious water wars. Owens Valley was a prosperous

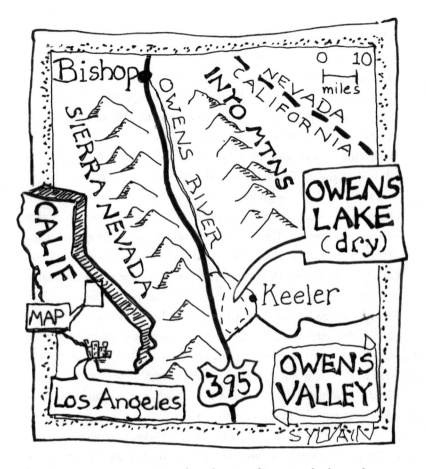

farming community in 1905, when the city of Los Angeles began buying up water options. Over the years, the city bought out hundreds of farmers and businessmen to obtain complete control of the valley's river system.

Instead of flowing through grassy meadows into Owens Lake, the water traveled 233 miles to Los Angeles in a concrete ditch.

Local residents fought the diversions through litigation and sabotage, including a 1924 "picnic" at the Alabama Gates that used dynamite to spill hundreds of thousands of gallons of water onto the desert floor. Owens Lake became a national symbol for the environmental devastation visited on rural communities by urban absentee landlords.

Now, Los Angeles officials have been forced to take some responsibility for the consequences of the city's thirst. The dustbowl of Owens Lake is by far the single largest source of particle air pollution in the United States, federal officials say, and it's a hotspot for PM10, the tiny particles that penetrate deep into the lungs. The federal Environmental Protection Agency ordered a plan for reducing the emissions in 1994, but the fight between Los Angeles and Owens Valley continued. The Great Basin Air Pollution District, charged with enforcing the federal Clean Air Act, wanted the city to restore thirty-five square miles of the lake by 2001. The city balked, threatening to sue over violation of its water rights.

But in the 1990s, a growing environmental consciousness brought changes in philosophy and management to the Los Angeles Department of Water and Power. S. David Freeman, who became the general manager of the department in 1997, shifted the focus from the city's out-of-pocket costs to the health risks for Owens Valley residents. Instead of continuing to refuse to give up any of the city's water supply to abate the dust, Freeman decided to negotiate with the Great Basin district.

The 1998 agreement, incorporated into Great Basin's implementation plan adopted last summer by the Environmental Protection Agency, establishes a schedule for meeting air-quality standards that avoids decades of litigation, says Richard F. Harasick, a Department of Water and Power engineer in charge of the Owens Valley project.

"We're over the kicking and screaming. We want to be good stewards of the environment that's been given to us. It's a change in our way of thinking," he says.

The $100 million plan calls for flooding sections of the lake. By the end of next year, saturated surfaces and shallow pools of water will cover thirteen square miles of the lake. By 2003, sixteen square miles of the dry lake will be treated for dust emissions, mostly by flooding. After that, the department will treat two square miles of lakebed a year for three years until it meets federal air quality standards, Harasick says.

What's remarkable about the recent dust-abatement agreement is that some of the water used will come directly out of the Los Angeles Aqueduct that transports Owens River water to the city. At $350 an acre-foot for up to forty thousand acre-feet annually, that's a big bite out of Water Department revenues, says Harasick.

"This is all about quality—air quality, environmental quality, the quality of life," he says. "The trick is to do it as affordably as possible, using as little water as we can."

Prodding the city in its self-proclaimed conversion are a litany of legal actions threatened or filed by the Lone Pine Shoshone-Paiute Tribe. Los Angeles missed deadline after federal deadline while members of the tribe continued to breathe in the dust and get sick, says Dorothy Alther, a Bishop-based attorney with California Indian Legal Services.

"It was clear that L.A. was going to do nothing unless someone complained," Alther says. "We became the gorilla in the closet, continually threatening to sue everyone."

The tribe will be monitoring the flooding project for progress and compliance with federal law. There are many more battles to be fought, says Alther.

For now, however, the federal order and the agreement it produced between Los Angeles and Owens Valley is "the best thing possible," she says. "The day the first drop comes out of the aqueduct to fix the problem, I'll be out there with champagne glasses."

April 24, 2000

Freelance journalist *Jane Braxton Little* writes about natural resource issues from a century-old building in Feather River country of California's northern Sierra Nevada.

A Dusty Lake Is Plumbed Halfway Back to Life

Matt Jenkins

The dry bed of Owens Lake has a primal, wind-wracked sort of gestalt. With the Sierra crest towering almost eleven thousand feet to the west and the blazing eye of the sun high overhead, it's easy to believe you're standing on the salt-rimmed edge of the sky.

Owens Lake hasn't actually been a lake for three-quarters of a century, its waters diverted south and the dry playa baked to an alkaline crisp. Four miles from here, the Los Angeles Aqueduct sparkles under the desert sun, funneling Owens Valley's water two hundred thirty miles across the desert and straight down L.A.'s thirsty maw.

Today, though, I'm sinking up to my boot tops in the long-dormant gumbo that underlies the lake bed. In front of me, a row of bright green "bubblers" drizzles water onto the playa. Five thousand three hundred of them, arrayed thirty feet apart across the northern half of the lake, are slowly filling the curving furrows disked into the lake bed.

Nineteenth-century descriptions of Owens Lake frequently note its beauty and abundance of wildlife. The lake was a migratory stop for ducks and geese, eared grebes, American avocets, and sandpipers moving between South America and the Arctic on the Pacific flyway. Local birder Mike Prather says that when ornithologist Joseph Grinnell visited the area in 1913, "He described wakes of birds as far as you could see across the lake."

That same year, L.A. water superintendent Bill Mulholland spiked the vein of the Owens River, which fed the lake, and diverted the water out of the valley to L.A. It took more than a decade for the lake to dry up, but when that finally happened the results were grim. Over the course of almost a million years, cadmium, arsenic, and other heavy metals had concentrated in the lake; now the lake bed lay exposed to the winds that howl through the valley. Those winds can blow up to seventy tons of dust per second into the air, creating a gritty airborne mixture that, with prolonged exposure, can cause lung damage, respiratory disease, and even premature death. Forty thousand people in the old mining and railroad towns along the lake, and in towns south into the Mojave Desert, found themselves breathing in the biggest source of particulate air pollution in the country.

Prather, who teaches in nearby Lone Pine, says that when the wind blows, "we don't let our kids out for recess anymore."

The air is crystal clear two days after Christmas, when I ride out to the lake bed with Terry Williams, a Los Angeles Water & Power supervisor, and Chris Plakos, a department spokesman.

"We don't deny what happened in the past," says Williams. "But it's different now."

The change of heart, and the solution to the dust problem, have been a long time coming—and are propelled in part by arm-twisting from the Environmental Protection Agency. But last November, Water & Power breached the L.A. Aqueduct and turned water out to Owens Lake so it could do something it hasn't done in almost ninety years—flow into the desert.

"You could almost water-ski on that," says Plakos as we roll past a flooded area off the edge of the road.

But the newly watered Owens Lake isn't meant for water-skiing; in fact, it isn't even meant to be a lake. The company that built the system has four more days to get it up and running, and crews are working fast to make final adjustments. When the system is functioning as intended, the lake bed will become an eighty-six hundred-acre mud flat.

So far, the city has committed up to forty thousand acre-feet of water a year—a bit more than 10 percent of the aqueduct's average annual flow. "But we'll see what's really needed as it goes," Plakos says.

"The idea," he adds, "is to saturate the ground, not create a lake."

More crudely put, the idea is to just barely get the job done—and Water & Power is making a Herculean effort to do that.

The agency's expertise at squeezing the valley dry may be locally reviled, but that skill comes in handy here, where getting as much as possible from every drop of waylaid water is a pragmatic imperative.

Water & Power will monitor weather conditions on the lake and adjust water flows to precisely match evaporation rates. Engineers have divided the lake bed into sections, and water that drains to the downhill edge of each section is captured and pumped back into the system for reuse. Under a separate program, the agency is rewatering the lower stretch of Owens River. "If the lake bed doesn't need [that] water," says Williams, "We can pick it up, pump it into the ditch, and send it on south."

The system is immense: two massive turnout structures on the aqueduct, a pump-back station at the lake, three hundred miles of pipe and another twenty-three million feet of drip tube, fifty-three hundred bubblers, twenty-five hundred acres of planted salt grass, and a system of sensors and fiber-optic cables to monitor water flow rates, solar radiation, and weather data. It will probably end up costing a quarter of a billion dollars.

Texas historian Walter Prescott Webb described the West as "a semidesert with a desert heart." It's not too hard to see the dust-control project as an artificial heart, a massive life-support system. Not, ironically, for the lake, but for the forty thousand people it affects.

For all its controversy, the construction of the L.A. Aqueduct and the tapping of Owens Valley stand alongside feats like the construction of Hoover Dam as proof of human ingenuity's power over nature. But this latest chapter in the history of Owens Valley may be one in a line of exhibits with another theme. It's part of the second, secret history of the West, the one where we re-engineered the world to our specifications and then had to go running back to stanch the fallout. Not before it killed salmon or desert tortoises, but before it killed us. The half-revived Owens Lake might just be the face of the next wave of habitat restoration, restoration for our sake, where the best we'll be able to do is split the difference with the birds.

Mike Prather, the birdwatcher, had pressed Water & Power for something more, but as Richard Harasick, the department's assistant director of water resources, told the L.A. *Times*, "We're not there to operate a bird sanctuary." The birds, said Harasick, "will be a happy byproduct."

In other words, L.A.'s need for water still trumps the habitat needs of wildlife.

Prather concedes that point. "We can't fill the lake up, realistically and politically, in this era," he admits. But he has a hunch that the birds might still find a place in this halfway-resuscitated ecosystem.

A small test run of the dust-control system in 1999 hinted at the possibilities. After a few months, says Prather, algae began growing on the re-wetted playa. Then brine flies colonized the algae, and birds arrived to feed on the brine flies.

"There's a good chance that the dust-control area could begin growing algae as things start warming up this spring," says Prather.

Then, he says, the birds will come again.

March 18, 2002

Matt Jenkins is a *High Country News* contributing editor.

L.A. Bets on the Farm

Matt Jenkins

On the south edge of the Union Station plaza, in the heart of Los Angeles, a twelve-story office tower stands swarmed by the constant stream of police helicopters that troop in and out of the L.A.P.D. air base a couple of blocks away. This is the headquarters of the Metropolitan Water District of Southern California, the most powerful water agency in the West.

On the first floor, in an expansive boardroom that evokes the ambience of the U.N. Security Council chambers, a ring of leather chairs waits for Metropolitan's directors, representatives of the twenty-seven agencies in the Los Angeles and San Diego area that buy water from Met. Eighteen million people—half of California's population and one of every sixteen people in the United States—get their water from Metropolitan. That water powers a $927 billion regional economy that accounts for 35 percent of the gross domestic product of the entire western U.S. If its service area were a separate nation, Met would fuel the eleventh-biggest economy on the planet.

Metropolitan is the apparatus that has enabled Southern California to grow beyond the limits of its local water supply, and the agency's name has become synonymous with limitless power. Metropolitan pumps its water hundreds of miles, from the Colorado River to the east, and the Sacramento and San Joaquin River Delta, located far to the north. The agency has always been determined to control its future: in more ambitious times, Met's stealthy hand seemed to guide grand plans to pump water from even farther north, in the Pacific Northwest and Canada, to its dry corner of the West.

Yet Metropolitan now faces a gathering crisis, and beyond a tightly guarded front desk and a bank of elevators, the view from general manager Jeff Kightlinger's top-floor office is terrifying. This has been the driest year on record in Southern California. The Colorado River

208

has been gripped by drought for eight years running. Snowpack in the Sierra Nevada, which feeds the Sacramento-San Joaquin Delta, was just 29 percent of average this year. And, in an effort to preserve the Delta's disintegrating ecosystem, a new federal court ruling dramatically cut pumping levels there. Next year, Metropolitan will have to ration water to its member agencies, raising the specter of a watery version of the California electricity crisis.

"It's amazing how fast things have moved. It's like being run over by a freight train," says Kightlinger. "We're being outstripped by the events and we can't keep up with them."

That crisis is, in broader form, one that the entire West will soon confront. Bedeviled by climate variability and change, water managers are struggling to provide a rapidly growing population with reliable sources of water. Surprisingly, Metropolitan may, in its moment of crisis, offer promising lessons for the rest of the region. Two decades ago, the agency embarked on a quiet endeavor to break out of the hidebound traditions of western water, partnering with farmers spread throughout the length and breadth of the state and experimenting with increasingly sophisticated ways of managing risk. That effort—despite some mistakes along the way—is now helping Metropolitan counterbalance the rising uncertainties it faces.

Two hundred miles east of Los Angeles, in the Colorado River town of Blythe, Ed Smith runs the Palo Verde Irrigation District. He works out of a low-slung office whose interior is painted avocado green and has the grim sixties feel of a Civil Defense shelter. The creepy ambience is further heightened by a high-definition aerial image of the irrigation district—taken by a Soviet spy satellite in the waning years of the Cold War—that's tacked to the wall of the building's bunker-like boardroom.

"The scary thing," Smith says, "is that you can see—this supposedly came from Russian stuff, OK?—and look: you can see friggin' cars and trucks on the freeway."

Looking at the satellite photo, it is hard not to get the sense of the irrigation district in the crosshairs of an evil empire—even more so because several such images made their way into Smith's hands via

Metropolitan, which has used the now widely available photos to assess the irrigation district's potential water yield.

Outside, the fields that appear in the satellite photo lie flat and lush, hemmed in by desert mountain ranges, jagged heaps of dusky slag that call to mind Luke Skywalker's home planet of Tatooine. After a five-mile trip over roads whose painted striping has warped beneath the ferocious sun, Smith stops his pickup at a dry field full of gigantic dirt clods. Earlier this year, the field was taken out of production. To keep the dust down from the fallowed field, "they wet it," Smith says, "and then go in there and disc it, it so it makes these big ol' nasty clods."

The cloddy field makes up a couple of the roughly fifteen thousand acres of ground that farmers scattered throughout the valley have fallowed to provide water to Metropolitan this year. It also represents the latest round in an ongoing and occasionally uneasy alliance between Met and farmers throughout the state.

In 1986, Metropolitan dispatched an emissary, a sometimes-pugnacious Ph.D. economist named Tim Quinn, to the Palo Verde Valley to cut a fallowing deal. The farmers' initial reaction was cold. One person close to the negotiations related that Quinn "set down with these guys like a schoolteacher, and got his little chalkboard out, and explained to them why they weren't making any money in farming, and why they should be just tickled to death to have Met come and save them and take their water."

Finally, however, after years of negotiations, the Palo Verde farmers agreed to test-drive the fallowing concept from 1992 to 1994. Farmers laid out about a fifth of their land—land they otherwise would have planted in alfalfa, cotton, and melons—in exchange for $1,240 per acre, an amount calculated to cover what they would have earned had they used the water to grow crops, plus a little extra.

For western water bosses, the standard denomination for water is an acre-foot: about 326,000 gallons, enough water for two families in the Los Angeles area for a year. Metropolitan got 185,000 acre-feet of water out of the deal—but not for long.

The agency stored the saved water in Lake Mead, upstream on the Colorado River near Las Vegas. But the winter of 1997 was so wet that it seemed likely the river would flood. To make room in Lake Mead for the coming floodwaters, the federal government emptied all $25 million worth of Metropolitan's water out the bottom end of the reservoir, from whence it flowed onward into the Gulf of California and floated away to sea.

For Met, the deal had not been an auspicious adventure, but it was hardly the end of the agency's pursuit of farm water.

In 1984, Carl Boronkay became Met's general manager, and he inherited a pledge the agency had made, thirty years earlier, to provide whatever water was necessary to supply the growing needs of Southern California. For decades, Met kept its pledge by importing water from the Colorado River and the Delta. But two years before Boronkay took charge, California voters defeated the Peripheral Canal, which would have been capable of siphoning the entire flow of the Sacramento River around the Delta and south to Los Angeles.

Boronkay set out to transform Met's thinking, and he soon hired Quinn, who had been working at the RAND Corporation, a Santa Monica-based public-policy think tank. One of the first things Quinn did was analyze the reliability of Metropolitan's water supply. He delivered his findings to the board from behind an overhead projector, the first of many times that the Nebraska native would induce a little heartburn among those he dealt with.

"I compared our reliability to other sectors like electricity and telephones and natural gas, and all those places were virtually 100 percent reliable all the time," he says. "And it turned out that we were about 50 percent reliable.

"It caught the board's attention." But more important, Quinn notes, "it really energized where Boronkay wanted to go."

Spurred by a serious drought in the late eighties, Boronkay set Metropolitan on a path toward diversifying its water-supply portfolio. No longer would the agency rely solely on massive engineering projects, such as dams, for its water. Met began giving its member agencies incentives to increase water conservation. Those agencies also began to increasingly "recycle" water by treating their wastewater for reuse. And they added a long-neglected asset back to the portfolio by working to clean Southern California's notoriously contaminated groundwater so that it could be made usable again.

But increasingly, the state's farms came to occupy a prominent place in Metropolitan's vision for the future. In one sense, the Peripheral Canal defeat marked a break between Met and agriculture. For decades, Metropolitan had joined the state's farm lobby in calling for new dams and water infrastructure. But as the prospects for more projects dimmed, Boronkay realized that agriculture represented a tremendous reservoir from which Met could potentially draw: 80 percent of the water in California goes to the state's farmers.

"I thought, just 5 percent of that agricultural water would make a hell of a difference to us," Boronkay says. "We could use just a little of the massive amount of water that's devoted to agriculture to save ourselves."

Boronkay, who is now seventy-seven, has perfected the habit of delivering radical observations with a disarming grin, but the idea of transferring farm water to the city put him on perilous ground. The notional conflict between cities and farms stands at the center of the West's rip-roaring saga of water wars—thanks largely to William Mulholland and the Los Angeles Department of Water and Power's infamous raid on the Owens Valley early in the twentieth century.

Boronkay knew in his bones that simply buying farms to take their water was a political nonstarter. But he saw promise in experimenting with fallowing programs as a way to free up water. "Farmers can pull back: they fallow land if markets aren't good," he says. "So it's nothing strange." He and Quinn set to work puzzling out whether farming communities and urban areas might be able to forge a symbiotic, rather than a parasitic, relationship.

In the late 1990s, California came under increasing fire from the six other states that share the waters of the Colorado River for taking more than its 4.4-million acre-foot allocation of the river. The river dispute made the ag card an even more important piece of Met's portfolio. Palo Verde's farmers watched as several agencies negotiated a complex set of deals to get water from the nearby Imperial Irrigation District, and they sensed that it wouldn't be long before they heard from Met once more themselves. "Met kept going to all these meetings and giving these PowerPoint presentations, and it always included a hundred thousand acre-feet from Palo Verde," says Smith. "They never bothered to tell us that, but we knew they were gonna come after it." Palo Verde was particularly attractive to Met because it had the oldest recognized rights on the entire Colorado River, which, in the first-in-time, first-in-right hierarchy of water law, also makes them the most dependable.

By that point, Palo Verde's farmers had resigned themselves to the inevitability of Met's presence in their lives. "We know there's eighteen million people over there, and twenty-seven thousand of us here. They're gonna come get some water," Smith says. "And we want to make a deal that's best for us."

In late 2000, one of the irrigation district's board members called Smith and instructed him to drive out to the Blythe airport to pick up a couple of representatives from Metropolitan. The two sides began negotiating an agreement that would take water transfers to a higher order of sophistication. As in the earlier deal, farmers in the irrigation district would generate water for Met by fallowing their lands. Unlike the previous arrangement, however, this one would stand in place for thirty-five years.

"Both sides spent a lot of time trying to look for bogeymen," Smith says. "If you're going to be in this thirty-five years, you have to think about a lot of things."

Simply taking land out of production for that length of time would have been tantamount to drying it up permanently. But by crafting a "rotating" fallowing program, in which any given field would be idled for no more than five years in a row, the new deal makes the impacts temporary and distributes them throughout the district.

The negotiations were not without their rough spots. Met, for instance, initially insisted on approving the yearly plan that each participating farmer submits to his bank for loans. "That was an absolute deal killer," Smith says. "We will guarantee that if you tell us to fallow some ground, we will fallow some ground. The rest of that ground, you have nothing to do with it. It's none of your damn business."

Finally, after nearly three years of negotiations and a set of meticulously written contractual protections, the Palo Verde Irrigation District agreed to be drawn within Met's orbit. Farmers idle between 7 to 29 percent of the land in the district each year. In exchange, they received a sign-up bonus of $3,170 per acre, plus about $630 for each acre they fallow in any given year. (In each subsequent year of the deal, that amount will increase to cover inflation.)

The fallowing program allows Metropolitan to draw a steady "base load" of at least twenty-five thousand acre-feet from the district each year. During dry years, Met can call for a maxed-out "peak load" of one hundred eleven thousand acre-feet. For the valley's farmers, the deal allows them to continue farming the majority of their acreage during normal years and compensates them for income lost from any fallowed acreage.

When Metropolitan's managers talk about the agency's diversified water-supply portfolio, they tend to emphasize the interplay between Met's water-conservation programs and its massive expansion of storage projects. Per-capita water consumption in Metropolitan's service area has been decreasing since 1990, while Met has expanded its water-storage capacity by a factor of ten over the same period. The agency can stash whatever water its efficiency efforts save during wet years.

But wet years are increasingly rare, and farm-water transfers play a critical role in the total mix; during droughts, they're the one reliable way Met can "backfill" shortfalls and make good on its pledge of 100 percent reliability. To ensure access to that water, Quinn—who was rising through Met's ranks on his way to becoming deputy general manager— began working to establish relationships with irrigation districts in other parts of the state.

"It wasn't like there was a long line of people wanting to talk to us," he concedes. "My nose got broken eighty-six times with agricultural district doors slamming shut on it, saying, 'What part of "no" don't you understand?' "

But Quinn learned. Eventually, he began touting the ways that Met could use its considerable financial resources to help farmers hedge their own risk, by providing them a supplemental source of income that was more dependable than variable crop prices.

Quinn also got better at sniffing out people like Van Tenney, who ran the Glenn-Colusa Irrigation District, more than four hundred miles north of Los Angeles. The district supplies water to rice farmers near Sutter Buttes, the eerily beautiful carcass of an extinct volcano that sits smack-dab in the center of the Sacramento Valley. In spring and fall, the sky is alive with ducks and geese winging their way in and out of several wildlife refuges in the area.

In 2001, Glenn-Colusa banded with other local irrigation districts to sell water to the Westlands Water District, an agricultural powerhouse in the San Joaquin Valley, south of the Delta. "That was a pretty major deal," says Tenney, "and I think Metropolitan was watching."

Still, in the years after Boronkay left Metropolitan in 1993, Met's top brass did little to help Quinn's cause. In the late nineties, Boronkay's successor, John "Woody" Wodraska—who, not long afterward, would go on to work for Enron's water subsidiary—delivered an incendiary speech to the area's rice farmers. "He basically came up and told the audience, 'If you guys don't cooperate with Metropolitan, we're gonna take your water,'" says Tenney. "It was the most in-your-face thing I've ever seen."

Wodraska's departure from Met, and a series of conversations with Quinn, finally convinced Tenney that the agency was, as he puts it, "going through a fairly significant attitudinal change." He agreed to talk.

Quinn, meanwhile, had been thinking about how to move beyond the simple first-order strategy of portfolio diversification as a way to manage risk. He set out to hedge two of Metropolitan's biggest risks—running short of water, and spending heavily on backup supplies that it might not need.

"The really bad years don't happen that often," Quinn says. "We had enough water most of the time." Metropolitan might only need to backfill its supplies one year in five. "I wanted to find some sort of mechanism that would solve that one-in-five-year problem," Quinn says, a way that Met could ensure itself access to backup water, but only in the worst drought years.

As a graduate student at UCLA, Quinn had been interested in stock-options trading. Electrical utilities had adapted that tool to put together portfolios that supplemented their "firm" supplies—such as power plants that they themselves owned and operated—with options to buy power from other producers on an as-needed basis. Quinn borrowed that idea and tailored it to the rusticated world of western water.

In the winter of 2002, Quinn arranged a series of meetings with farmers in Glenn-Colusa and ten other Sacramento Valley irrigation districts and began negotiating one-year options contracts for part of the farmers' water. Initially, says Tenney, "Probably half my farmers would've strung me up. [Shipping] that water south for money was just viewed as a terrible moral thing to do." But for the farmers, the options deals opened up a wider array of—what better way to put it?—options than just growing a crop with their water.

Under the terms of the contract, Met paid the irrigation districts $10 an acre-foot for the option to buy sometime before the following March. If Met called the option, it would pay an additional $90 per acre-foot to buy the water. The irrigation districts would then "float" it down the Sacramento River and into the Delta; State Water Project pumps at the Delta's southern edge would transfer the water into the California Aqueduct, which would then carry it to Southern California.

If Metropolitan didn't need the water, it wouldn't exercise the option. Farmers would pocket the option fee and then use the water on their farms. For Met, the arrangement was attractive because the agency could keep extra water on-call, but pay just a fraction of what it would have cost to buy the water outright and run the risk of not actually needing it.

It was an elegant idea—on paper. All told, Met signed options for more than 146,000 acre-feet of water. The winter was dry, and that spring, Met called the options. Almost immediately afterward, the heavens opened, and it rained like hell. "April was off the charts," says Quinn. "April and May combined were one of the biggest flows in history."

Because so much water had fallen on Northern California, the State Water Project pumps were running day and night, sucking water into the California Aqueduct. "The pumps were so busy that they didn't have any room for option water," Quinn says. And, in a sort of déjà vu, $8.3 million worth of water floated down the Sacramento River and out to sea. "We watched tens of thousands of acre-feet of water go out to the Golden Gate Bridge," says Quinn, "because we had to call it too early."

Undaunted, Quinn tried again the next year. He began negotiating another round of options contracts, with a call date on April 1. But he added a new provision. "I learned in 2003 to put your call date really late," Quinn says, so he sweetened the new round of contracts: if farmers would hold on until May before Metropolitan decided whether to exercise its options, the agency would pay an additional $20 per acre-foot premium. "We offered them more money if they kept the call going longer," Quinn says. "That's valuable to you as the buyer, because it reduces the probability of your making a mistake."

With such adjustments, Quinn slowly stacked the odds in Met's favor. At the beginning of every "water year," which starts on October 1, there is a fifty-fifty chance that Metropolitan will have enough water to meet its demands. The potential spread at the start of the year is huge: Met may need to store as much as a million acre-feet of excess water each year, or it may need to scare up a million acre-feet to cover shortfalls. It all depends on how much precipitation falls over the course of the winter. Only as summer approaches do water managers finally have a solid idea of how much water will really be available.

In early 2005, Met signed options for one hundred twenty-five thousand acre-feet of water. But by February, after a relatively wet winter, there was only about a 10 percent chance Met would need it. "And then when April hit"—in a repeat of what had happened in 2003—"the [supply] curve shifted up," Quinn says. "All of a sudden we had no [water] problem."

This time, Met let the options expire without exercising them. Although the agency lost the $1.25 million it paid for the options, that was just a fraction of the nearly $16 million it would have lost had it bought the water but not ultimately needed it.

"Some people say, 'Well, you wasted money—you paid the ten bucks [per acre-foot],' " Quinn says, shrugging. "But it's like paying health insurance: even if you don't get sick, you don't feel like you wasted the premiums you paid."

This summer, Quinn left Metropolitan for a new job just as the biggest crisis in years hit the agency. In June, the state shut down its Delta pumps for nine days to protect endangered Delta smelt, whose populations have plummeted in recent years. Then, in September, U.S. District Judge Oliver Wanger ordered the state to protect the smelt by throttling down the pumps from late December until June, when the fish spawn in the Delta. The restriction could reduce by up to a quarter the amount of water pumped out of the Delta.

Metropolitan kicked into crisis mode. The agency maintains an office on the ninth floor of The Senator Hotel, across the street from the state capitol in Sacramento, and high-level Met managers have been on rotating deployments there throughout the fall. In October, the agency joined the list of supporters for a proposed ballot initiative that would approve a multibillion-dollar project to route Sacramento River water around the Delta.

Exactly what form that project will take is, for the moment, unclear. But it could turn out to be a scaled-down version of the Peripheral Canal, which would protect Met's water supply and, the project's supporters say, be paired with a substantial program to restore the smelt's habitat. (Despite that apparent reversal of its Boronkay-era decision not to seek new infrastructure, Met did, quite prominently, decline to support a competing measure that enjoys the spirited support of the farm lobby; it would authorize both a canal and two new dams.) Even if voters approve either of the measures—something that many capital veterans say is unlikely—it will be at least fifteen years before an around-the-Delta canal is completed.

That has left Met scrambling to assess how vulnerable its water supplies will be next year. Metropolitan has significant quantities of water stashed around the state in its various storage projects. But as that water is drawn down, farm-water transfers will become critical. Deep within the agency's L.A. headquarters, its Water Surplus and Drought Management group—

known in Metspeak by the pronunciation of its acronym, WSDM, as "the Wisdom group"—has been assessing whether Met needs to begin doing drought-rationing triage and lining up options contracts.

When the state shut down its Delta pumps in May, the WSDM group began calling in Met's chits. The agency immediately asked the Palo Verde farmers to fallow the maximum amount of land allowed under their contract. "We put them on notice," says Kightlinger, Met's general manager, "and we'll be going full-bore next year."

Meanwhile, in an office just past the reception area in the ninth-floor Sacramento office, Steve Hirsch has maps pinned on every available patch of wall. Hirsch is Met's program manager for water transfers and exchanges, and he has an order from WSDM to find and buy two hundred to two hundred fifty thousand acre-feet of water next year - 9 to 11 percent of Met's annual average deliveries.

Judge Wanger's ruling is forcing Hirsch into unexplored territory. In the past, when Metropolitan negotiated dry-year options with farmers, Hirsch says, "it's always been smarter to go north of Delta," in the Sacramento Valley, where water is cheaper. But Wanger's decision considerably complicates efforts to move water from the Sacramento River through the Delta and into the pumps.

Because of the pumping limits, Hirsch will have to thread his water transfers through needle's-eye windows of opportunity that may open at the pumps from next July through September. Only if next year is extremely dry will Met have any chance of getting water transfers across the Delta, through the State Water Project pumps and into the California Aqueduct.

That has left Hirsch pursuing a two-pronged strategy. In addition to buying options north of the Delta, he is making contacts with an entirely new set of irrigation districts, south of the Delta in the San Joaquin Valley. There, it's more likely that Met can actually take delivery of whatever water it buys—but the prices are higher, too.

Met is not the only agency seeking emergency water. Several San Francisco Bay Area urban water agencies will also see their supplies cut by Judge Wanger's ruling and are scouting out their own water-transfer deals. They will likely work cooperatively to find water. But at the end of

September, the directors of the San Diego County Water Authority—a member of Met that has been increasingly insistent on lining up its own dedicated supplies—voted to seek a deal for thirty thousand acre-feet from the Butte Water District in the Sacramento Valley.

The increased competition for water could drive prices up significantly. "If the prices get too high, we have the ability to say we'll sit out a year," Hirsch says. Metropolitan has enough water in storage that it could draw that down further to make up any shortfalls. "That's what we'll do if things get too crazy," Hirsch says, although he points out that such a tactic would result in less water in storage to cover shortfalls in future years.

In addition to the logistical challenges Met faces in the coming year, it will have to overcome some substantial lingering perceptual issues. "They've done a very good job of changing their approach and seeking cooperation," says Van Tenney, who retired from the Glenn-Colusa Irrigation District last year. But, he says, to many irrigation districts, "they're still suspect, even today. A lot of people in the north wouldn't give them the time of day."

In October, Hirsch did not seem particularly overwhelmed by the complex juggling act he'll be facing this winter. Still, he allowed, "this year's tough, because we're entering into a lot of new scenarios."

As evidence continues to mount that climate change will further reduce water supplies in California and throughout much of the West, Hirsch's tough new scenarios will likely become the norm for the entire region. It may not be long before Met's quiet, two-decade-long experiment in risk management proves useful to far more than the eighteen million people whose faucets the agency will try to keep full next year.

Back in L.A., in his office on the twelfth floor of Metropolitan's headquarters, Kightlinger says that the state's farms are as important to the agency now as they were in Carl Boronkay's day. "In those critical years, we need everything we can get hold of," he says. Then he circles back to the abiding question, "How do we make it work so we can both survive?"

November 12, 2007

Matt Jenkins is a *High Country News* contributing editor.

LAS VEGAS

The Water Empress of Vegas

Michael Weissenstein

There are few facts of life in Las Vegas more constant than breakneck growth and sunshine. The dry, bright afternoon of January 22, 2000, was no exception.

Gamblers laid down their shares of that month's record-breaking $866 million casino win. Tourist-laden airplanes landed at the nation's seventh-busiest airport. Suburbanites shuttled children between birthday parties and soccer games.

And on a sun-dappled, narrow island in Lake Mead, a crane lowered Democratic Senator Harry Reid and Republican Governor Kenny Guinn, awkward in hard hats and safety harnesses, into the mouth of southern Nevada's newly opened, $80.9-million "second straw" into the Colorado River.

Watching from the edge of the crowd, Patricia Mulroy was elated. "I can't remember a day when I've been happier," the Southern Nevada Water Authority's general manager told a reporter.

Mulroy had good reason to be happy.

Western cities have never stopped growing because of lack of water, but in the early 1990s, Las Vegas began to look like an exception. The first mega-casinos had begun to rise on the Strip. Cheap homes, warm weather, and well-paying service-industry jobs were drawing three to six thousand people a month: Mexican immigrants, downsized blue-collar workers, retiring baby boomers from across the nation, and refugees from California's receding economy and high home prices.

The Las Vegas Valley's population ballooned from 741,459 people in 1990 to 1,375,765 people in 2000, an 85 percent surge roughly equivalent to every man, woman, and child in Santa Fe moving to Las Vegas each year. The boom made Las Vegas the nation's fastest-growing metropolitan area.

New homes and lawns sprawled across a valley floor touched by four inches of rain a year. Southern Nevada's annual consumption of Colorado River water spiraled toward the three hundred thousand-acre-foot ceiling imposed in the 1920s by the Law of the River, the powerful series of interstate compacts and Supreme Court decisions governing Colorado River water.

Southern Nevada's cities started guarding their shares of Nevada's annual allocation of Colorado River water. Governments and businesses made contingency plans for 1995, when the valley would hit its water limit. Headlines nationwide declared that Las Vegas, the water-guzzling Sodom on the Colorado, was about to run dry.

But the headline writers had not reckoned with Patricia Mulroy, a rising talent in the bureaucracy of Clark County, which includes the Strip and the other unincorporated parts of the valley. The German-born former court administrator was appointed general manager of the Las Vegas Valley Water District in 1989. Within ten years, the outspoken, politically savvy operator had gotten her hands on enough water to carry the metro area through the growth foreseen for the next half century.

She did it without building dams, and without importing water via large aqueducts from distant rural areas. She changed the rules so that the water would come to her, and she gambled on victory. When the second straw was completed, Mulroy still wasn't sure that Las Vegas would get enough water, but with the help of Interior Secretary Bruce Babbitt, she won her bet.

These successes have a dark side. Mulroy has delivered water to some of the region's worst water-wasters. Some say her approach is poisoning Lake Mead, which supplies water not only to Las Vegas but also to users farther downstream, including farmers in the Imperial Valley and some Southern California urbanites. But so far, these seem small considerations in Las Vegas, where the power structure is focused on a single objective: growth.

According to census maps, the Las Vegas metropolitan area stretches from central Nevada to California and into western Arizona. But its demographic heart is the Las Vegas Valley, a broad basin framed by soaring sandstone escarpments and black volcanic slopes.

The Las Vegas Valley Water District serves much of this valley. Mulroy recalls that in her first years as deputy general manager in the mid-1980s, annual increase in water consumption soared from 5 percent a year into double digits. "When we started seeing 17 and 21 percent, we were in trouble," Mulroy says of the early 1990s. "The slumberland that we had been in forever was over. The balloon popped."

A metropolis built on virtual reality had run into the central reality of life in the desert: water. "The bankers were starting to get squeamish about giving out loans," Mulroy says. "It was looking like it was going to undermine the whole economic fiber of southern Nevada."

The growing water scare led to the ouster of the Las Vegas Valley Water District's general manager in 1989. Mulroy was given the mess.

She became one of the water warlords in a lawless region. Although Las Vegas is well known, the city is only one of five municipalities within Clark County that form a nearly unbroken stretch of urban development from the Colorado River to the foothills of the Spring Mountains on the far northern end of the Las Vegas Valley. In 1989, the Las Vegas Valley Water District, the former dam workers' camp of Boulder City, gritty North Las Vegas, and the bedroom community of Henderson divided Nevada's meager allocation of water with other, smaller cities and some aging industrial sites.

"Use it or lose it" was the order of the day, and there were reports of one small city opening its fire hydrants and pouring water into the streets to use its full municipal allocation before year's end.

"It was really not fighting [each other] as much as trying to position each of our entities strategically to prepare for our continued growth," says Phil Speight, Henderson city manager.

Mulroy set about corralling North Las Vegas, Henderson, and Boulder City into union with the city of Laughlin's Big Bend Water District, the Clark County Sanitation District, and her Las Vegas Valley Water District.

Her goal was to form a regional water agency, the Southern Nevada Water Authority.

It only took her two years to accomplish the task. In 1991, the once-warring water and sewer agencies approved agreements that charged the water authority with tackling southern Nevada's water-supply and -quality problems.

"My job was always the politics, to take the analytical and translate it into political terms," she says of her bureaucratic career.

In order to persuade the municipalities to pool water, she built trust by sharing proprietary hydrological information with them. The water pool was managed by Mulroy and her loyal team of deputies, with oversight from what has turned out to be an almost entirely compliant board of elected officials from the Authority's member cities.

Phil Speight argues that Mulroy has earned members' compliance. "Whether or not she could ... put on another hat and become the regional czar was something that she had to establish with all of the entities," Speight says. "She was able to develop trust with all of the administrators as well as the political leaders of each of the entities through her work ethic. She basically picked up the gauntlet when the time was right."

North Las Vegas, Henderson, Boulder City, and Laughlin still run their own water utilities. But water conservation, interstate negotiations, infrastructure construction, groundwater management, wastewater planning, and other regional responsibilities fall to the Southern Nevada Water Authority—which is, in all but name, the same as the Las Vegas Valley Water District run by Mulroy and her deputies.

Mulroy's team then took aim at Nevada's Colorado River Commission. That body was supposed to get more water for Nevada out of the Colorado River, but it had been unsuccessful. In 1993, Mulroy and her allies persuaded Nevada's legislature to give Las Vegas-area elected officials serving on her water authority board three of the seven seats on the commission. That shifted the commission's negotiating power to the Authority, and therefore to Mulroy.

With the commission in its pocket, says Mulroy, the Authority became "a different critter than had ever been created in the West." Local water agencies are usually at war with one another. In Las Vegas, they formed a powerful united front.

In a region where politics is marked by petty intrigue and little significant decision making, Mulroy became known for tough honesty, bold moves, and a willingness to work closely with the powerful.

Rather than curry favor with the casino operators or homebuilders, Mulroy made it clear that she would use her skills to obtain what every businessman wanted—water—and distribute it without questioning southern Nevada's ethic of pedal-to-the-metal growth.

After Mulroy consolidated her power in the Southern Nevada Water Authority and took over the Colorado River Commission, her first act was to stake a claim to hundreds of thousands of acre-feet of upstate, rural groundwater. This sparked a backlash against what the "cow counties" called a water grab. Mulroy didn't help matters by pointing out that one hotel in Las Vegas employed more people than all the ranches and farms in rural Nevada.

The reaction wasn't confined to Nevada. Hundreds of organizations nationwide protested what the Authority optimistically called its "Cooperative Water Project." Mulroy was vilified by farmers, ranchers, rural officials, and environmentalists.

"I will grant you that the way we did it caused a lot of fear," Mulroy says today.

Then she opened a second front. On the heels of a report predicting that Las Vegas would run out of water in 1995, she revoked hundreds of the Las Vegas Valley Water District's commitments to serve future developments with water. She also stopped issuing new commitments. With urban developers now added to her list of enemies, it looked as if the new water empress had a death wish.

But Mulroy says she and her deputies did not stumble blindly into these moves. The rural water filings and canceled commitments were meant to remind the West that southern Nevada was rich, running out of water, and not about to go away.

"We only knew that it would create the necessary debate of, 'Where is southern Nevada's future water supply going to come from?'" she says.

It's part of how she operates. Mulroy has often proposed unpopular ideas to win support for a more sensible solution that would never be considered if not for the harsh alternative she first puts forward.

A perfect example is the thousands of acre-feet of water the Authority has purchased from agricultural areas in northern Clark County over the past two years. The legal, brute-force way to get that water to Las Vegas is to dam the tributaries and build a pipeline.

The other way—the illegal way—is to let the water flow naturally via tributaries into Lake Mead, where her Authority could withdraw additional water through existing intakes. But that way would require significant change in the Law of the River, which does not allow so-called water wheeling. If you own water, you have to put it to use at that point, rather than let it flow downstream to some more convenient point, such as Lake Mead.

She describes her presentation to the Department of Interior this way: "There are your options. You choose. I can go either way."

Over and over again, she posed those kinds of alternatives to her opponents—rural Nevada, environmentalists, the Department of Interior, and Arizona and California. Did they want her to do things the hard, destructive way, or would they help her do it the easier way?

Authority insiders are close-mouthed about the immediate prospects for water wheeling, but it seems almost certain that Mulroy and her deputies are applying the same tough tactics to the new Interior administration. Their chances of success are uncertain.

In a very short time, Mulroy has added supply and softened urban-rural acrimony through small-scale, amicable acquisitions from Nevada farmers, neighboring states, and the federal government.

"If it's wet, we go get it," is how David Donnelly, Mulroy's deputy general manager, puts it.

The water plan depends on many new water sources rather than one blockbuster project. A major part of the portfolio is "return-flow credits," which allow a Colorado River water user to use and reuse the same water until it finally evaporates or sinks into the ground. In the case of the Las Vegas Valley, it means that every acre-foot of wastewater that flows back into Lake Mead can be credited toward the amount of water that southern Nevada withdraws from the reservoir. If Las Vegas withdraws four hundred twenty thousand acre-feet of water from Lake Mead, which is exactly what it does, but dumps one hundred twenty thousand acre-feet of effluent back in, which is also what it does, it has stayed within its three hundred thousand acre-foot quota.

Every state on the Colorado River has the same right: they all divert more than their quotas, but are only "charged" for the amount that doesn't return to the Colorado River for use by a downstream state. But in Nevada, no agency was using those credits until 1992, when the Southern Nevada Water Authority signed a contract with the Bureau of Reclamation. With that agreement in place, the water commitments began flowing to developers again, and they and their bankers calmed down.

There's a rub. The return flow is more than accounting. The flow back into Lake Mead—made up of everything from the discharge from wastewater-treatment plants to lawn-sprinkler runoff from the streets— takes place at the Las Vegas Wash. At one time, this wetland covered two thousand acres, and supported an array of wildlife. Today, erosion and down-cutting caused by growing runoff has reduced the wash to two hundred acres. The fact that the wetland was created initially by the return flows hasn't stopped its destruction from being controversial.

Some environmentalists say return-flow credits discourage Las Vegas from reusing its wastewater. Mulroy, who has recently launched efforts to restore some of the Las Vegas Wash wetlands, argues that "we'd still be having the problems" without return-flow credits. "I don't have any regrets," she says. "[The wastewater] was going to be there anyway."

Once she'd gotten the return-flow credits, Mulroy turned to enlarging Nevada's base-right to Colorado River water of three hundred thousand acre-feet per year. She is quick to depict California as the West's most egregious water guzzler. But she has fought for concessions similar to those that allow California to take eight hundred thousand acre-feet per year more out of the Colorado than allowed under the decades-old Law of the River that governs the Colorado.

The key here was her relationship with former Interior Secretary Bruce Babbitt, the water master of the Colorado River and the man who, in theory, could have told California that it had to live within its legal allotment. Mulroy describes her relationship with Babbitt as cooperative and cordial, and Babbitt has praised Mulroy and her Authority. Mulroy traces the relationship to her first meetings with Babbitt, when he was an attorney representing rural Nevadans trying to stop Mulroy's raid on northern Nevada's groundwater.

Babbitt says his close-up view of Nevada's problems strengthened his commitment to loosening the restrictions that prevented flexible use of Colorado River water.

Mulroy recalls, "When Bruce Babbitt became secretary, he said, 'I will solve southern Nevada's problem with Colorado River water.' He was always a firm believer that change needed to occur along the Colorado River."

Just before leaving office this January, Babbitt signed a document that gives California, Arizona, and Nevada access to so-called surplus Colorado River water for the next fifteen years, even if they have to draw down Lake Mead to create that surplus. As a result, Las Vegas' second straw into the river, which had so elated Mulroy when it was completed in early 2000, is finally full of water.

Southern California will use its surplus water to get through each year, but Nevada will store much of its surplus in Arizona aquifers through a water-banking deal, also made possible by changes Babbitt helped bring to the Law of the River. Remaining supplies will be banked in Las Vegas Valley aquifers depleted by decades of overdraft. The banked water will be used toward the end of the next fifty years, to allow southern Nevada to continue to grow in that period.

Mulroy is also getting involved in city planning. In April 2000, she laid out a bold plan to build by 2005, the year of Las Vegas' centennial, a $171 million "Central Park" on one hundred eighty acres of land owned by the Las Vegas Valley Water District she continues to manage. That would create the largest park in this city that has only an acre of open space per one thousand people, less than a quarter the national average.

What's wrong with this picture? A great deal, according to environmentalists and a small group of local critics. They say Mulroy's successes are bolstering Las Vegas' culture of water waste.

Part of Mulroy's strategy is to demonstrate that her Authority prefers to be as light on the land and the water as possible. Mulroy and her staff have launched a unified, media-savvy effort to remake the image of Las Vegas as water wastrel, a place that sends both lives and precious water down the tubes.

The conservation effort is aimed as much at other states as local residents. If southern Nevada wants to be a player on the Colorado River, it needs to gain the respect of the other states in the basin.

In the past two years, the cities of Las Vegas and North Las Vegas and unincorporated Clark County, which contains the Strip and many of the metro area's fastest-growing neighborhoods, have passed ordinances restricting turf grass on lawns and golf courses.

To show its toughness, the Authority shelved plush, kid-friendly conservation mascot Deputy Drip last summer in favor of stark television and print ads warning Las Vegans to conserve. Its programs have produced a 17 percent conservation rate, meaning that residents are using that much less water than they would have without conservation, agency officials say. Mulroy promises a 25 percent conservation rate by 2010.

But a drive through Las Vegas neighborhoods shows something else.

A central icon of Las Vegas is the oasis, the pool of clear water in the heart of the desert. Steve Wynn, the Strip's best-known casino developer, built his Treasure Island, Mirage, and Bellagio around flamboyant public water shows. Now he plans to build four hotels, a vast lake, and a "water stadium" on the site of the shuttered Desert Inn. Other developers say their valley is "undergolfed." Subdivisions and office parks echo the water theme, with names like The Lakes and Desert Shores, and with endless decorative ponds, fountains, and swimming pools.

As a result, the metro area is a vast stopping grounds for migratory birds flying to and from their winter roosts in Mexico and California's San Joaquin Valley. Mallard ducks, Canada geese, and other waterfowl have settled by the thousands in backyard pools and the "water features" of golf courses. Bird waste has become a common complaint of pool owners, and Nevada Department of Wildlife officers spend days relocating wild birds from urban suburbs to rural wildlife refuges.

Profligate water use doesn't stop with backyards and golf courses. Streams of runoff from lawns flow nightly through city streets. The Authority has three "water cops" patrolling the metropolis of 1.4 million people, but despite rivers of wasted water in the streets, the Authority had not written a single citation as of February 2001.

Mulroy has proven she is willing to enrage the entire state to implement her policies. But in the case of "wasted" water, nothing is at stake for the valley's water supply. It will all flow into the Las Vegas Wash, the eroding wetlands that channel an estimated 153 million gallons a day of wastewater and treated urban runoff into Lake Mead. And that 153 million gallons will all be credited back to Las Vegas under the Law of the River.

Water in the streets may not bother Mulroy and her Authority, but it disturbs Larry Paulson, a retired University of Nevada, Las Vegas, biology professor who has spent much of his career studying the Las Vegas Wash. Paulson is a charming but quick-tempered former Air Force staff sergeant, and an oft-quoted Mulroy detractor who can quickly veer from trenchant criticism to conspiracy theory.

Many dismiss him in public as a gadfly but acknowledge in private that he has been on target in his observations about the wash's rapid erosion, which is destroying its ability to naturally filter Las Vegas' wastewater. Initially, the city's wastewater created the wetlands. But as the flows grew, they rapidly degraded the channel by cutting down through the crumbly southern Nevada soil.

Paulson argues that return-flow credits have encouraged Las Vegas to destroy the wash and blindly poison its own water supply. He wants to see the area clean and reuse the water rather than dump it into Lake Mead and then reuse it. On a recent Sunday evening, Paulson stood at the top of a hill overlooking the spot where Las Vegas Wash empties into Las Vegas Bay.

"See under that bridge? That's where the wash was in 1971, when I started working out here," he says, pointing to a point about forty feet higher than the wash's current bed. "Nevada's been for the past twenty, twenty-five years taking every opportunity to maximize the amount of treated sewage it puts back into Lake Mead, a mere six miles upstream from our drinking-water intakes."

There are serious signs of trouble. Las Vegas' drinking water was linked by the Centers for Disease Control and Prevention to the metropolitan area's 1994 outbreak of illnesses caused by cryptosporidium, a parasitic microorganism contained in human and animal waste. Thirty-two people died and seventy-eight were sickened in that outbreak, according to CDC figures. Recent studies have also found perchlorate, which is a rocket fuel component, mutated fish, pharmaceutical residue, and human hormones in the wash and the bay.

Authority officials say the wastewater is diluted by the time it reaches the intakes, and argue that Las Vegas' drinking water is perfectly safe. Water-quality problems, they say, are simply a matter of public misconception.

Paulson has a simple response: "Why don't you ask the people what they think?"

Residents are voting with their dollars. It is nearly impossible to find a local resident who can afford a tap-mounted filter or a bottled-water dispenser and doesn't have one. Las Vegas Mayor Oscar Goodman has publicly stated that a person would be crazy to drink his city's tap water. Patricia Mulroy has successfully used the Law of the River to fuel her city's insatiable growth, but she may one day face a rebellion in her water empire.

April 9, 2001

Michael Weissenstein is editor for The Associated Press living in London.

Squeezing Water from a Stone

Matt Jenkins

Few parts of the nation are drier than the Las Vegas Valley. Yet, like a circus performer catching bullets in his teeth, the city here flouts the terrors of the desert and has achieved its own sort of rowdy transcendence.

Las Vegas "owes nothing to its surroundings," wrote historian Hal Rothman in his 2002 paean to the city, *Neon Metropolis*.

Today, 1.7 million people—70 percent of Nevada's population—live in Las Vegas and its suburbs. Unlike more traditional western resource-extraction economies, which reach far out into the countryside for their fuel, Las Vegas tends to generate its wealth in place: the city's $60 billion-a-year economy is dominated by the service industry—casinos and tourism—and its environmental footprint is remarkably small.

In fact, as the city has grown, its economy has come to serve as a life-support system for much of the rest of the state: thanks to Las Vegas, ten of Nevada's seventeen counties are guaranteed a fixed amount of tax revenue from the state, far more than they actually generate themselves.

Las Vegas' phenomenal success has led boosters such as Rothman, a University of Nevada, Las Vegas, history professor, to tout it as a model for the New West. But the city's economy, powerful as it is, is perched atop a precarious pedestal: a tiny slice of the Colorado River's water.

That doesn't particularly concern Rothman. "No American city has ever ceased to grow because of a lack of water," he wrote in *Neon Metropolis*, "and it's unlikely that Las Vegas will be the first."

"The only genuinely determining factor in acquiring water," he argued, "is cost." And money, Rothman wrote, "is no problem in Las Vegas."

As if to prove him right, Las Vegas is now pushing forward with what will be the biggest groundwater-pumping project ever built in the United States: a $2 billion effort that will pump more than fifty-eight billion gallons of water out of the ground every year. The project will reach far beyond the glitter of Las Vegas into the valleys of eastern Nevada's Basin and Range country, ultimately extending as far north as the area around the high-desert town of Ely.

When the play of light across the Great Basin is just right, it reveals the pockets of water that seem to disappear in the glare of the midday sun: stingy seeps, shy rivulets that poke their way across the desert, great limpid pools of water bubbling into the light. Those are all mere hints of the watery treasure trove that lies beneath the entire area: an enormous aquifer that spreads across some hundred thousand square miles of eastern Nevada and western Utah.

Las Vegas has always pushed the limits harder than any other place, because it has had to—and because it can. "When you've got a city the size of Las Vegas, that's growing as fast as it is, it's hard to estimate what's going to be economically infeasible," says Mike Dettinger, a U.S. Geological Survey hydrologist who authored some of the first comprehensive studies of the aquifer. "Anything's possible if you have a big-enough city at the other end of the pipeline."

Las Vegas may, however, have reached the tipping point, beyond which its continued growth can only come at the expense of the rest of the state. The groundwater project in the Basin and Range will pry open a place of tremendous biological diversity that includes Great Basin National Park, three national wildlife refuges, at least three state and five federally listed threatened and endangered species, and a host of rural farming and ranching communities. Tapping the aquifer could unravel the tenuous hydrologic, ecological, and political equilibrium in the Great Basin, giving the lie to boosters' claims that Las Vegas is the city of the future. And, ultimately, the water project may be a prelude to an all-out war for the waters of the Colorado River.

The fight building over Nevada's groundwater might never have started, if not for a space-age nuclear-weapons program. In the late 1970s—at the same time he was hoping to create a legacy as a champion of arms control—President Jimmy Carter backed the MX missile program, a plan to shuffle two hundred intercontinental ballistic missiles between forty-six hundred shelters in the Great Basin. The shell game was essentially a bluff, meant to force the Soviets to the negotiating table or risk blowing their entire nuclear wad shooting missiles at empty bunkers.

To the rural Nevadans who were going to be on the receiving end of a project designed to draw Soviet fire, the MX program made less sense. Environmentalists, Indians, ranchers, and academics allied to mount a fight that swept the state. Steve Bradhurst, who directed the fight against the MX program for the governor's office, says, "Wherever you went, particularly in rural Nevada, you'd see stop signs … you'd see 'STOP,' and then people would paint on 'MX' underneath."

In 1981, Nevada Senator Paul Laxalt, a close friend of and the campaign chairman for Ronald Reagan, prevailed upon the newly elected president to ax the program.

Although the program never put a single missile in the desert, the search for the water it would have required significantly advanced scientists' understanding of the desert's aquifers.

In most of the eastern Great Basin, there are two aquifers, one on top of the other. For more than a century, farmers have tapped the one closest to the surface, which is made up of water caught in the sand and gravel that has filled in the valley bottoms. But below that lies the real prize: the deep carbonate aquifer, so called because the water is contained within massive bands of limestone. Several million years ago, the geologic faulting that created Nevada's Basin and Range province took what was then a fifty-mile-wide band of limestone, broke it into splinters, and smeared it out across the Great Basin. The fractures in the rock are packed with water.

As part of its investigations for the MX program, the Air Force drilled a series of wells that reached down into the carbonate aquifer. Those wells soon became fodder for the kinds of legends normally associated with deranged conquistadors seeking cities of gold in the desert. Dettinger, the USGS hydrologist, says one MX well, north of Las Vegas, "hooked into some sort of crack that went God knows where, and it produced like crazy." After that, he says, "there was a tendency to imagine that if you put a well into the carbonate, it would just make water."

Back in 1922, the seven states along the Colorado River met to negotiate the Colorado River Compact. The Compact divvied up the river's water and came to serve as the foundation for a complex set of agreements and legal rulings known among water managers, with a sort of Ten Commandments reverence, as "The Law of the River."

At the time, Nevada (which, practically speaking, meant Las Vegas) had less bargaining power than any of the six other states—California, Arizona, Utah, Colorado, Wyoming, and New Mexico. Las Vegas was just a miserable little rail stop back then, and in all the years since, the city has been bedeviled by one stark fact: it walked away from the negotiations with just three hundred thousand acre-feet of water per year, a measly 4 percent of the water in the Compact. (One acre-foot is about 326,000 gallons, or enough water for two homes in Las Vegas for a year.)

By the 1980s, when a string of record-breaking growth years began, Las Vegas was beginning to feel the pinch. In 1989, the metropolitan area, whose population was just shy of three-quarters of a million people, grew by more than sixty-one thousand—an astounding 8 percent.

The same year, Vegas hired Patricia Mulroy as the general manager of what would become the Southern Nevada Water Authority. Mulroy immediately made it a personal crusade to ensure that the city had enough water to continue growing. And on October 17, 1989, she made her first move toward the Basin and Range. Mulroy filed water-rights applications with the state for over eight hundred thousand acre-feet of groundwater—more than twice the city's Colorado River allocation, and enough to supply almost 1.7 million new homes.

Rural Nevadans reacted as if they were under Soviet attack, filing more than four thousand protests with the state engineer and assembling a legal team that included former Arizona governor Bruce Babbitt, who would go on to serve as U.S. Secretary of the Interior.

In response, Mulroy turned her attention elsewhere, and put the project on hold. Over the next decade, Vegas proved itself more adept than any other city in the West at digging change out of the couch. The Water Authority worked to increase water efficiency in Las Vegas, and began offering a dollar-a-square-foot bounty to the city's residents to rip out their lawns, an effort that has resulted in the removal of sixty-four million square feet of grass. The city has also perfected a watery sleight of hand to stretch its meager share of the Colorado as far as possible: it pumps far more than three hundred thousand acre-feet out of Lake Mead each year, but treats its wastewater and returns it to the reservoir for re-use by California and Arizona.

During the 1990s, Mulroy also began talking with the six other Colorado River states. She called for a "major rethinking" of the way the river is managed, and she courted the other states in an attempt to buy some of their water. Mulroy won the ability to "bank" some water in Arizona for drought years, but her call for changes on the river met a cool reception, particularly from Colorado, which has long styled itself as the enforcer of order on the river.

At the time, Colorado was in an enforcing kind of mood. For more than forty years, California had been using more than its share of the river. Finally, in the 1990s, Colorado successfully led the Upper Basin states—which also include Utah, Wyoming, and New Mexico—in demanding that it stop.

Las Vegas' relentless growth was proving equally worrisome. In 2001 alone, the city added more than ninety thousand residents. The Upper Basin began to talk about forcing Vegas to live within its Colorado River allocation; when Mulroy came knocking, asking for more water, the other states sent her home to deal with her own problem.

Mother Nature, meanwhile, was putting a finer point on things. A major drought had started on the river in 1999, and 2002 brought a frying-pan-to-the-head moment. That year, the Colorado River received only a quarter of its average runoff.

Mulroy says that when river managers ran computer models during the 1990s to predict the likelihood of drought, "there was zero probability that a drought of this magnitude would hit. Nobody anticipated it."

It was clear that Mulroy was running out of options. Once again, she turned her attention to the Basin and Range country, and the hundreds of thousands of acre-feet of water that the city had claimed.

The project in the Basin and Range, as currently proposed, will use 115 to 195 pumps, spanning seven valleys in eastern Nevada, to fill a 235-mile-long, six-and-a-half-foot diameter pipeline that follows U.S.

Highway 93 to Las Vegas. It won't pump a single drop of water for at least a decade, but it has already kicked off what is sure to be an epic struggle between Las Vegas and rural Nevada.

The rural counties are at a phenomenal disadvantage. The Water Authority's budget this year is $642.7 million. Meanwhile, White Pine County, home to Ely, was forced to ask the state to step in to manage its finances after it went broke earlier this summer. In addition to its economic might, Las Vegas holds 70 percent of the votes in the state Legislature. One potential champion for the rural counties—U.S. Sen. Harry Reid, the Democratic leader in the Senate—has made only a tepid commitment to their cause, and critics are quick to point out that Reid's son Rory is a county commissioner in Clark County, which includes Las Vegas, and that he also sits on the board of the Southern Nevada Water Authority.

Nonetheless, rural Nevadans are rallying around the cry that this is a repeat of Los Angeles' infamous water raid on the Owens Valley in the early 1900s, when the city secretly bought out farmers and shipped their water south, turning the valley into a dust-storm-ravaged wasteland.

Many of the project's most thoughtful opponents are veterans of the MX fight. One is Dean Baker, who runs a ranch in Snake Valley, on the Nevada-Utah border. Baker's ranch stands in the shadow of Wheeler Peak and Great Basin National Park, on the northeasternmost fringe of the water project, in what he calls "the driest part of the driest state in the Union."

In the 1970s, Baker began buying center-pivot irrigation systems to water his land, then watched as the water they sprayed out simply evaporated without ever hitting the ground. He experimented for years, souping up his center pivots with a wizard's array of special nozzles, and pushing more water through the machines, before he was finally able to put enough water on the ground to grow a crop.

Baker is one of three rural representatives on the twenty-six-member advisory committee created by the Water Authority, where he's one of the few voices questioning whether farmers' irrigation water will disappear as Vegas pumps down the aquifer. Once a month, he flies his Cessna 182 to Las Vegas for committee meetings: "I keep asking them, 'Is there any other project in the world at this elevation, with this precipitation, with this humidity, [that is] sustainable?' "

Jo Anne Garrett, another MX veteran, has also been involved. Back in 1989, when Las Vegas first filed its water-rights applications, she helped convince White Pine County residents to tax themselves to underwrite the opposition's legal efforts. Last year, after two White Pine county commissioners and the district attorney attempted to negotiate a water deal with Las Vegas, Garrett and two other county residents took to the streets with a recall petition. They got less than half the signatures needed to hold a recall, but voters ousted the two commissioners in that fall's election; the district attorney is up for re-election next year.

The county hasn't met with Las Vegas since, but the fight has begun to border on the desperate. There's a little more than $100,000 left in the fund to fight Las Vegas, and earlier this year, White Pine county commissioner Gary Perea took the unusual step of asking Pat Mulroy for money so the county could hire somebody to fight her water project. Mulroy, not surprisingly, declined.

The science and the landscape are full of questions. A series of U.S. Geological Survey reports released in the 1990s raised concerns that, in spite of the immense size of the aquifer, only a fraction of its water can be sustainably pumped without permanently depleting it. The Water Authority originally applied for more than eight hundred thousand acre-feet of water per year. Now, it says it can sustainably pump 125,000 to 180,000 acre-feet, skimming off only the pulse of "recharge" that the aquifer receives each spring and summer as snowmelt percolates down into the limestone.

This spring, the federal Bureau of Land Management began work on an environmental impact statement for the pipeline, noting that the project could affect desert tortoise, sage grouse, pygmy rabbits, and several species of endangered fish. Nevada state engineer Hugh Ricci will hold public hearings to help him decide whether to approve Las Vegas' water applications, something that could happen within the next few months.

The U.S. Geological Survey is also working on a new estimate of how much water can be sustainably pumped from the aquifer. But that study won't be finished until November 2007, and it won't model the potential impacts of the Water Authority's pumping on existing well users. Nor will it address the risks to the springs that dot all of eastern Nevada, and are some of the most ecologically important—and sensitive—places in the Great Basin.

"From an evolutionary standpoint, it's just absolutely fascinating," says Jon Sjöberg, a Nevada Department of Wildlife supervisory biologist, describing the world of life that the aquifer supports. About ten thousand years ago, as the climate warmed, the salty lake that covered eastern Nevada began drying up. But a few vestiges of the saltwater ecosystem were caught by the freshwater springs as everything else evaporated away. In these isolated springs, a remarkable array of fish, snails, and amphibians survived and evolved, creating the Great Basin's legendary biological diversity.

Sjöberg offers the example of the White River springfish, a tiny creature averaging slightly more than an inch in length, which was placed on the federal endangered species list in the 1980s. There are five different subspecies of White River springfish in five springs strung over more than one hundred miles between Ely and Las Vegas.

With such small populations in such isolation, "it doesn't take much to affect them," says Sjöberg.

"We're in a constant crisis mode, running from one disaster with one species to another. All you're trying to do is keep them from going extinct," he says. He talks about using pickle buckets to rescue Pahrump pool fish from springs northwest of Las Vegas when they dried up after farmers started pumping nearby.

"We're used to that," he says, but the groundwater project "has the potential to affect all of those resources collectively"—not just fish, but also mammals such as desert bighorn sheep and elk that depend on isolated water sources.

One big concern is that, in the fractured carbonates, water-level declines from the project's wells can "propagate" along the fractures like cracks spreading across a windshield, possibly affecting springs hundreds of miles away.

The Department of Wildlife was an official "cooperator" in the BLM's environmental impact statement until this June. Then, at the direction of Governor Kenny Guinn's office—and for reasons that the office has never convincingly explained—the agency withdrew from the process.

That has left Sjöberg sidelined, with plenty of questions. "This has to be done right, because you're looking at something that is happening on a landscape scale. And that's where it just kind of takes your breath away," says Sjöberg. "We spend a lot of time just staring at the wall going, 'Oh shit. What do we do?'"

Only a little more than a century ago, groundwater hydrology was seen as something of the occult, and despite great advances in the science, it still requires a certain willingness to feel your way forward toward the answers.

"The bottom line," says Mulroy, "is even the most sophisticated hydrologic modeling is nothing more than an educated guess."

Jeff Johnson, the Water Authority's senior hydrologist, says that "the next step is going in and actually developing the resource, through wells and a pipeline, in order to try to refine some of those numbers."

The Water Authority is already part way into a small-scale trial run in Coyote Spring Valley, an empty expanse of Joshua trees and creosote bush fifty miles northeast of Las Vegas, on the edge of the Desert National Wildlife Range. The state engineer is requiring the Authority to test-pump for several years to determine the effects on the aquifer before he'll consider granting full rights.

"Right now, the philosophy is we're going to start slow, pump a certain amount of water, and see what happens to the springs," says Bob Williams, the U.S. Fish and Wildlife Service's field supervisor for Nevada. Williams is responsible for the bevy of federal wildlife refuges in the state, and for protecting plants and animals on the federal endangered species list such as the White River springfish.

The Water Authority, Fish and Wildlife Service, and several other parties are funding studies of the Moapa dace, another endangered native fish in the area, as well as restoring habitat and removing predatory invasive fish. "We're trying," says Williams, "to reduce one threat as we bring another on."

The Water Authority says it will use a similar pump-and-monitor strategy for the groundwater project in the Basin and Range. "We don't want to go in and pump for ten years and then, gee, it dries up and is gone. That doesn't serve anybody's purpose," says Johnson. "The idea here is go in, develop the resource, do it conservatively, and then manage it for long-term viability, indefinitely."

But the strategy is not without risk. "The but," says Williams, "is if you start pumping, and in maybe two years or five or ten, you start seeing [a water-level decline], can you turn it off fast enough to actually stop the effects?"

Dean Baker doubts that "turning it off" will even be an option. He talks about the tremendous investment that Las Vegas is making in the pipeline, and is skeptical that the Water Authority would happily walk away if the project were found to adversely affect water levels.

"If they build that pipeline," he says, "the urge will be overpowering to keep it full."

Clearly, there are simpler—and far less expensive—solutions on the Colorado River. Even six years into a drought, there is still a lot of water on the river. Some is water that the Upper Basin has rights to but still doesn't use. Much is water being used by farmers—whether on alfalfa fields in Wyoming or asparagus farms in Southern California's Imperial Valley—that Las Vegas could conceivably buy. The Imperial Valley alone receives 3.85 million acre-feet a year.

"If we could work out some deal, or some agreement, between the basin states where Nevada could get more water," says Williams, "that would be better than to build this pipeline and run the risk of so much environmental—I don't want to use the word 'damage'—but potential for environmental concerns."

For now, however, that water remains beyond Pat Mulroy's reach. Mulroy maintains that the Basin and Range groundwater project is simply an effort to develop "a plumbing system that is separate and apart from the Colorado River." But she is largely being forced to pursue the project, with all its uncertainties, because there are problems on the Colorado that she hasn't yet been able to crack.

At the same time, the groundwater project itself is beginning to show signs of strain, albeit subtle ones. The environmental impact statement on the pipeline, originally due out next spring, is, according to Mulroy, "kind of in a stall mode right now." The study will likely be revamped to assess the impacts of another water project to the south in Lincoln County; the manager of the study announced that he is quitting this fall, after it became clear that it will probably take at least three more years to redo it.

Meanwhile, the pressure is growing. Last year, Las Vegas added more than thirty-five thousand houses and nearly ninety-five thousand people. New projections, released this August, show that the population will grow even faster than previously anticipated. Based on those updated numbers, the Water Authority says that its existing supplies will allow Las Vegas to continue to grow until 2013. But the Authority is now facing a widening gap between that year and when it can lay its hands on its next big shot of water. Under the most optimistic projections, the groundwater project was scheduled to come online in 2015; now, it may not do so until several years after that. Mulroy is pursuing other options, but those are even more politically fraught.

That raises two scenarios. Las Vegas, contrary to Hal Rothman's claims, could be the first American city to stop growing because of a lack of water. But a far more likely scenario is that Mulroy will be forced back to the Colorado and its as-yet-uncracked challenges.

In the past, she urged the other states to "rethink." This time, she may invoke the Colorado River equivalent of the nuclear option, and file a lawsuit asking that the Colorado River Compact be declared null and void. "If there is no way that the Compact can accommodate Nevada, then Nevada has no choice but to consider the Compact broken," she says. "I think we're all trying to avoid going to court, but in truth of fact, Nevada is backed into a corner."

Because the Compact is essentially a treaty between states, any challenge to it will go directly before the U.S. Supreme Court. That's the absolute last place any of the states wants to be: while every state would like a shot at a bigger slice of the river, no state is willing to risk losing some of its entitlement in court—especially in the Supreme Court, beyond which there is nowhere to appeal.

But Nevada has almost nothing to lose. Because Las Vegas has, far and away, the tiniest cut of the river—that paltry 4 percent—it has far more incentive than anyone else to go for broke. "What are you gonna do?" asks Mulroy. "Take our three hundred thousand acre-feet away?"

In past negotiations, the other states have insisted that Mulroy leave no stone unturned at home before she seeks more Colorado River water. The groundwater project may, then, be Mulroy's effort to show that Nevada has exhausted every option within its borders, a sort of pre-emptive strike to neutralize the other states' arguments before the Supreme Court. But it may also be Mulroy's own MX-worthy stratagem, one final effort to force the other states to the negotiating table.

The prospect of a date in court gives the six other states tremendous incentive to help Las Vegas find a solution to its problems. The states' representatives have been meeting at least once a month since January in an effort to do just that.

They are, however, also hedging their bets. Colorado has long maintained a special $2 million fund to defend its Colorado River water rights. Now, Arizona is preparing a comparable war chest.

Nevada, oddly, is making no such special preparations. But as Hal Rothman is so fond of pointing out, while Las Vegas may be short on water, it has plenty of what really matters.

"If we have to go to court," Mulroy says archly, "we've got the money."

September 19, 2005

Matt Jenkins is a *High Country News* contributing editor.

DENVER

Water Pressure

Ed Marston

Ten years ago this month, the George H. W. Bush administration killed a massive Denver-area dam called Two Forks.

Dams had been defeated in the past, but not by a Republican president elected with strong support in the Rocky Mountains. Stopping western dams usually required national campaigns. But the South Platte River and its gold-medal trout fishery in Cheesman Canyon didn't have a national constituency. And even if it did, Congress couldn't stop it, because Denver and its forty or so suburban partners were going to pay the $1 billion cost of the five hundred fifty-foot-high dam out of their residents' pockets.

All the dam builders needed from the federal government were regulatory permits.

In 1989, after six years and $25 million, the Army Corps of Engineers had completed an environmental impact statement, and was poised to issue the key permit. Only a signature from the U.S. Environmental Protection Agency was needed.

Denver got the signature, but it was at the bottom of a veto.

How did this stunning defeat happen? And what has the blockage of a major new source of drinking water meant for metro Denver, which added almost five hundred thousand residents during the 1990s, and is projected to add another one million persons to its 2.3 million population by 2020?

The first answer is easy. The veto was the work of William K. Reilly, President Bush's newly appointed head of the EPA. He initiated the veto over objections from his top staff and the powers that be in Colorado.

Then, after nineteen months of political pressure, he turned his intent to veto into a veto.

How the metro area will continue to cope without Two Forks is a harder question. Metro Denver skated through the ten years following the veto. Conservation performed especially well. In 1990, Denver served eight hundred ninety thousand people within Denver and its surrounding suburbs. In 1999, it served an additional ninety-five thousand people with the same amount of water.

Denver can continue to take care of itself and its inner suburbs. The fast growth is at the sprawling, ever-expanding edge in the counties to the south and east of Denver. Think of metro Denver as you think of the universe in the wake of the big bang: the farther from the center, the faster the expansion and the thinner the population.

Thus far, the outer suburbs have been drilling wells and buying up farmers' irrigation water to supply their new subdivisions. But aquifers get pumped out, and there's just so much available agricultural water. Back in 1990, Monte Pascoe, who was then head of the Denver Water Department, opposed Reilly's veto and still believes it was a mistake.

Pascoe recalls that when Reilly called him the day after Thanksgiving 1990 to say he had just vetoed the project, "I told him: 'This makes it easier for the Denver Water Department. Now taking care of the people [in Denver's outer suburbs] is the EPA's job.' " With the defeat of Two Forks, Pascoe was telling Reilly, Denver was no longer taking responsibility for the outer suburbs' water needs.

Pascoe remembers that the phone conversation was not pleasant; Reilly, he says, "got testy."

There was no testiness on October 27, 2000, when Reilly came to Denver to talk to a celebratory crowd of one hundred at a dinner put on by Environmental Defense, a group that was at the center of the anti-dam effort. Activists from the veto fight, dressed in jeans, mixed with high donors, consultants, a Colorado Supreme Court justice, a former governor, and others at the downtown Oxford Hotel. The crowd, many of whom had not seen each other in years, was hungry, but not for food, and for awhile it seemed people would never stop talking and sit down to eat.

Reilly's welcoming remarks added to the mood: "We should savor our victories. Life doesn't have that many."

Reilly opened his after-dinner speech by saying: "I have never talked about Two Forks before. It was in the courts through 1996. The proponents alleged I came to office prejudiced. But I came to the office with complete ignorance."

Nevertheless, after only six weeks on the job, he set the veto process in motion. The paperwork he immersed himself in had been done under the Reagan administration, and its political appointees were still his top staff. When an assistant realized Reilly was going to dig into the project, she told him: "Your timing is bad." Reilly replied: "No. Your timing is bad." If the eight-year process had been a few months faster, Two Forks would have been approved by the time Reilly came to office.

The first person Reilly called to discuss the project was Colorado's former three-term Democratic governor, Richard Lamm, who told him: "It's not a good project, but I will understand if ... you don't stop it. I know what happens when you're identified early on as an opponent of growth."

Lamm's successor, and the then-current governor, Democrat Roy Romer, told Reilly the metro area didn't need water from Two Forks, but it needed the economic boost construction would bring. The end of the energy boom in the early 1980s had left 25 percent of Denver's office space empty.

The environmentalists whom Reilly called stressed the damage Two Forks would do by removing more water from the Platte River, further threatening the whooping crane in central Nebraska. Just as bad, environmentalists said, some of the Two Forks water would come by tunnel out of the upper Colorado River basin, further threatening that river's endangered fish, like the pikeminnow. The environmentalists also had some good news. Reilly, they said, could safely stop Two Forks because there were cheaper, less damaging ways to provide Denver with water.

In weighing the pros and cons, Reilly told the audience he was impressed by Governor Romer's economic argument until he realized Denver was asking for eighteen years to complete the project, which didn't indicate plans for quick construction. He also questioned the project's population projections. And he learned that Denver, with high per-capita water use, was serving eighty-eight thousand unmetered homes and had not met earlier commitments to conservation. Finally, he said, he didn't accept the proponents' argument that Two Forks "was none of my business."

Reilly also indicated he was taken aback by a callousness about the Platte River's Cheesman Canyon and its trout stream. "I never heard the Two Forks proponents acknowledge that we had an exquisite natural resource at stake. They didn't try to justify the loss."

In the end, Reilly decided Two Forks would violate Section 404C of the Clean Water Act. That was the straightforward part, he said. Much harder was divining the politics. Could he veto the project without being reversed by President Bush or inciting Congress to revoke the Clean Water Act?

Finally, "I asked myself: Why did the president choose the head of the World Wildlife Fund to run EPA?" He decided that Bush had meant it when he campaigned as the "environmental President," and had appointed Reilly to turn that promise into a reality.

That "gave me confidence. I told the White House the project was questionable. I told [John] Sununu [Bush's very aggressive chief of staff]: Stay out of it. Blame me. Say it was my solitary decision."

Reilly got his wish. Sununu held Reilly responsible for angering Colorado's Republican congressional delegation. So there followed a stream of Colorado heavyweights to Washington, all ushered into George Bush's office by his chief of staff to lobby against the veto. Reilly said Republican Sen. Bill Armstrong told Bush that a Two Forks veto would mean the end of Denver as a "green city."

Reilly also got support. Public hearings in April 1988 were packed with Two Forks opponents. Letters to the White House ran seven to one for the veto. One writer was a part-time Vail, Colorado, resident and former president, Gerald Ford. Vail was for the veto; the western Colorado ski town would suffer dry stream channels if Two Forks were built.

During those nineteen months, Reilly never heard from the one man who could have reversed him—George Bush. All he got were encouraging signals in the form of invitations to state dinners at the White House. So on the day after Thanksgiving 1990, with both Sununu and the Colorado congressional delegation out of town, the final veto order was signed by an EPA official; Two Forks was dead.

The veto was challenged in court by most of the water utilities and by those interested in land development, including the Colorado Cattlemen's Association. But a transformed Denver Water Department, with a new manager and a changing board, did not join the appeal. The litigation ended in 1996, when the judge threw out the case, saying that even if Denver had joined the case, the plaintiffs would probably have lost. The suburban water providers decided not to appeal.

Reilly could make his initial veto decision in six hectic weeks because a major chunk of Colorado's environmental community had spent six years collaborating in the elaborate public process intended to pave the way for a Two Forks permit. They had met monthly with Denver and the suburban water providers, they had done economic and hydrologic analysis, and they had produced a low-impact alternative to the Corps of Engineers' preferred solution: the 1.1 million acre-foot, twenty-fiv-mile-long Two Forks reservoir.

Environmentalists were in a position to give Reilly an alternative because of Lamm and the thirty-person Governor's Metropolitan Water Roundtable he had created. Like Reilly, Lamm, in 1981, had gone against some of his advisors, who warned him to stay clear of water. That was conventional wisdom. Colorado did not then and does not now have a state water plan. Each river basin, each drainage, each city, each ditch company, each shovel-wielding farmer, is so jealous of their water that no governor or legislature has dared create a plan for the state.

Among Lamm's thirty appointees were two environmentalists: Dan Luecke, then and now head of Environmental Defense's Rocky Mountain office, and Bob Golten, then an attorney with the National Wildlife

Federation. Behind them stood the Colorado Environmental Caucus, a statewide coalition of environmental groups that met monthly. Although the environmentalists were outnumbered, the group, with Lamm chairing every session from 1981 to 1986, operated by consensus, which gave everyone a veto.

The environmentalists had not come to the table to help build a large dam on the South Platte River. They were looking for a forum at which to present alternatives to dams. According to Luecke, the alternatives they hoped to present did not include stopping water development in order to stop growth: "The mythical link between water and growth doesn't exist. You can't stimulate growth with lots of water, or stop it by depriving an area of water."

Instead, the environmentalists wanted to provide the water needed for growth in the least damaging way. But to create alternatives, they first had to understand the details of the metro-area water system: Which utilities could be hooked together to share resources? How many homes and businesses were wasting water because they were unmetered or paying a flat or declining rate? How much water did each diversion take out of a stream? How much water could be pumped from underground?

One player had data, teams of specialists and lawyers, and a computer model that could take the data and run out different water supply scenarios. But the Denver Water Department wasn't about to share its data or its model. Luecke recalls, "They told us in so many words: We're the experts. You're little environmentalists. Get out of the way"—and let us build a major dam on the South Platte.

When Luecke and Golten wouldn't let the Governor's Roundtable reach consensus by joining the other twenty-eight members in support of a large dam on the South Platte, Luecke says, "They called us obstructionists and tried to convince Lamm to remove us. To his credit, he didn't. But to prove that we weren't obstructionists, we said we'd come up with a plan to supply water, and it would have a reservoir on the South Platte."

They made that promise in spring 1982. By October 1982, they had their plan. It would provide one hundred forty thousand to one hundred seventy thousand acre-feet of water a year from a small South Platte River dam, conservation, sewage reuse, a mixing of groundwater and surface-water sources, and other means.

They created the alternative with the help of a computer model of the metro water system that Luecke wrote and hydrologist Lee Rozaklis loaded up with numbers: the size of reservoirs, their evaporative losses, the ability of the Roberts and Moffat tunnels to convey water beneath the Continental Divide to the Denver area, stream channel capacities, likely precipitation, aquifer yields, and so on.

The model got nowhere with the Roundtable. Luecke says, "I don't see how we ever thought we could convince most of them of anything." But he believes the model helped convince the EPA staff and eventually Bill Reilly that there were alternatives to Two Forks.

Was Reilly right to veto Two Forks? So far, it looks like a good decision. Hamlet "Chips" Barry, who was appointed to head the Denver Water Department after the veto, gives full credit to Reilly's veto for transforming his department's culture and operation. He told a rural, western Colorado audience in 1994, "Beliefs that belonged to the environmental fringe in the 1960s have become mainstream values today." As a result, the department has shed its "earlier adolescent personality."

For starters, the once-imperial organization now cooperates with two of its traditional enemies: rural western Colorado and environmentalists. With the support of both, Denver has built a small reservoir in western Colorado. And it is about to adopt another environmentalist suggestion and build a large project to reuse some of its sewage to provide water for several large projects within Denver, including the redevelopment of the former Stapleton Airport.

Barry says, "We can't re-plumb the whole city. But we can use it [the reclaimed sewage] in new construction. This reuse will provide about fifteen thousand acre-feet of water. Two Forks was only going to provide us with twenty thousand acre-feet." The other eighty thousand acre-feet per year were to go mainly to outer suburbs.

The veto didn't hurt Denver in part because the water out of Two Forks was never the city's main concern. Instead, Two Forks was about the city's place in the metropolitan region. Until the 1970s, Denver had seen itself as the undisputed leader of the area, annexing surrounding land whenever it wanted to grow and providing all who wanted it with water diverted from the Colorado River Basin. That future was shattered in 1974, when Colorado voters passed the Poundstone Amendment, locking the city within existing boundaries. Suddenly, Denver saw itself sharing the fate of other cities, with an aging infrastructure and disproportionate numbers of poor, elderly, and disabled residents.

And so Denver, armed with its formidable water system and its future claims on the Colorado River, came to the Governor's Roundtable with a non-water agenda. Luecke remembers, "They would bring in lists of the people who were using its emergency rooms," or going to the main Denver library or museums. And half of these users, Denver's representatives told the Roundtable, were from the suburbs. Out of its diminished resources, Denver was subsidizing suburbanites. Luecke continues, "They weren't at the Roundtable just to build this dam. There was a larger agenda. They were aggrieved."

Denver hoped that by welding together an urban-suburban partnership based on Two Forks, it would begin to solve some of the urban problems caused by the metro area's political divisions.

In the end, Denver didn't get its dam, but it did get some of the cooperation it had been after. Monte Pascoe, head of the Denver Water Board at that time, recalls: "One of the good things about the Two Forks discussions was that it created cooperation. That was when we got the cultural facilities tax passed, and a large number of other cooperative arrangements."

Denver and the eighty entities around it, the close-in suburbs and water companies it supplies with water, are cooperating and have water for the future. But that is not true of the new, prospering, sprawling outer-ring suburbs. It is here that the downside of the Two Forks veto is most visible, especially because what seemed like outlandish population projections ten years ago now look much closer to the mark.

Parker, Erie, and Cherry Hills Village are the kinds of places that Pascoe told Reilly were now the EPA's responsibility, or at least they were no longer Denver's responsibility. The booming of this ragged ring of outer suburbs has led the Washington, D.C.-based Fannie Mae Foundation to recently name Denver as the fourth-worst case of urban sprawl in the nation, after Atlanta, Miami, and Detroit. Perhaps Reilly's knowledge of this growth and his memory of Pascoe's remark ten years ago led him to also tell the celebrating audience in downtown Denver: "There is no final resolution of this issue."

Eric Kuhn, who heads the Colorado River Water Conservation District, agrees with Reilly. The district's job is to protect the water of the west side of the state and the Colorado River from the Front Range to the east, and from California and Arizona and Nevada to the southwest.

"The veto changed the point of attack rather than the ultimate outcome," Kuhn says. "The south metro area is over here in western Colorado, looking for large transmountain diversions. The veto set up a situation of haves and have-nots. Denver and the inner suburbs it serves don't need more water. But the suburbs around it are still hanging onto the notion that a billion-dollar project is the answer to their future."

The environmentalists who helped defeat Two Forks foresaw this, and have been working for the past decade to drive yet more stakes through the heart of Two Forks. Luecke said that after Reilly's veto, "We asked ourselves: What could cap future diversions out of the Colorado River and prevent Two Forks from rising again?"

The answer, they decided, was the federal Endangered Species Act, and endangered fish like the pikeminnow (formerly called the squawfish) in the Colorado River near the Utah line. And so Environmental Defense, this time with The Nature Conservancy's Robert Wigington as partner, participated in years of tortuous, low-profile negotiations and maneuvering with water developers and with the U.S. Fish and Wildlife Service. This work culminated in 1999, when the Fish and Wildlife Service issued an opinion governing water flows in a fifteen-mile stretch of the Colorado River between DeBeque and Grand Junction.

This federal document limits future takes out of the river to an initial total of sixty thousand acre-feet. If the fish thrive in the face of this depletion, then another sixty-thousand acre-foot depletion would be allowed, with the one hundred twenty thousand total acre-feet to be split between the fast-growing West Slope and the faster-growing Front Range.

But Two Forks was only going to be partially filled with diverted Colorado River water. The rest of its ninety-eight thousand acre-foot per year yield was to come from the South Platte River. Here, too, the Endangered Species Act comes into play. A memorandum of agreement between the three states and the federal government bars any additional net depletions of the river to protect the whooping crane in central Nebraska. The Platte River Whooping Crane Maintenance Trust and Environmental Defense participated in these negotiations.

Would-be water diverters are also blocked to the south. Congress just elevated the Great Sand Dunes National Monument to a national park. And the law creating the park will ban water diversions out of the Rio Grande in the San Luis Valley to the Front Range.

Eric Kuhn of the River District says it appears that the federal government has done what several generations of Colorado elected officials refused to do, or couldn't do: "Federal law is basically creating a state water plan." And that plan appears almost to have been designed to prevent the metro Denver area from taking much more water out of the three large rivers that originate in its mountains.

Former Gov. Lamm, who now runs a public policy center at Denver University, and who attended the October 27 celebration, isn't ready to celebrate.

"There is no greater force on earth than thirsty people. Where is the metro area going to get its water? When water interests on the Front Range get thirsty, I don't think the Endangered Species Act and its minimum stream flows will keep them from knocking on western Colorado's door."

He predicts the outer suburbs will use the Denver Water Department to do that knocking. Lamm calls Denver Water Department head Chips Barry "an unsung hero." But Lamm worries about what happens after Barry and the current Denver Water Department. "Denver has the water rights and infrastructure to supply the outer suburbs, and the economic interests that run Colorado will use the Denver Water Board to get additional water."

Kuhn, sitting in the district's headquarters in Glenwood Springs on the Colorado River, agrees with Lamm, although he sees the suburbs using a different weapon to get their water. Kuhn suggests that if the outer suburbs get thirsty enough, they may move against the doctrine of prior appropriation itself. The doctrine is the fundamental law of water use in Colorado and in most of the West. It allocates water to those who first put it to use.

So when it comes to claiming water, population is not a factor. Miners, farmers, and older cities like Denver have the most senior claims on the West's water. Newer cities, and the suburbs which grew up later, have had to make do with what was left. First-comers get to use the steady base flows out of a river or a stream. Late-comers who want dependable water supplies have to build reservoirs to store spring runoff for later use. Users who come after them are generally out of luck.

Western water use generally goes 80 percent or more to agriculture, with urban areas using a relatively small amount. The saying is that "water runs uphill towards money," but it is also true that it is expensive and time-consuming to make it do so. And in some cases, it is impossible.

For example, twice now corporations with lots of money have sought to divert the Rio Grande out of the San Luis Valley in southern Colorado. And each time, the poorest county in the state turned the developers back.

In the past, environmentalists have been the major critics of the doctrine of prior appropriation, as they seek to return water to streams for fish and wildlife. Now, Kuhn predicts, the doctrine has a new enemy: "If anything will cause prior appropriation to break, it will be the new suburbs' thirst for water."

If Lamm and Kuhn are correct, then the shape of the next Two Forks battle is already visible. It will pit the outer suburbs against Denver and the West Slope, with traditional water law and control of Denver's water system as the prizes.

Lamm hopes such a struggle can be avoided because he knows who usually wins. "I turned sixty-five recently, and looked back, asking: What did I do wrong? I kicked my way in the door by helping to stop the Olympics, and then won the governorship because of Watergate. I thought I had a mandate [to stop growth]. But I didn't. I should have come to an understanding with the dominant economic interests." Instead, Lamm fought them and, more often than not, lost. "I almost got impeached for saying that instead of the C470 highway, we should build mass transit. If we had mass transit, I'd be more impressed with the argument that we can add growth by infilling. As it is, I think all the Two Forks veto did was buy us twenty years.

"All of the land north and south of Denver has been spoken for—north to Fort Collins and south to Colorado Springs. It's platted and zoned. There's tremendous momentum in that. Stopping growth is like stopping an automobile. You need time. You need braking distance."

If Lamm is right, Colorado has ten more years before water once again becomes a hot topic. In control, for the moment, is a new old-guard. The Denver Water Department under Chips Barry is a progressive force. Environmentalists are key participants within Colorado and federal water-planning negotiations. And the metro area has a plan for meeting metro-wide water needs, prepared over the last few years by Hydrosphere, a consulting firm whose principals cut their water teeth by fighting Two Forks.

But the power of sprawling growth was shown on November 7, in Colorado and in Arizona, where the two states trounced initiatives that would have confined development within urban-growth boundaries.

If the fight over water returns to Colorado, it will make Two Forks look like a warm-up act.

November 20, 2000

Ed Marston (emarston@hcn.org) is former publisher for *High Country News*.

Drought Unearths a
Water Dinosaur

Allen Best

Ralph E. "Butch" Clark is the unlikely author of what some view as the most preposterous water idea ever conceived in Colorado: a two-hundred-mile pipeline with a ten-foot girth that would carry water from the Colorado River near the Utah border east along Interstate 70, over the Continental Divide, eventually spilling into Denver's swelling suburbs. When Clark, an environmental planner from Gunnison, Colo.rado presented the idea to the Denver Water Board in 1988, it was promptly thrown on a heap of similarly impossible, mega-hydro-engineering projects.

Even Clark, at the time, admitted his idea should be undertaken only "if all other alternatives to new transmountain diversion are exhausted."

Now, twelve years later, it's back. This summer, Grand Junction water attorney Greg Hoskin dusted off Clark's proposal, retitled it "The Big Straw," and presented it to a surprisingly responsive group of Colorado politicians. The timing is right as the entire state grapples with dwindling water sources and a growing population during an extended drought. In July, Gov. Bill Owens announced he would ask the state legislature for a half-million dollars to study the feasibility of Clark's dream.

But not everyone thinks it's a great idea.

"Before we invest billions of dollars in old-time solutions to water problems, we need to figure out whether that's the right answer," says David Getches, a law professor at the University of Colorado and former director of Colorado's Department of Natural Resources.

Regardless of the opposition—past or present—The Big Straw is very much alive. Some say it has opened the door to other projects that were once deemed too big, too damaging to the environment or too costly for serious consideration. Others wonder if the feasibility study may have the opposite effect: The plan's audacity could steer officials away from expensive water projects toward more practical solutions, such as conservation.

Butch Clark developed The Big Straw, hoping to end the water battles between Colorado's west and east slopes with an environmentally friendly alternative to the high-impact water projects then on the drawing board. It was also a bit of a bluff, Clark says, meant to show officials that their only alternative to changing water-use behavior was sensational and unaffordable.

"In 1988, Western Colorado's Gunnison River was targeted for three transmountain diversion proposals," Clark says. "I was trying to suggest that there were a lot of other, cheaper alternatives: conservation, conjunctive use ..."

But the Front Range and its politicians wanted a faster solution than conservation. About 85 percent of Coloradans live east of the Continental Divide, mostly in Denver and its suburbs. But at least 75 percent of the state's moisture falls west of the divide, where, in the Colorado River, some of the state's last unclaimed water remains.

For years, Front Range cities and suburbs have tried to get at this water through diversions from high mountain valleys. The most ambitious of these plans was the Two Forks project, which would have diverted Colorado and South Platte river water into a twenty-five-mile-long reservoir southwest of Denver. But in 1990 it was vetoed—surprisingly— by the head of the Environmental Protection Agency under the George H. W. Bush administration.

That veto forced Denver to rely entirely on existing water supplies, with the city's suburbs left to face an uncertain future. Today, the pinch is most acute in the thriving communities built around Colorado's information-technology industry, which depend on two main aquifers that, at current rates of depletion, could go dry in as little as forty years. As officials with the Denver Water Board consider drilling new wells in this finite water source, at an estimated $1 million a well, the climate is perfect to seriously consider Clark's proposal.

After all, The Big Straw addresses much of what Two Forks would have: it would annually take about two hundred eighty thousand acre-feet of Colorado River water from the Utah border, respecting existing Colorado water users who draw from the river as it moves west across the state. The stream flows in the Colorado and its tributaries would remain untouched, preserving wildlife—down to the state line. And, finally, the pipeline would be built along Interstate 70, so the construction impact would be negligible.

But regardless of The Big Straw's appeal, it's extremely expensive and environmentally dubious.

Bar-napkin estimates peg the costs of a pipeline along I-70 to Dillon Reservoir, Denver's Western Slope reservoir, at up to $5 billion. And costs could run even higher, because new reservoirs at one, the other, or both ends of the pipeline may be necessary to regulate the release of water.

"Everybody seems to think this is some kind of environmental panacea," says Brent Uilenberg, with the U.S. Bureau of Reclamation, "but in fact, it has some potentially disastrous consequences." The endangered Colorado pikeminnow, for one, could be devastated by the diversion, a fact that would most certainly surface during the feasibility study.

Still, after a summer of severe water restrictions in the suburbs, dead rivers, and strained livestock, Colorado politicians are under the gun to do something. Eric Kuhn, general manager of the Colorado River Water Conservation District, which monitors water use on the Western Slope, says he fears "a political minefield" when state legislators convene in January, intent on returning home to constituents with "The Answer" to their water woes.

Some members of the Owens administration concede an ulterior motive: if the state doesn't claim its water allocated under the 1922 Colorado River Compact, California may eventually lay claim to it.

Greg Walcher, director of the state's Department of Natural Resources, predicts quick action. "Within the next year or two, we're going to begin building water projects and new storage."

Even those who are skeptical of The Big Straw hope the study will introduce more productive discussion of the state's water needs. "My own impression is that the economics may be distressing news to people," says Chips Barry, manager of the Denver Water Department, "but until the study, anybody's off-hand guess—including mine—is probably not of great value."

As for the idea that The Big Straw is simply a political Band-Aid for drought-worried Coloradans, Barry disagrees.

"All old and semi-dormant water projects get new life in times of drought," he says. Barry says there's plenty of room for conservation, but adds that the Front Range will ultimately need a new water source, drought or no drought. With the state's exploding population, he says, even the most outrageous projects deserve a second look.

September 16, 2002

Allen Best has been writing about water issues in Colorado since 1977.

Colorado's Thirsty Suburbs Get the State into Trouble

Allen Best

Denver's southern suburbs have a rich, new-car smell. Emboldened by information-technology employers, Douglas County during the nineties was the nation's fastest-growing county. It also ranked among the nation's elite in per-capita income, education, and other measures of affluence.

In short, this region of sleek and slinky subdivisions looks and feels an awful lot like the sprawling suburbs of Los Angeles in the 'sixties and seventies. In fact, many of its new residents during the nineties came from California.

But for all their luxuriant golf courses that roll up toward the Colorado Rockies, Denver's southern suburbs in Douglas County and unincorporated Arapahoe County are in a pinch. Their hurried growth is based on an exhaustible water supply. Wells for this oasis civilization are running dry.

Some say this underground body of water, called the Denver Aquifer, will hold out for a thousand years, others say only 3thirty or forty. What is known is that existing wells produce steadily diminishing volumes of water every year, sometimes only a third as much. Wells must be dug deeper and deeper. Replumbing this subterranean water supply could be enormously expensive.

But in the West, who pays their own way in water? For most of the twentieth century the federal government played the role of an uncommonly generous banker to westerners in need of water.

The largest project, what the late historian David Lavender called a "massive violation of geography," was the Colorado-Big Thompson diversion. That project, launched during the dusty, hard-bitten 1930s, takes water from the snow-clogged headwaters of the Colorado River through the Continental Divide onto the rich but dry lands of the high plains, creating irrigated farms even to the Colorado-Nebraska border. Now, those farms are being steadily converted into subdivisions around Boulder, Greeley, and other small cities. Colorado Big-Thompson water that once grew grains and vegetables now grows lawns and flushes toilets.

After another drought, in the 1950s, a similar project occurred elsewhere in Colorado. Launched by President Kennedy in 1962, the Fryingpan-Arkansas moves water from streams near Aspen to Colorado Springs and Pueblo, on the Denver side of the Rockies. In both cases, water destined to flow west via the Colorado River is now used along the Front Range.

Today, after yet another drought, there's a cry for more storage. The latest scheme is called Referendum A, which would authorize state-backed bonding of some $2 billion for water projects to be determined by the governor. Not surprisingly, Governor Bill Owens is also the chief lobbyist for Referendum A.

The suburbs that Referendum A is designed for have several options, none easy. They can seek to convert water now used for agriculture for their subdivisions. Call this trading beef steaks for survey stakes. Altogether, 93 percent of Colorado's water is devoted to agriculture, and 80 percent of that is used to grow alfalfa, corn, and other crops used to feed livestock. In other words, about two-thirds of Colorado's water goes to steaks and hamburgers. It would seem that the water could easily be diverted from farms to cities.

But Coloradans' self-image is grounded in pastoral pleasantness. Buying farms for their water is only a step above selling your sister into the sex trade.

A second option for Denver's southern suburbs is to bore tunnels and lay pipelines for the hundreds of miles necessary to access what little water is not already claimed on the western side of the Continental Divide. This also would prevent water from getting to Las Vegas and California. Like the cry of "The Utes must go" of 125 years ago, the common refrain of any successful politician in Colorado is: "No water for California."

Still, even the bogeyman of California hasn't united Coloradans. With few exceptions, Colorado's Western Slope residents see Referendum A as an uncouth guest, the kind who moves in but fails to chip in for groceries. Even most Republicans from these more rural areas have broken ranks to oppose Referendum A.

Support is stronger in eastern Colorado, but the large cities of Denver, Aurora, and Colorado Springs see nothing in this for them. Democrats actively oppose it, and many Republicans have remained quiet. Yet this scheme could get approved. Proponents have a large campaign chest, and not least, they have highly visible enemies to blame for the trouble— drought and California.

But the real enemy remains the build-now, pay-later mentality of these suburbs. Government authorities for two decades routinely approved subdivision after subdivision, predicated only on exhaustible, underground supplies. It would be, they correctly surmised, somebody else's problem.

Well, they were right. It is now our problem.

October 13, 2003

Allen Best has been writing about water issues in Colorado since 1977.

SALT LAKE CITY
Suburbanites Compete for the Lake's Fresh Water

Matt Jenkins

Great Salt Lake's fate largely turns on three rivers that flow out of the Wasatch and Uinta mountains. But as population booms along the Wasatch Front and water-use rates remain among the highest in the nation, development pressure is mounting on the Bear, Weber, and Jordan rivers, which together provide about 70 percent of Great Salt Lake's freshwater inflows.

Activists recently declared victory in a fight against dams on the Bear River, and they're pushing for stricter water conservation and a drastic change in thinking about how water is used along the Wasatch Front. But the future seems certain to hold more challenges in keeping rivers running to the lake.

"It's going to be fights and fights and fights," says Zachary Frankel, head of the Utah Rivers Council and a longtime champion of the Bear River.

In 1991, the Bear River Development Act targeted the river for six dams and a whopping two hundred twenty thousand acre-feet of water development. That touched off a battle, spearheaded by Indian, agriculture, and environmental interests, concerning the dams' impacts on the river and the seventy-four thousand-acre Bear River Migratory Bird Refuge on Great Salt Lake's northeastern shore. Conservation groups such as the Utah Rivers Council warned that new dams on the Bear could drop the lake's level anywhere from one to six feet and starve the refuge of the water it needs to harbor birds.

The activists' push convinced Utah Gov. Mike Leavitt to sign a bill in February that removes the two most promising dam sites on the Bear River from future consideration.

"There are still four other dams on the books," says Frankel. "But this is a huge victory because these are the two most actively proposed dam sites for the last ten years."

Political realignments beyond the Great Salt Lake watershed may bring new water to the basin, buying even more time for the Bear.

The Central Utah Project (CUP), first proposed in 1951 as part of the Bureau of Reclamation's last big dam-building push on the Colorado River, harnesses water from the upper Colorado River Basin and brings it west for use on the Wasatch Front. Over time, the CUP has gone through a chameleon-like series of reconfigurations and has shrunk dramatically. In 1992, Congress turned the CUP over to the Central Utah Water Conservancy District (CUWCD); since then, the project, whose original beneficiaries were supposed to be farmers, has been reworked for the benefit of the urban Wasatch Front.

One big shot of water is on its way from Strawberry Reservoir via the Diamond Fork System; more may soon be available. In 1998, the CUCWD scrapped a project to send water south to Juab County for irrigation. This February, the District announced plans to bring that water north, toward the Wasatch Front, instead. Now, an additional seventy thousand acre-feet of water is up for grabs.

How the water is divvied up may be tempered by lingering discontent—and lawsuits—from agricultural interests, but the Salt Lake Valley cities have a good shot at most of the available water.

"It's going to buy a whole new era for us," says veteran water observer Daniel McCool, director of the University of Utah's American West Center. "It certainly places any discussion of the Bear River project far into the future."

But the pressure to supply Salt Lake City and its growing suburbs with water won't go away.

The Utah Division of Water Resources has considered simply siphoning about seventy-five thousand acre-feet of Bear River water into the Willard Bay Reservoir, north of the lake, for use in urban Salt Lake and Davis counties. Although a diversion won't have as big an impact on the lake as the dams and a full two hundred twemty thousand acre-foot depletion, its effects would still be significant.

Wasatch Front cities are also looking at Great Salt Lake's other feeder rivers. The Jordan Valley Water Conservancy District, which supplies water to cities such as Sandy and West Jordan, is in the process of buying up fifty to seventy thousand acre-feet of agricultural rights to notoriously dirty Jordan River water. But the district won't use that water, says general manager David Ovard. Instead, it plans to ask the state engineer to approve permit changes that would allow the district to pump an equivalent amount of cleaner water out of the shallow aquifer that partially feeds the river.

Environmentalists like Great Salt Lake Audubon president Mary Gracia worry that pumping nearby groundwater will actually suck water out of the river, drying up wetlands and reducing inflows to Great Salt Lake.

"Nobody is saying, 'We need to look at streamflows; what does wildlife require?'" says Gracia. "They're just looking at people numbers."

Ovard says that the district doesn't want to pump the river dry; in fact, he says, he's trying to engage environmental groups' help in drafting a pumping plan.

In the long run, groups like Great Salt Lake Audubon and Utah Rivers Council are working to bring about a shift in thinking that will take Great Salt Lake's ecological needs into account and move away from what McCool calls "an infinite-growth model applied to a very finite resource."

Already, says Frankel, "The small-town mindset of Utah is smashing up against the urban reality that we are a giant suburb."

April 29, 2002

Matt Jenkins is a *High Country News* contributing editor.

The Great Salt Lake Mystery

Tim Westby

Something's fishy about the offices of Great Lake Artemia. It hits you the moment you step in the door of the company's nondescript building on Salt Lake City's industrial north side: The air smells vaguely of the ocean. An employee repairs a rubber pontoon while others clean two large, circular dryers. The floor is scattered with canvas bags filled with what looks like wet sand. More sacks are stored in a walk-in cooler nearby. In the lot behind the building sit eight shallow-draft fishing boats.

A thousand miles from here, on a wharf in Seattle or San Francisco, this scene wouldn't warrant a second look. But here, in the middle of the Great Basin, it's perplexing.

Owner Mark Jensen's explanation is as odd as his location. Those canvas bags aren't filled with wet sand, but with thousands of pounds of microscopic eggs. The eggs come from the only creatures that can survive in the brutal environment of Great Salt Lake, which lies, purple-gray, on the western fringe of this desert city. They're the eggs of brine shrimp, half-inch-long invertebrates that look like a cross between a scorpion and a cocktail shrimp. *Artemia* is their Latin name.

In the front office, Jensen places a petri dish filled with eggs under a microscope. Even through this lens, they look like tiny pencil dots. They're so small it would take two hundred fifty thousand to fill a teaspoon. But they're big business for Jensen and for thirty-one other Great Salt Lake brine-shrimp companies, which harvest them by the billions and ship them to Asia, where aquaculture farmers hatch them out and feed the brine shrimp to prawns.

In the last decade, Utah's brine-shrimp industry has attracted colorful characters from around the world to a game that is as competitive and high-stakes as any ocean fishery. Jensen, for his part, spent more than twenty years as a Grand Canyon raft guide before becoming a shrimp harvester in the 1980s. "It was something I could do in the winter that involved boats," he says.

These days, Jensen's crew harvests hundreds of thousands of pounds of brine-shrimp eggs each winter in a mad-dash, round-the-clock flurry. Most of his employees are Grand Canyon guides: "They're not afraid of big water—wind and waves, winter storms," he says. "The smart mariner gets off the water before that stuff hits."

The brine-shrimp industry has done more than provide its two hundred or so employees a way to make a living on the water. It has also helped put Great Salt Lake—one of the West's least-understood ecosystems—under the microscope.

Utahns have long regarded Great Salt Lake with a shrug. You can't blame them. In the middle of some of the West's more surreal and lonely desert, a very salty lake nearly the size of the Grand Canyon doesn't exactly invite intimacy. You can't walk out to the water's edge without slogging through a moat of muck. In warm months, it swarms with brine flies and can stink like rotting eggs. Unless it's duck-hunting season, people generally steer clear.

When the lake hasn't been ignored, it's been abused. Agricultural and government agencies have dammed and sucked water from the three main rivers feeding the lake. Suburbs and industry have crept to the edge of the lake's wetland fringe, spilling millions of pounds of pollutants into the water every year. Mineral companies have constructed elaborate dike systems and evaporation ponds to extract vast reserves of minerals, including magnesium and sodium chloride.

But now, Great Salt Lake is finally getting some respect. In the last decade, local and national environmental groups have taken new interest. An international coalition of public and private organizations has designated the lake a Hemispheric Shore Bird Reserve.

The Great Salt Lake Bird Festival draws thousands of people every May to celebrate the arrival of an estimated five million migratory birds that stop here each year.

Perhaps most significantly, the state of Utah is conducting the first ever long-term study of the lake's ecosystem, funded entirely by the

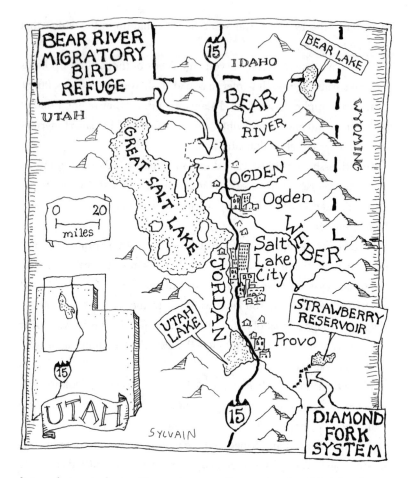

brine-shrimp industry. Researchers are discovering that this inland sea—Salt Lake City's neglected namesake—is far more complex and vulnerable than previously thought.

But the Wasatch Front is undergoing a wave of unprecedented growth, and some worry that all the attention is coming too late.

"The data that's available is very shallow. As a result, we're making very major decisions based on a very lean offering of research," says Lynn de Freitas, president of the conservation group FRIENDS of Great Salt Lake. "It's promiscuous behavior. It's not safe sex in my book."

The late historian Dale Morgan called Great Salt Lake a lake of paradoxes. "In a country where water is life itself and land has little value without it, Great Salt Lake is an ironical joke of nature—water that is itself more desert than a desert."

Writer Terry Tempest Williams calls it "the liquid lie of the West."

It wasn't always so. During the last glacial era, fifteen thousand years ago, Lake Bonneville, Great Salt Lake's freshwater predecessor, covered twenty thousand square miles of western Utah and parts of Nevada and Idaho, an area nearly the size of Lake Michigan. About fourteen thousand years ago, an ice dam gave way at Red Rock Pass in southern Idaho. The resulting torrent crashed down the Portneuf River past present-day Pocatello, then roared downstream across the Snake River Plain, carrying boulders the size of cars. Geologists say it was the second-largest flood known to have occurred in the world. Within a year, the lake dropped four hundred feet.

By eight thousand years ago, the lake looked a lot like it does today: a shallow pool in the desert, fed by three rivers. The Bear and Weber rivers tumbled down from the Wasatch and Uinta mountains. The Jordan River linked Great Salt Lake to its freshwater sister, Utah Lake, to the south. The lake got its famous salinity because it has no outlet. Like other terminal lakes in the Great Basin it is the equivalent of an enormous bathtub without a drain; water that flows in can only evaporate, leaving dissolved minerals behind.

Native Americans and early explorers hunted ducks and geese and trapped beaver and mink in the lake's freshwater marshes. Mormon pioneers, who arrived in the Salt Lake Valley in 1847, hunted on the lake's fringes and extracted salt from the water; otherwise, they ignored it. They turned to the region's rivers to water crops and create cities. Ever since, the driving mission of state and local water policies has been to capture as much water as possible before it reaches the lake, where it becomes undrinkable and unusable.

Great Salt Lake has had a few moments in the limelight. During the late 1800s and early 1900s, resorts popped up along its southern shore, attracting people from around the world with the chance to swim in water so salty they could float like corks. The grandest of these resorts was Saltair, built in 1893 by the Mormon Church. The resort, touted as the "Coney Island of the West," saw its height in the Roaring Twenties, and featured the world's largest dance floor, a roller coaster, touring Vaudeville companies, bullfights, and hot-air balloons.

But Saltair was subject to the lake's infamous ups and downs. In 1925, the resort burned to the ground. It was rebuilt only to be marooned as the lake level dropped and the water receded. It burned a second time in 1970, and was rebuilt again more than a decade later. This time it was flooded during a four-year wet period in the mid-1980s.

It was then that Great Salt Lake forced its way, literally for some, into Utah's living rooms. It rose twelve feet, spreading out across the flat valley around it, flooding six hundred thousand acres. The lake swamped suburbs, causing hundreds of millions of dollars in property damage, and threatened Salt Lake International Airport and two interstate highways.

Then-Governor Norm Bangerter's solution was highly controversial: pump lake water over the Newfoundland Mountains and into the West Desert. Taxpayers footed the $55 million bill only to watch the weather turn to drought. After two years of operation, the state shut down the pumps, and "Lake Bangerter," as the West Desert evaporation ponds became known, dried up. The pumps now sit unused.

While ever-fluctuating Great Salt Lake is little more than a nuisance to some humans, it's a bonanza for birds, says biologist Don Paul, sitting in a converted closet he uses as an office at the Antelope Island State Park Visitor's Center. After thirty-three years with the Utah Division of Wildlife Resources (DWR), Paul is one of the top experts on the more than 255 species of birds that spend part of the year here. Great Salt Lake is "probably the single most important water bird habitat in the inland West," he says.

Paul's crammed office is stacked high with toilet paper, paper towels, and plastic soap dispensers for the visitor center's public restrooms. But at one point, he nods toward the room's only window, which overlooks the lake, and says without irony, "Isn't this a great office?"

Only a fellow biologist—or a birder—would agree. Because Great Salt Lake is one of the few reliable bodies of water in the Great Basin, it offers a critical stopping point for waterfowl and shorebirds migrating between nesting grounds in the north and winter habitat down south. Each spring and fall, birds gorge themselves on brine flies and brine shrimp. On the avian equivalent of Highway 50, it's a pit stop with an all-you-can-eat seafood buffet.

The numbers are stunning. In the average year, says Paul, Great Salt Lake sees over eight hundred thousand Wilson's phalaropes, the second-largest population in the world; twenty thousand white pelicans; over a thousand wintering bald eagles; the world's largest populations of California gulls and cinnamon teals; sixty thousand tundra swans; over one million eared grebes; and the entire Intermountain West population of white-faced ibis.

Paul uses the eared grebe, which starts arriving from Canada in August, as an example of the lake's importance to birds. With long slender necks and stubby beaks, eared grebes are designed more for swimming than flying. Once they test the water for food, they start to molt, or shed their feathers, becoming flightless for several weeks before leaving for the Sea of Cortez. While they're at Great Salt Lake, however, they devour fifteen thousand brine shrimp a day, more than doubling their weight.

Wilson's phalaropes, which nest in the pothole country of the Northern Plains, are another example. Sandpiper relatives with long, needle-like bills and streaks of cinnamon down their silver backs, Wilson's phalaropes come to Great Salt Lake in the summer to molt and feast furiously on brine flies. The flies are fuel for a long fall journey: in early August, they fly almost non-stop to wintering grounds in Argentina, Bolivia, Chile, and Peru.

Great Salt Lake's waterfowl have inspired much of the conservation work here over the past century. In the early 1900s, duck and goose hunters realized that growing water use by farmers and settlers was draining the lake's wetlands. Duck clubs sprang up to preserve—and develop—marshes at the lake's edges. Many of these duck clubs survive today. Some offer the pampered hunting experience (your annual membership dues could run as high as $75,000, but the staff will pluck, clean, and even prepare your quarry a l'orange). Others offer the rough and stubbly (it costs just $150 to be a member, but you'll sleep in a tent and may even get your feet wet).

Great Salt Lake has also been on the forefront of public hunting opportunities. The Public Shooting Grounds, opened in 1923, may be the first marshes built for the use of the average-Joe hunter. And in 1928, Congress established the Bear River Migratory Bird Refuge on the lake's eastern shore. It was one of the first wildlife refuges in the country, and is now perhaps best known as the setting for Terry Tempest Williams' book, *Refuge: An Unnatural History of Family and Place.*

Today, much of Great Salt Lake's four hundred thousand-acre fringe of wetlands is protected under some form of federal, state, private, or nonprofit control. These wetlands are the hatching grounds for five hundred to seven hundred fifty thousand ducks each year, according to the DWR. But, say conservationists, many of these wetlands are deepened and "enhanced" for waterfowl at the expense of shorebirds, which forage in mudflats or salt playas.

"The bottom line is I'm glad [the duck clubs] are there," says Wayne Martinson, Utah wetlands coordinator for the National Audubon Society, "and I hope they can continue, because I worry what would be there if they weren't."

While much has been done to protect Great Salt Lake's halo of wetlands, little would be known about the lake itself it weren't for the brine-shrimp harvesters. And to understand the harvesters, it helps to know a little more about the shrimp.

Some may know brine shrimp as "Sea-Monkeys"; back in the 1970s and eighties, brine shrimp were sold to kids through ads in the back of comic books and magazines, and today they're hocked online. They look nothing like the grinning sea people in the ads, but they're perfect for mail order: their winter eggs, or cysts, go dormant for several months, so they can survive long-distance shipping. "Just add water," and they'll hatch.

It's this quality that makes the brine shrimp industry possible—this, and the fact that Great Salt Lake brine shrimp are the best, most nutritious food for cocktail shrimp, or prawns. Asian prawn farmers realized this thirteen years ago, and in short order, their demand sparked a rush on the lake's "black gold."

During the 1986-87 season, four companies harvested a little less than 1.9 million pounds of biomass, a messy mix of brine shrimp eggs and flotsam and jetsam. Within five years, there were eleven companies operating twenty-six boats that pulled 13.5 million pounds from the lake. By 1995, twenty-one companies held sixty-three permits, with more wanting in on the action.

There was now fierce competition for the long streaks of salmon-colored eggs that look like oil slicks on the surface of the lake. Harvesters started using spotter planes to find them. The pilots radioed down to boat captains, who raced across the lake, surrounding the eggs with "containment booms" developed for cleaning oil spills before pumping them on board in a kind of water and egg slurry.

In the early days of the brine-shrimp boom, harvesters and state managers believed it was impossible to over-harvest brine shrimp eggs. But the influx of fishermen, many of whom had watched other fisheries crash from over-fishing, brought a new environmental ethic to the lake. A group of them formed the Utah Artemia Association.

Getting such a competitive crowd to talk to one another was tough at first, says Mark Jensen with Great Lake Artemia. "It was like a bunch of cowboys coming together for their first meeting," he says. "Guys that used to give each other the one-finger salute suddenly had to sit down at the table together." Harvesters pushed the DWR slowly, and in some cases grudgingly, for more oversight.

The agency eventually responded in 1996 by capping the number of permits at seventy-nine and the number of companies at thirty-two. DWR also started shutting down the harvest when egg density dropped to a certain point, to keep shrimp populations healthy. But despite the closer regulation, the brine-shrimp harvest went through a series of roller-coaster fluctuations. In 1999, DWR virtually cancelled the harvest after a two-year decline. Some scientists warned that the ecosystem was seriously out of whack.

The truth was that no one really knew what the lake's natural cycles looked like. To better understand the dynamics that drive the lake and its shrimp, harvesters had agreed in the early 1990s to steep increases in the cost of permits—from $3,000 to $10,000—to fund a research program. But it wasn't until 1996 that the DWR established the Great Salt Lake Ecosystem Project. With just three years of data, researchers didn't have much to go on.

As if to prove this point, the brine-shrimp populations bounced back the next year. Harvesters pulled in a record twenty million pounds of biomass. This winter's harvest was strong, too. The brine-shrimp industry's problem has flip-flopped; with a glut of eggs in the freezers, and weak demand, the price per pound has plummeted.

This is little consolation to some observers, who say such wild fluctuations in brine shrimp—one of the foundations of the ecosystem—could be a sign that the lake is on the verge of collapse.

"Everything is in flux—that's how you characterize the Great Salt Lake ecosystem," says Joel Peterson, of the Nature Conservancy of Utah. "But we can't continue to keep taking away water sources, wetland areas, food resources for birds."

The Great Salt Lake Ecosystem Project's lead researcher, Notre Dame University Professor Gary Belovsky, cautions against predictions of doom. "We're just beginning to understand and learn about it [the lake]," he says. "We've made tremendous strides already. But as you answer one question, there are often two other questions that arise."

Researchers have been able to identify one culprit in the brine-shrimp bust of 1997 through 1999. The Southern Pacific Railroad out of Ogden crosses an earthen causeway that effectively splits the lake in half and blocks its natural circulation. As a result, the south arm, which receives freshwater from the three rivers that feed the lake, is diluted, while the north arm maintains an unnaturally high salt concentration.

Brine shrimp survive in a relatively narrow salinity range, so when the lake's salt balance is off kilter, shrimp populations suffer. Clay Perschon, who heads the Great Salt Lake Ecosystem Project for the Division of Wildlife Resources, says the railroad causeway has caused many of the lake's salinity problems. It's one of several causeways, however, "so the lake really isn't one lake, it's several," he says.

Two years ago, after the state adopted a new management plan for the lake, the railroad deepened and widened a breach under the causeway, and saline levels have slowly started to rise in the south arm.

Perhaps the most fundamental and important finding of the ecosystem project is that the lake is much more complex than anyone used to believe. It had been argued for years that Great Salt Lake was a simple ecosystem founded on a single species of alga: the shrimp ate the alga, and birds ate the shrimp.

But researchers have discovered many kinds of algae that vie for dominance. While brine shrimp feed on a number of algal species, they thrive on one particular species. The dominant alga—and therefore the entire ecosystem—depends on water temperature, salt levels, and nutrients coming into the lake. "That means humans may have more unforeseen impacts then we used to believe," says Belovsky.

This in itself is a minor revolution in thought. Conventional wisdom says because wetlands act as a cleaning filter and salt can break down some nutrients, the lake can accept a limitless amount of pollution. Magnesium Corp. of America, which sits on the lake's western shore, was rated for years as the nation's number one toxic-chemical polluter. The Brigham Copper Mine, the largest open-pit copper mine in the world, dumps tens of thousands of pounds of toxic chemicals into the lake every year. Farmington Bay on the southeast side of the lake could be one of the most polluted water bodies in the state, thanks to years of sewer discharges.

Great Salt Lake isn't the first lake to be used as a sewer and dumping ground. In the 1960s, following years of industrial pollution, Lake Erie was declared dead. Erie has been cleaned up, and is now considered an environmental success story, says Belovsky. But there's a key difference. Lake Erie "flushes itself out every thirty years or so," he says. "The Great Salt Lake doesn't flush itself out. What goes in is going to stay there."

This has implications that go far beyond the lake to logging and mining in the watershed and development across the floodplain. Can we rein in these impacts in time to avert ecological crisis? "We'd better," Belovsky says. "Given the amount of growth and the demand for water, we'd better or we're going to be caught off guard. I personally wish these issues had been addressed fifteen or twenty years ago."

Fifteen or twenty years ago, just more than one million people lived along the Wasatch Front. Today, just shy of two million people live on the strip of land between the lake and the Wasatch Mountains, from Brigham City in the north to Provo in the south. The state estimates there will be another one million by 2020, driven largely by Utah's top-in-the-nation birthrate. By 2050, five million people will live along the lake's eastern shores. And as the population skyrockets, so do assaults on Great Salt Lake.

Salt Lake City already uses more water per capita than any other city in the U.S., and the region's largest water provider, the Jordan Valley Water Conservancy District, says it will need more sources within ten years. By some estimates, the lake would be at least six feet higher today if it weren't for all the water use by humans. That means salt levels—and shrimp populations—fluctuate even more than they would naturally, something that will inevitably have an impact on the lake's birds.

While many of the wetlands surrounding the lake are more or less protected, wetlands above the lake are being converted into roads and housing developments. So are the region's farmlands, where birds forage for food, especially in times of high water. And even "protected" wetlands are vulnerable when they get in the way of progress.

But the outlook for Great Salt Lake isn't entirely bleak. Environmentalists and others are championing the ecosystem's basic needs, which Audubon's Martinson sums up as, "drink, breathe, and circulate." In other words, the lake needs an adequate supply of clean river water; a buffer zone around it to protect wetlands and to allow for constantly shifting water levels; and reworked dikes and causeways to even out saline levels.

"Can we do all this with five million people?" asks Martinson. "Maybe, but only with a whole lot of planning."

In the last decade, mitigation money from the Central Utah Project has helped numerous preserves along the lake. The National Audubon Society established a two-thousand-acre preserve on the lake's south shore and is working on acquiring another sixteen hundred acres. The Nature Conservancy, which has a thirty-five hundred-acre preserve on the lake's eastern shore, is making a major push to protect upland habitat and sensitive areas throughout the lake's watershed.

Last year, Davis County developed a shoreline protection plan that spells out where development should occur along the lake's edge. The shorelands plan is really just a "wish list," says Lynn de Freitas with FRIENDS of Great Salt Lake, but it's a start, and the other three counties that border the lake are developing similar plans.

In 2000, the state adopted a new comprehensive management plan for the lake. Environmentalists say the plan falls short in many areas: it stays within the arbitrary "meander line," a high-water line established by the state at 4,217 feet, and fails to set any quantifiable water standard. But it goes much further to protect than did past plans. For the first time, for example, the state said the lake should be managed in the public trust.

These are humble beginnings for what someday could become a comprehensive management plan for the lake's entire twenty-two thousand-acre watershed, says University of Utah law professor Bob Adler. He suggests modeling such a plan after similar efforts on the Chesapeake Bay, the Great Lakes, and the Columbia River Basin.

"If we can start to act now, it will be cheaper in the far run and the result will be much less restrictive," he says.

State officials are guarded about the idea, however. Perschon acknowledges that managing at the watershed level is best for any system, but he worries that such a complex and controversial undertaking would give short shrift to short-term problems such as water quality and salt balance. "I'm just anxious to see something done," says Perschon. "I don't feel like we can wait twenty-five years to make this really big thing happen when some of the problems we face are this year and the year after."

Some say only a major catastrophe will get the lake the attention it needs. "If the building's not burning down, what's the use of having a fire-prevention system?" asks brine-shrimp harvester Mark Jensen sarcastically. "We're going to have a real ecological crisis before anything is done."

But with so little basic knowledge of Great Salt Lake, it's anyone's guess when, or even if, that crisis will come. "The insidious thing is that it is not just going to go 'boom'—where all of a sudden the system crashes," says The Nature Conservancy's Peterson. "It's been slowly degrading over the last hundred years, and we're not going to see drastic changes overnight."

When all is said and done, the biggest threat to Great Salt Lake may be lack of understanding—and lack of foresight. Peterson wonders how things might have turned out if people had recognized the lake's natural values years ago. After a long pause, he says quietly: "This thing could have been a national park."

April 29, 2002

Tim Westby writes from Salt Lake City, Utah.

BAY AREA

Delta Blues

Susan Zakin

There was nothing out there on the water—no towns, no light, no signs of civilization at all. Fog rose from the Delta; it covered the sky and inhabited every corner of cold distance.

Twenty years ago, Marc Reisner wrote words similar to these in *Cadillac Desert*, his landmark book about western water. Looking down from his cramped seat on a jet traveling from Utah to California, what Reisner saw—empty desert ticking by for eleven minutes at five hundred miles per hour, then the suddenness of crowded cities—is still the West today.

But something has changed. Reisner's book altered the way westerners think about water. We know now that water is not merely fuel for our ambitions, but fragile, and finite.

A large part of *Cadillac Desert* is devoted to California. The superlatives are familiar: the world's fifth-largest economy, a population bigger than Canada's, the richest agricultural state in the country. California is also the ultimate example of the American West's trillion-dollar, century-long effort to, as Reisner put it "maintain a civilization in a semidesert with a desert heart."

Since Reisner wrote his book, California has had to face the reality that while its profligate use of water had built an empire of astounding proportions, the state's environmental checking account was badly overdrawn. Even if nobody cared about protecting the environment, the tap would eventually run dry for farms and cities, too.

Nowhere was that more apparent than in the California Delta, the five hundred fifty square miles of water, marshes, and wetlands that lie at the heart of this enormous state but are virtually invisible to most people who live here.

Half of California's rain and snowmelt runs into the Delta, funneling down from the Sierra Nevada, through the Feather River, the Yuba and the American, the Mokelumne, the Stanislaus, the Tuolumne and the Merced. These tributaries feed the Sacramento and the San Joaquin rivers, which meet the Pacific Ocean at the Delta, just northeast of San Francisco Bay.

Carrying water away from the Delta are the pipes and aqueducts of the Central Valley Project and the State Water Project, two enormous systems of dams and water diversions. Together, they send water south, supplying drinking water for twenty-two million people in and around Los Angeles—about two-thirds of California's population—and irrigation water for the Central Valley farms that grow 35 percent of the country's fruits and vegetables.

Almost ten years ago, people in California began the most ambitious effort in western history to make peace between warring water interests and to restore the Delta, which had been diked and developed and starved of the freshwater runoff that keeps its ecosystem alive. Now, the result of their work, a painstakingly negotiated $8.7 billion plan called CALFED, is threatening to die with a whimper, as the Bush administration turns its back on many of the major environmental initiatives undertaken during the Clinton years.

If California can't solve its water problems, the state's environment and economy will both suffer. And as the bursting of the dot-com bubble taught us, California's economic ills reverberate through the rest of the country. This is particularly frightening as the U.S. faces budget deficits and high-priced military adventures with no end in sight.

On the other hand, they say that if you can make it in New York, you can make it anywhere. If California can solve its water problems, perhaps the other western states can, too.

The California Delta in winter destroys every sun-drenched, hedonistic, surfer-dude fantasy I ever had about this state. I am trapped on a boat in the most unrelenting cold I have experienced in years.

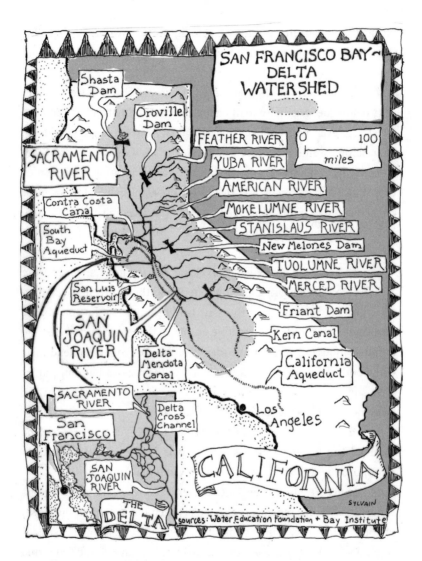

"I grew so cold and numb, finally, that I ceased to shiver," wrote Jack London in *The Fish Patrol*, a 1905 collection of maritime adventures in the San Francisco Bay Area. California may have changed since then, but the weather hasn't. If the Delta is the heart of the state's circulatory system, it is frozen.

I'm spending the day with Fish and Game biologist Derek Stein and Delta native Bob Buker, cruising through ghostly pale fog that has scared off the party boats that congregate here in warmer weather. We imagine how the Delta looked before it became a sponge squeezed by farms and cities.

Along the shore, black-crowned night herons roost in a tree; I count sixty before they frighten and fly. We see them twice that day, in numbers. Hawks are everywhere. Buker slows the boat for snowy egrets and great blue herons. Some have speculated that the Pacific Flyway—the route followed by millions of migratory birds—came into being thousands of years ago because of the Delta and enormous Tulare Lake, near Bakersfield, which provided stopping points and feeding grounds. These birds are the skeletons of those migrations, these waters a ghost of the old Delta.

Before European settlement, the Delta's marshlands "stretched from Willows to Bakersfield in a continuous swath of green," according to a history published by The Bay Institute, a San Francisco-based environmental group. The Institute estimates that there once were nine hundred thousand acres of tule marsh—tules are sedges that lend their name both to a native species of elk and to the region's blinding winter fog—and fourhundred fifteen thousand acres of vernal pools in the Sacramento and San Joaquin river watersheds.

In her 1903 book, *The Land of Little Rain*, Mary Austin described the southern San Joaquin Valley as "ghostly pale in winter, in summer deep poisonous-looking green—full of mystery and malaria."

Now, after a century of engineering, less than 5 percent of the region's historical wetlands remain. The Delta has been reduced to, in the words of The Bay Institute, "a quilt of disconnected patches too small to sustain dependent species" such as winter-run Chinook salmon, the California clapper rail, and the saltmarsh harvest mouse.

The Delta's farms are struggling, too. This is where agriculture started in California, on drained marshland, before massive water projects made it possible to farm the desert. But these relatively small-scale operations find it difficult to compete with agribusiness. The rambling network of dikes and levees that make it possible to farm here is wearing out, and so is the Delta itself. The peat soil oxidizes when it is exposed to the air; in other words, it changes chemical composition, dries up, and blows away.

Many of the human-made islands that once held farmhouses and fields have subsided, some as much as fifteen feet below sea level. Others have simply disappeared, swallowed by winter storms.

We reach Liberty Island, a gray sheen beyond a broken levee made of rock and earth. In the 1970s, a heavy storm burst the levee surrounding the island and let the Delta's waters rush in. The once-fertile farming island is now a ruin, a lake of lost possibilities.

A line of power poles stretches into infinity, or what appears to be infinity in the white haze. The bases of the poles are submerged in at least ten feet of water. They tilt ominously, a surreal reminder that water is the baseline of existence here.

Buker, who just retired from Pacific Gas and Electric, tells me that the wires are probably live, still providing electricity. "If it falls, it just shorts out," he says. "There are a lot of places in the Delta like this."

In the Delta, the boomtown past is still visible, its bones scattered where they fell. Historic towns like Locke look frozen in time, the homes and businesses of Chinese workers abandoned. Giant gates hold back the arms of rivers that once alternately meandered and rushed through this giant riverine estuary.

After a century of hard use, it was inevitable that the Delta would lose its resilience. In the 1930s, the federally funded Central Valley Project, an enormous system of dams and water diversions, had been built to rescue farmers in Southern California. After the completion of the State Water Project in the 1960s, which helped spur the growth of the city of Los Angeles, signs of a breakdown began to appear.

By the 1990s, the Delta's tributaries were so altered that more than 90 percent of Central Valley salmon spawning habitat had been destroyed. Winter-run chinook salmon were placed on the endangered species list in 1990, after the population declined to only 533 fish.

The Delta itself was in trouble, too. In 1993, a coalition of environmental groups sued the U.S. Environmental Protection Agency for failing to establish water-quality standards. The lawsuit did not concern industrial pollution, but saltwater; too much freshwater was being siphoned off, pulling the line of saltwater farther into the Delta.

Concerns about the altered ecosystem were confirmed in 1994, when the tiny Delta smelt, once prolific enough to be caught and grilled for lunch by Derek Stein's predecessors at the Fish and Game Department, was listed as endangered. The three-inch-long, translucent smelt is a resident here. Unlike the migratory salmon, the loitering smelt is "susceptible to being in the wrong place at the wrong time," in the words of one U.S. Fish and Wildlife official.

As the Fish and Wildlife Service moved to protect the smelt, the State Water Project and the Central Valley Project faced crippling shutdowns. With the lawsuit over water quality and the listing of the smelt, things seemed to reach critical mass. For the first time, cities and farms in Southern California confronted the possibility that the days of Chinatown were numbered: long-term water shortages could end a century of empire-building.

Someone had to give up water, or so it seemed. Environmentalists said it was time to retire inefficient farms. Farmers said the food supply couldn't be compromised. Cities knew they represented the state's future; surely they couldn't be expected to give up any water.

Timing, as they say, is everything. Several months earlier, California Gov. Pete Wilson had abandoned state water reform to gain support from traditional agricultural interests. The Clinton administration realized that Wilson, a Republican, would use this perennially divisive issue in a presidential bid.

In early December 1994, Betsy Rieke, assistant secretary for Water and Science at the U.S. Department of Interior, headed to California to defuse the crisis. Rieke, who had a strong track record dealing with Arizona's water issues, was known for her strategic prowess. She realized that the various interests—agriculture, urban, and environmental—were aligning in a way that might make an agreement possible.

With a forty-eight-hour deadline looming— a federal judge had set a December 15 ultimatum for a resolution of the water quality lawsuit— Rieke got the water warriors into a room, and told them they couldn't come out until they had agreed to agree.

It may have surprised everyone when they actually did it. Rieke's formidable personality may have had something to do with it. Or perhaps the Republican takeover of Congress made environmentalists eager, even desperate, to make a deal. Maybe someone just had to go to the bathroom.

In any case, environmentalists said they would stop suing, at least for a while. Government officials promised agricultural and urban interests that water needed for endangered species would be purchased only from willing sellers. And everyone agreed to spend several years figuring out a way to manage California's enormous plumbing system so it fulfilled the needs of fish as well as farmers and city-dwellers.

On December 15, Gov. Wilson stood on a podium to announce, "Peace has broken out." Interior Secretary Bruce Babbitt, EPA chief Carol Browner, and representatives of the agricultural, urban and environmental communities stood beside him as he unveiled the agreement, called the Bay Delta Accord.

"It was one of those hair-stand-on-end moments," said Rieke.

Over the next six years, Californians spent thousands of hours in intensely public "stakeholder" meetings. When it was all over, a small group retreated behind closed doors to come up with a final plan. It wasn't a popular way to do it, but officials believed it was the only way to sift through the cacophony of interests, ideas and ultimatums.

When they emerged in August 2000, they had a 1,199-page plan to restore the Delta, while inflicting minimal pain on agriculture and cities. It was called CALFED because it was designed to satisfy the requirements of both state and federal environmental laws.

CALFED is not the largest ecological-restoration effort ever attempted. That dubious honor probably falls to the Florida Everglades. But it is the only such undertaking that balances restoration with the need to supply water to one of the world's most heavily irrigated agricultural regions and enough urbanites to overpopulate a small European country.

Over the next three decades, CALFED—a program involving twenty-three state and federal agencies—will install fish screens, replant marshes, tinker with the operation of dams, improve levees, conduct millions of dollars' worth of scientific studies, defend itself from lawsuits, fund water-conservation programs, buy land, set up regional water councils, buy water for fish, and maybe even build a few new dams or reservoirs. The cost of the program's first seven years is $8.7 billion, to be split among federal, state, and local authorities.

This enormous win-win scenario will also vindicate the Clinton-era approach to resolving environmental conflict—the "let's all hold hands and agree or at least agree to disagree," touchy-feely alternative to the region's more familiar dig-in-your-heels western warfare.

Unless there isn't enough money. Or enough water.

In theory, at least, water shouldn't be a problem. The great irony is this: there is no shortage of water in California. The average freshwater runoff to the Delta is about twenty-three million acre-feet, with 30-60 percent diverted to cities and agriculture.

But that average is misleading, because California's rain and snowfall gyrate wildly from year to year. In the record-breaking storms of 1982-83, more than sixty million acre-feet barreled down from the Sierra into the Delta. In 1979, in contrast, only six million acre-feet flowed into the Delta.

The solution to California's water problems has always been to stockpile water during wet years for use during dry ones. But the state doesn't have enough dams and reservoirs to hold all of the runoff in wet years, inspiring an old California phrase that drives environmentalists crazy—people talk about water that is not "used" as being "wasted to the sea."

It all seems so simple. If California could hold back just a fraction more of those winter storm bonanzas, the state's farms could still be irrigated and lawns could stay green—there might even be some water left for fish—when the inevitable punishing drought arrives.

The CALFED plan recommended studying the feasibility of water-storage projects, but did not call for any action until the project's second phase, which begins in 2010. The most controversial option for new storage is raising Shasta Dam near the headwaters of the Sacramento River. Raising the dam would flood a portion of the McCloud River, a world-class trout river that has already lost fifteen miles to the dam.

Other possibilities include dramatically increasing the storage capacity of the Los Vaqueros Reservoir in suburban Walnut Creek, building an offstream water-storage facility north of the Delta called Sites that would divert 1.9 million acre-feet of the Sacramento River during wet years, and constructing a reservoir south of the Delta.

CALFED officials have even revived the idea of a peripheral canal, an aqueduct that would haul water around the Delta instead of letting water flow through it. In the 1970s, a similar plan caused one of the epic battles of California water history.

Some members of the environmental community, like Gary Bobker, program director of The Bay Institute, seemed willing to consider some of these projects. Others, like Tom Graff of Environmental Defense and Steve Evans of Friends of the River, criticized CALFED for considering raising dams when the rest of the country was tearing them down. "There is a finite amount of water," said Graff. "If you want to deliver more, the environment is going to suffer."

Last winter, as CALFED was in danger of running out of money, the critical question of water storage nearly landed all 1,199 pages of the plan in the recycling bin. Faced with the task of authorizing CALFED—and providing roughly one-third of its funding—the California congressional delegation seemed to fall back in time, splitting along all-too-familiar ideological lines. Ken Calvert, a Republican congressman from Riverside, introduced a CALFED authorization bill that would give Bush's Interior Secretary, Gale Norton, the power to jet-propel water-storage projects through Congress.

Environmentalists and taxpayer advocates viewed the Calvert bill as a return to the bad old days of rubber-stamped dam projects and handouts to agribusiness. "The best dam sites are taken," said Aileen Roder of

Taxpayers for Common Sense. "We're just recycling the same garbage—these dinosaur projects—over and over again, instead of looking at solutions."

Calvert's supporters, like California Farm Bureau spokesman Dave Kranz, argued that without new storage, CALFED couldn't succeed.

Congress approved a temporary funding package, and Calvert has been forced to remove most of the provisions in his bill that environmentalists found objectionable. Still, supporters have yet to get CALFED formally authorized by Congress, a threshold that would make long-term funding much easier to come by.

This fall, the House version of CALFED authorization is being held up by Republicans who oppose a provision inserted by Representative George Miller, Democrat-California, a staunch advocate for the environment and labor, which requires the use of union labor on CALFED projects. At the same time, powerful western senators John Kyl, Republican-Arizona, and Pete Domenici, Republican-New Mexico, are threatening to add $10 billion of antiquated western water projects to the Senate version of the CALFED authorization bill.

Despite the infighting, observers expect CALFED authorization to pass before Congress adjourns for Christmas. The big change is that funding for the program is likely to drop. Although Calvert's bill still contains the full $3 billion, which is the federal share of the plan, the Senate version is expected to call for $800 million in funding. When it comes to the actual appropriations, the amount could be far less.

With time running out before Congress adjourns in December, CALFED's supporters must weigh the advantages of authorization with the price of pork—Democratic or Republican.

The Bush administration, for its part, recommended spending only $15 million next year for all environmental work in the Bay Delta region, including CALFED.

The Interior Department's lead man on CALFED, Assistant Secretary of Water and Science Bennett Raley, chafes at the suggestion that he hasn't supported the program. He blames the downturn in the economy for the funding cuts. "There's enormous good in CALFED," he says, "But it's one thing to negotiate a deal for the future with the assumption that money is no object. It's another thing to implement that deal when you have [fiscal] limitations."

Meanwhile, on the ground, CALFED is moving ahead in fits and starts. So far, its record is marked by successes ranging from the subtle to the dramatic—and a few devastating failures.

In its first year of operation, and in the years leading up to its creation, the focus was on restoration. In 1999, four dams were removed from Butte Creek, a tributary of the Sacramento River south of Mount Lassen, and fish ladders were installed on five other Sacramento River dams. Spring-run salmon numbers shot up to six thousand, from a low of ten a few years earlier.

But this was followed by an ugly glitch. One of CALFED's cornerstones is something called the "Environmental Water Account," which allows CALFED to buy water to hold in reserve for emergencies that threaten fish. This water is crucial, because the whole Rube Goldberg contraption of CALFED is based·on assurances to Central Valley farmers and Southern California cities that they won't suffer unexpected cutbacks in water supply because of endangered species.

During winter storms in early 2001, officials held back water while winter-run Chinook salmon, the most endangered fish in the Delta, died in droves at the state and federal water projects. In the end, 18,503 juvenile fish died, far exceeding the 7,404 permitted under the Endangered Species Act rules set by the National Marine Fisheries Service.

To place the issue in perspective, it helps to know that the previous year's entire population of adult winter run Chinook salmon in the Delta was a mere twelve hundred fish.

Environmentalists were critical of the managers' decision not to release water to save fish. But CALFED had not yet devised a plan for such extreme situations. Managers may have been overly cautious because they were afraid that they would need the water for other species of fish expected to hit the pumps later in the year.

The astonishing part was that everyone stayed on board. While farmers were practically rioting in the Klamath Basin, both environmentalists and agricultural interests in California remained involved in CALFED through its early, sometimes rocky years.

Then, in early February 2002, CALFED got a nastier jolt when its Environmental Water Account lost between two and three hundred thousand acre-feet of water. In 1992, the Central Valley Project Improvement Act, backed by Miller and Senator Bill Bradley, Democrat-New Jersey, had promised a revolution in California water policy. For the first time, a law put nature into the equation of California water use. The law set aside eight hundred thousand acre-feet of water to double anadromous fish populations.

In 1997, the Clinton administration came up with a plan to put that law into effect. That plan is full of arcane details, but they don't matter much now. In early February, a federal judge struck it down, gutting the Environmental Water Account and throwing off all the calculations, computer models, and spreadsheets painfully constructed by water wonks.

CALFED executive director Patrick Wright says there was enough water this year that water users still received the assurances promised by the Environmental Water Account—guarantees that their water won't receive further cutbacks for environmental reasons. What happens next year? Nobody knows.

Wright, a former U.S. Environmental Protection Agency official, isn't deluding himself about his job. California's water system is a Persian rug that must be carefully picked apart and painstakingly rewoven. "Around the West, people have been saying the era of big dams is over," says Wright. "But in California, the fight is [still] very, very real."

Tom Graff of Environmental Defense thinks he knows the future of CALFED—it doesn't have one. "The plan doesn't have any coherence. It's just sort of a big, muddled mess, so nobody can get too mad at it," he says. "The good thing from my point of view is that the Bush administration has come along and defunded it."

Gary Bobker of The Bay Institute has been deeply involved in California water issues for more than a decade. He believes that the water-storage projects envisioned in the CALFED plan will be too expensive to build.

He foresees the program turning into what he calls "CALFED Lite," a massive ecosystem-restoration project.

But planting willows along rivers won't solve the problem of ensuring a water supply for California industry. This is no small matter; without water, the California dream fades from boomtown to ghost town.

To free up more water, Bobker is willing to talk about the great CALFED taboo—retiring farmland. "There are parts of the Central Valley that are a thriving economy that everyone's interested in keeping viable," Bobker says. "But then there are parts of the valley that should never have been farmed."

In particular, he points to the west side of the San Joaquin Valley, where pollution problems prohibit food crops, and farmers grow subsidized cotton that costs seventy cents a pound to produce, but sells for only thirty-five to forty cents a pound on the world market. "The question is not whether this land will be retired, but when," he says. "Should we really be turning cartwheels and doing things that cause environmental harm to prolong a terminal patient?"

In the last days of the Clinton administration, officials came close to making a deal to buy out San Joaquin Valley farmers most affected by pollution. The clock ran out on that attempt, but many view a buyout, which would free up water for other uses, as inevitable.

Bennett Raley says the Interior Department is again looking at buying land and conservation easements. "Most people recognize that in the long run, retiring farmlands is going to be a piece of the equation," he says.

But the Farm Bureau is resisting. Although it is still participating in CALFED, the group has two lawsuits pending against the plan, claiming that it fails to evaluate the environmental consequences of the program on agricultural land. "We just think that's a bad idea," says Bureau spokesman Dave Kranz. "This program focuses all on water, almost exclusively on fish. We have a population that's headed toward fifty million in the next twenty years, and those people need to eat."

CALFED's architects may have been wise to temporarily sidestep the question of retiring farmland. Confronting the volatile question might have threatened the fragile coalition on which CALFED depends. And by delaying construction of water projects until at least 2010, CALFED officials may have chosen to let history take its course.

But, as Tolstoy believed, sometimes history needs a strong leader to move it forward. So far, in the Bush administration, that leader has not appeared. Some theorize that the administration simply refuses to hand out largesse to California, where voters overwhelmingly supported Al Gore in the 2000 election.

Whatever the reason, Central Valley farmer Paul Betancourt says the Bush administration has shown no interest in buying out farmers whose land is too polluted to grow food crops. "A lot of nothing has happened," says Betancourt, a registered Republican and local Farm Bureau official. "Under a Gore administration, it probably would have gone much faster."

Many Clinton-era initiatives—from the Columbia River to the Sonoran Desert—are withering because of inertia on the part of the Bush administration. Whether or not one believes, like Clinton's Interior Secretary, Bruce Babbitt, that "compromise is the answer all the time," one wonders how all the "stakeholders" who spent months sitting in meetings feel, now that their efforts are being discarded in this de facto fashion.

For CALFED, a bit of belt-tightening may not be fatal. A massive restoration project washing across the California Delta could create a version of the future that looks at least a little like the past. Perhaps it's possible that, with restoration alone, Californians can build a real and metaphorical nest for black-crowned night herons, and create refuges for fish like the Delta smelt, which could once again be plentiful enough to eat without a second thought.

September 30, 2002

Susan Zakin writes from Tucson, Arizona.

Death in the Delta

Francisco Tharp

Fish populations continue to tank in the Sacramento-San Joaquin Delta, according to figures released in early 2008 by the California Department of Fish and Game.

After tossing the trawl nets and tallying the numbers, the agency found a record low population of longfin smelt in the Pacific Coast's largest estuary. Populations of Sacramento splittail, American shad, striped bass, and the threatened Delta smelt also neared their lowest since the annual fall survey began in 1967.

"These data are just one more clear indication that the overall ecosystem of the Delta is in dire straits," says Christina Swanson, senior scientist at The Bay Institute, a nonprofit that protects the San Francisco Bay. "Longfin and Delta smelt are teetering on the brink of extinction. They could be gone next year."

The state's Department of Fish and Game agrees that the fish are in serious trouble. "We're very concerned about the trend that these data indicate," says Marty Gingras, supervising biologist. The department says it cannot determine exactly how close to extinction the five species are, because the survey compares current fish populations to past abundance rather than providing a precise tally of the number of fish. Nonetheless, says Gingras, "there is merit in listing longfin smelt under the California Endangered Species Act, and uplisting the Delta smelt from threatened to endangered."

A major factor harming the Delta's fish is the overdraft of water from Delta watersheds. State and federal records indicate that water-project diversions, which supply twenty-four million Californians and a $31 billion dollar agricultural industry, gulp an average of nearly two trillion gallons of Delta water per year. That's more than half of the water that trickles into the Delta in a dry year, and 20 to 30 percent of total flows in a wet year.

"Clearly these data are confirming that we regularly take too much water out of the Delta and rivers," says Swanson. The Bay Institute recommends that the state consider higher water efficiency, better management of groundwater, and water recycling to ease Delta demand.

Other problems threaten the Delta's fish as well. Non-native species, such as the overbite clam, tend to out-compete natives and create less suitable habitat for them. Additionally, the water contains unhealthy levels of herbicides and pesticides from upstream agriculture and ammonia from sewage.

Habitat loss is another important factor in the Delta. Over the past hundred and fifty years, most of its marshes and waters have been leveed, drained, and rerouted for agricultural and urban development.

A recent court ruling may provide some relief for the Delta's fish. Last August, U.S. District Court Judge Oliver Wanger of California's Eastern District imposed restrictions on export pumping from the Delta after ruling in favor of environmental groups. The groups had sued the U.S. Fish and Wildlife Service for failing to protect the federally listed smelt. Until the agency completes a new biological opinion on Delta management, the smelt and their ecosystem remain under interim protections.

January 17, 2008

Francisco Tharp is a former intern for *High Country News.*

Hold the Salt

Jennifer Weeks

Early on a bright fall morning, dozens of black-necked stilts pick their way across a shallow pond at the edge of San Francisco Bay, feeding on tiny floating brine shrimp. Each bird is about a foot tall, with a black face and back, white undersides, and spindly red legs. The water is so calm that they seem to walk on a mirror, bending down to admire their own reflections.

The setting is Eden Landing, a complex of human-made ponds next to the San Mateo/Hayward Bridge. It's a tranquil scene but hardly paradise: commuter traffic buzzes past, jets descend to nearby airports, and a rising breeze carries whiffs of rot from a shoreline landfill. The ponds themselves are industrial sites, built decades ago to make salt by concentrating and evaporating bay water. Viewed from the air, the progression of ponds look like colored tiles: first, algae tint the "starter" ponds green, then brine shrimp and salt-loving bacteria turn the thickening solution orange and finally red.

Before the Gold Rush, San Francisco Bay was bordered by two hundred thousand acres of tidal marshes that provided rich habitat for fish and birds. Today, 90 percent of those tracts have been filled in for farming, development, and salt making. This spring, state and federal agencies will launch a fifty-year program to convert up to fifteen thousand acres of salt ponds back into tidal wetlands.

Most wetlands in the West lie inland, but those in coastal estuaries (mixed saltwater and freshwater zones) like San Francisco Bay have special biological and economic value. They support millions of birds that migrate along the Pacific Flyway and provide spawning grounds for many fish and shellfish species. Wetlands also are natural sponges that soak up flood tides—a service that will become more critical as global climate change raises sea levels.

The salt-pond project dwarfs other wetland restoration initiatives in the West, which typically cover a few thousand acres at most. Working at this scale could yield major payoffs, says David Lewis, executive director of Save The Bay. "San Francisco Bay is part of a huge ecosystem," Lewis says. "Forty percent of California's watershed flows into it, so improving the health of the Bay can have a big impact."

Project managers are analyzing many intricate issues, such as sediment flows in the Bay and birds' foraging habits in ponds and marshes. But the biggest challenges are economic and political. No central structure exists to coordinate the many federal, state, and local agencies involved in the project or raise enough money to completely restore the salt ponds and other wetlands around the Bay.

Meanwhile, new shoreline development proposals divert energy and government attention from the slower work of bringing wetlands back to life.

The second-largest estuary in the nation, San Francisco Bay is ringed by highways and seven million people but still provides nesting and breeding grounds for birds, fish, and mammals. Dozens of endangered or threatened species use the estuary, including the brown pelican, Delta smelt, and northern sea lion.

Local advocates have been lobbying to clean up the Bay since the 1960s, when raw sewage flowed straight into it and only four of its 276 miles of shoreline were publicly accessible. Starting in 1972, groups like Save the Bay helped to build support for restoring some five thousand acres of tidal marsh. When Cargill Salt, which owned many of the area's salt ponds, decided to consolidate its holdings in 2000, advocates saw a bigger opportunity. With private foundation support, a partnership of state and federal agencies bought three tracts of salt ponds for $100 million.

Cargill sold the ponds as-is. Many are full of highly saline brine, so the first step in restoring them is letting water flow in to recreate natural tidal patterns. "We've simplified the ecology of the Bay over time by creating a very hard, diked edge," says Lynne Trulio, professor of environmental studies at San Jose State University and the project's science team leader.

"Restoring tidal action and marsh vegetation aims to remedy that and make the South Bay ecosystem richer and more self-sustaining."

In 2004, managers installed tidal gates to cycle water periodically through some ponds. Salinity levels fell, and the ponds supported growing numbers of shrimp, flies, and fish, which in turn drew dunlins, sandpipers, and many species of ducks. The change was bigger and faster than expected: counts of some species rose as much as sevenfold in the first year. When three isolated "island" ponds that had only been used by gulls were breached permanently in 2006, thousands of shorebirds and fish-eating birds immediately began feeding there.

The long-term restoration plan, which is jointly managed by the U.S. Fish and Wildlife Service, the California State Coastal Conservancy, and the California Department of Fish and Game, calls for converting 50 to 90 percent of the ponds to tidal wetlands. Some will remain as "managed" ponds that can be customized for certain bird species. By adding islands or changing water depths, wildlife managers can create different habitats for birds that forage or nest in and around the ponds, such as the western snowy plover, a threatened species that nests on salt-pond islands and levees.

The second ingredient in wetlands restoration is dirt—plenty of it. Before it became Silicon Valley, the area around the South Bay was an agricultural zone known as "The Valley of Heart's Delight." Farmers pumped out groundwater for decades to irrigate fruit and nut trees, lowering water tables. Some pond bottoms sank by as much as thirteen feet, too far below the water line to support marsh plants.

To start recreating marshes, workers will breach the dikes so that waves can carry in fresh sediment. In ten to fifteen years, when enough sediment has piled up, cordgrass and pickleweed will start to colonize the mud flats. Eventually the plants will thicken into habitat for species like the endangered California clapper rail and salt marsh harvest mouse.

But because the project covers such a big area, breaching ponds could interfere with larger processes in the Bay. "We know a lot about tidal marsh restoration, but there are questions that stem from the ecosystem scale of this project," says Trulio. For example, opening up the salt ponds could draw sediments from existing mud flats farther north in the Bay that provide crucial foraging areas for migrating water birds. "Losing all the mud flats and not gaining any marsh is everybody's nightmare," says executive project manager Steve Ritchie of the California State Coastal Conservancy. "We're pretty confident that we know how sediment moves in the Bay, but we're going to go slowly on opening up the southern ponds."

Mercury is also a concern. For over a century, mercury deposits from the New Almaden mines near San Jose and other sources have washed into the Bay, and stronger tidal circulation could stir them up. Bacteria found in wetlands can convert mercury to toxic methylmercury, the form that moves up through food chains. And high mercury levels have already been found in clapper rail and tern eggs in the area.

Yet another uncertainty is whether invasive species will move into new marshes. Many non-native species are present in the Bay, notably *Spartina altiflora*, a non-native cordgrass that was planted several decades ago to stabilize shorelines. Here as well as in Washington's Puget Sound, spartina is displacing native grasses and reducing water circulation despite energetic weeding by hundreds of volunteers. Breaching ponds may also displace existing colonies of California gulls. These large, aggressive birds prey on smaller species like snowy plovers and may compete with them for space on the remaining managed ponds.

Restoration agencies plan to tackle these uncertainties through adaptive management, an approach that uses careful trials—such as breaching specific ponds or moving dikes—to determine which actions succeed or fail. Results from one step will help scientists decide what to do next, and ultimately will determine what fraction of the salt ponds is converted back to marshes. Phase I of the project will restore about fifteen hundred acres of tidal habitat between 2008 and 2010.

All told, the salt-pond restoration is projected to cost nearly $1 billion over fifty years. A dozen other, smaller wetland-restoration projects covering more than twenty-three thousand acres are planned or under way around the Bay. Save the Bay estimates that all of these projects could be completed for a total of $1.43 billion, of which about $370 million has already been invested.

What's needed now is a cohesive strategy to raise the balance from federal, state, and local sources and target the projects that are the most scientifically sound. A 2006 survey of Bay Area residents found that about 80 percent were willing to pay $10 yearly in taxes or fees to improve the Bay. Save the Bay would like to see managers tap this goodwill through local funding measures rather than looking to Congress for most of the money. "Often politicians are behind the curve on how willing the public is to pay for environmental benefits," says Lewis. The funding process is especially complicated in San Francisco because nine counties and dozens of towns adjoin the Bay, and each has different concerns about flooding, infrastructure, land conservation, and other issues.

California has lost at least 90 percent of its wetlands, more than other West Coast states, but development and pollution are also stressing important estuaries like the lower Columbia River in Oregon and Puget Sound. Water-diversion projects have reduced river flows into these bodies, causing saltwater intrusion that changes the estuaries' chemistry and destroys fish habitat. And growth in areas like King County, Washington, and coastal Oregon creates constant pressure to dredge or fill in wetlands for other uses.

"Wetlands are inconvenient. If we want to build a road from point A to point B and there's a wetland in the way, it will always lose," says Robin Clark, habitat-restoration manager at People for Puget Sound.

If local agencies find a way to meld their budgets and agendas, the salt-pond project could energize similar efforts to restore other West Coast wetlands. "Hopefully, we can show that even with multiple jurisdictions, you can take a regional approach and find ways of collaborating," Lewis says. "Political boundaries have to recognize ecological boundaries. If the West had been required to develop based on watersheds and water realities, instead of artificial political lines and invented water boundaries, growth patterns would have been very different from what we see today."

February 4, 2008

Jennifer Weeks is a independent writer specializing in energy and environmental issues.

AFTERWORD
Welcome to the
Era of Scarcity

I have a classic western postcard tacked to the bulletin board above my computer. It shows two men in a field with shovels raised above their heads, locked in mock battle. Behind them runs an irrigation ditch. The caption reads: *Discussing Western Water Rights, A Western Pastime.*

The postcard always makes me laugh, because I know how worked up westerners can get over water. At last year's annual ditch meeting, my neighbors in western Colorado seemed on the verge of an insurrection when the volunteer members of the board sheepishly announced that a leak in the reservoir that supplies our late-season water had not been fixed. That meant the reservoir would not fill, and the ditches would run dry by early August. Our green patches of grass, alfalfa, and corn would quickly become as brown, bare, and cracked as the desert lands that surround them.

In years past, my neighbors and I might have shrugged off one shortened growing season; with the reservoir fixed, the following years would flow copiously all summer long with snowmelt from the mountains behind town. But something weird is going on with the weather. The snowpack— the source of nearly all of our water—has become unpredictable, with most years on the lean side; no matter how much snow flies in the winter, it seems to melt off ever more early in the spring.

Scientists confirm what old timers know by observation: the climate is changing, and the water supply is shrinking. This sobering reality— punctuated by a drought in the early 2000s that reduced the level of Utah's mighty Lake Powell to just 30 percent of capacity—has sent shockwaves around a region that has been growing as fast as a Midwestern cornfield after a summer rain. Suddenly, it is possible to imagine our one hundred-year experiment in desert civilization failing as quickly and decisively as that of the Anasazi or the great societies along the Nile River.

As we enter a new era of water scarcity in the West, it is instructive to remind ourselves of how we got to this point. Most of the past century has been about damming the great rivers of the region to siphon off water for farmers and produce electricity for the great urban centers; the federal government has led the charge, pumping enormous resources into water development for a sparsely populated region.

Then, in the 1960s and 1970s our society developed a belated ecological conscience. Dams, we discovered, not only drown canyons, but they also alter the timing and frequency of flows below, radically changing the conditions for fish and riverside vegetation. Our manipulation of the region's major river systems—the Columbia, the Colorado, the Missouri—had turned them into increasingly hostile territory for native species, from cottonwoods to salmon.

Pushed by lawsuits from environmentalists and Native American tribes, water managers began changing the way they release waters from reservoirs, trying to better mimic the natural seasonal cycles. In some cases, they proposed removing dams altogether. Although precious few dams actually came down due to stiff political opposition, those that did—in places such as Arizona's Fossil Creek—demonstrated Mother Nature's remarkable recuperative powers.

A citizens-based watershed movement also sprang to life. Around the West, people expressed their concern about deteriorating rivers and streams by donning rubber boots and gloves and diving into restoration. They re-contoured channels straight-jacketed by engineers, de-fanged fish-killing irrigation systems, ripped out exotic plants such as the tamarisk and Russian olive, and re-planted native willows and cottonwoods.

All of this activity and awareness led many of us to believe that we had entered a great new era of restoration. With a more careful allocation of water, we could have both thriving human communities and healthy natural communities. But climate change has thrown a deeply problematic wrench into the works. With a growing population and a climate-induced water recession, we may not have enough water for agriculture, cities, and wildlife to all thrive at the same time.

A difficult period of triage lies ahead, and there will be winners and losers. If the West's cities have their way, the rural areas and the Indian tribes—with some financial bribing—will hand over their water. It's already happening in places like southern California and Las Vegas, where deals are being cut to pump groundwater and divert traditional agricultural waters to the urban areas. The specter of dried-up fields and trickling rivers has already appeared in the Central and Imperial valleys and parts of Nevada, and it will undoubtedly spread further into the Interior West as the drought deepens.

This first round of belt-tightening has not been too painful. Agriculture, which accounts for some three-fourths of all water use in the West, has been sloppy with its liquid assets. To provide more water to the cities, farmers have simply become more careful; they are lining canals, laying pipe, and replacing flood irrigation with drip irrigation. Cities are also becoming more careful; low-flow toilets and showerheads, and limits on outdoor water usage in the summer have become normal and largely accepted features of life across the region.

But if the weird weather continues as predicted, more radiclal measures lie just ahead. Urban planners are already pushing to build one last round of dams in an attempt to capture every precious drop of moisture—this, despite the fact that a prolonged drought in the West would mean these new reservoirs might never fill up. Conservation practices will intensify. In places like San Diego, Calif., and Cloudcroft, New Mexico, plans to expand the recycling of sewage water are moving ahead; drinking former toilet water may seem gross, but many of us will have to close our eyes and swallow.

Then there is desalinization—turning salty ocean waters into freshwater supplies. Though few in number today, desalinization plants will soon dot the southern California coastline, pumping freshwater into coastal-city water systems. They will take some pressure off of a diminished Colorado River, giving states in the Interior West more room to grow.

How much room? Well, that is the trillion-dollar question of our times. I suspect that our region will be able to sustain, at least for a while, more people than we might ever want to imagine possible. But our technological ingenuity will be able to take us only so far; at some point, the West's enduring characteristic—aridity—will set a boundary beyond which we cannot grow.

When that day comes, ecologically healthy rivers may be a luxury that society isn't willing to afford. All those noble plans to remove dams to save the salmon or restore the Grand Canyon may be thrown out the door in favor of maintaining maximum water storage and relatively clean hydropower. Agriculture—the original reason the great dams of the West were built—will be a shadow of its former self. My neighbors and I will no longer be worrying about our hay crops; we will no longer wear rubber boots and carry shovels to direct muddy melt waters down furrowed fields. The great Western Pastime of arguing over water will be as intense as ever, but the fight will have moved to the cities.

Of course, I could be wrong. The mega-drought may not happen, or we may find a way to live more lightly on this fragile land. Though you won't find it on any postcard, the story of western water has been as much about cooperation as it has been about conflict. This desert society wouldn't have endured as long as it has without people setting aside their own self-interest for the common good.

Paul Larmer
Publisher of *High Country News*

Index